Author of PMP Exam Prep: Technical Project Manager

WHEN YOU ONLY NEED THE PMP MOCK EXAMS
THREE MOCK EXAMS - 800 TOTAL SAMPLE QUESTIONS

CONQUER THE QUESTION ASKED 80-85% OF THE TIME
AS A PROJECT MANAGER, WHAT WOULD YOU DO NEXT?

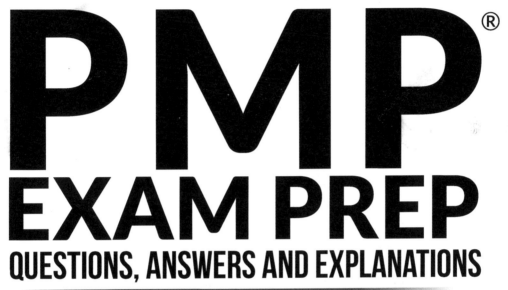

PMP®
EXAM PREP
QUESTIONS, ANSWERS AND EXPLANATIONS

Aligned with PMBOK Sixth Edition

Fully updated for the
2020-2021 PMP Exam

DARRON CLARK, PMP, BSCS, EMBA
Founder GPM Services LLC

ISBN- 978-1-7341334-4-8

Library of Congress Control Number:

Independent Publishing Platform, North Charleston, SC

PMBOK® is a registered trademark of the Project Management Institute.

Project Management Professional and PMP® are registered trademarks of the Project Management Institute.

Oracle®, Real Application Clusters, and Data Guard are registered trademarks of the Oracle Corporation.

Strayer University is a registered trademark.

Credits

This coursebook follows the PMBOK® Guide, Sixth Edition.

PMI®, PMBOK® Guide, Project Management Professional, PMP®, Certified Associate in Project Management (CAPM)®, PMI Agile Certified Practitioner (PMI-ACP)®, and PMI-ACP® are registered trademarks of the Project Management Institute, Inc.

Oracle® is a registered trademark of the Oracle Corporation

GPM LLC® is a registered trademark.

* Note that PMI reserves the right to test on materials not contained in the PMBOK® Guide. See the exam content outline at www.pmi.org under certifications (PMP)®.

Contents

About the PMP Exam

The PMP® exam is tricky—one of the hardest project management exams. Be prepared to study beyond PMBOK® and the classroom material.

The exam tests substantive and reading comprehension skills. Some questions are long and wordy, and you'll need to filter through irrelevant information to find critical facts for answering the question correctly.

What Can I Expect on the PMP Exam?

» Scenario-based questions

» Long, wordy questions

» Questions with more than one answer

» Common sense versus *PMBOK® Guide* answers

» Mathematical problems

» Long and complicated critical path diagrams

» Answers that are correct, but for a different question

» An innovative approach to a known topic

Current Exam Content Outline

Domain	Percentage of Items on Test
I. Initiating	13%
II. Planning	24%
III. Executing	31%
IV. Monitoring and Controlling	25%
V. Closing	7%
Total	100%
Total Number of Scored Questions	175
Total Number of Unscored (Pretest) Questions	25
Total Number of Questions	200

Exam Content Outline Updated for January 2021

Project Management Professional (PMP)® January 2020 Exam Update:[1]

The last day for candidates to take the current version of the PMP exam is now December 30, 2020.

The PMP examination is a necessary part of the activities leading to earning a professional certification; thus, the PMP examination must precisely reflect the practices of the project management practitioner.

PMI retained Alpine Testing Solutions to develop the global *PMP Examination Content Outline*. Alpine Testing Solutions provides psychometric, test development, and credential management solutions to credentialing and educational programs. The task force members were given responsibility for outlining critical job tasks of individuals who lead and direct projects based on their experience and related resources.

---

1   "PMP® Exam Change is Moving to June 2020," https://www.pmi.org/update-center/certification-changes/pmp.

Mapping Domains to Project Processes

The following table identifies the proportion of questions from each domain that will appear on the examination.

Domain	Percentage of Items on Test	Number of Exam Questions
I. People	42%	84
II. Process	50%	100
III. Business Environment	8%	16
Total	100%	200

About half the examination will represent predictive project management approaches, and the other half will represent agile or hybrid approaches. Predictive, agile, and hybrid approaches will be found throughout the three domain areas listed above and are not isolated to any particular domain or task.

Domains, Tasks, and Enablers

In this document, you will find an updated structure for the *PMP Examination Content Outline*. Based on feedback from customers and stakeholders, we have worked on simplifying the format so that the *PMP Examination Content Outline* is easier to understand and interpret.

On the following pages, you will find the domains, tasks, and enablers as defined by the Role Delineation Study.

- » Domains: the high-level knowledge areas that are essential to the practice of project management.
- » Tasks: the underlying responsibilities of the project manager within each domain area.
- » Enablers: illustrative examples of the work associated with the task. Please note that the enablers here are not meant to be an exhaustive list but instead offer a few examples to help demonstrate what the task encompasses.

Domain I	People—42%	How It Maps to PMBOK 6
Task 1	Manage conflict » Interpret the source and stage of the conflict » Analyze the context of the conflict » Evaluate/recommend/reconcile the appropriate conflict resolution solution	9.5 Manage Team 9.6 Control Resources
Task 2	Lead a team » Set a clear vision and mission » Support diversity and inclusion (e.g., behavior types, thought processes) » Value servant leadership (e.g., relate the tenets of servant leadership to the team) » Determine an appropriate leadership style (e.g., directive, collaborative) » Inspire, motivate, and influence team members/stakeholders (e.g., team contract, social contract, reward system) » Analyze team members' and stakeholders' influence » Distinguish options to lead various team members and stakeholders	4.2 Develop Project Charter 4.3 Develop Project Management Plan 4.4 Direct and Manage Project 4.5 Monitor and Control Project
Task 3	Support team performance » Appraise team member performance against key performance indicators » Support and recognize team member growth and development » Determine the appropriate feedback approach » Verify performance improvements	9.1 Plan Resource Management 9.5 Manage Team 9.6 Control Resources
Task 4	Empower team members and stakeholders » Organize around team strengths » Support team task accountability » Evaluate the demonstration of task accountability » Determine and bestow level(s) of decision-making authority	9.1 Plan Resource Management 9.3 Acquire Resources
Task 5	Ensure that team members/stakeholders are adequately trained » Determine the required competencies and elements of training » Determine training options based on training needs » Allocate resources for training » Measure training outcomes	9.1 Plan Resource Management 9.4 Develop Team 9.6 Control Resources
Task 6	Build a team » Appraise stakeholder skills » Deduce project resource requirements » Continuously assess and refresh team skills to meet project needs » Maintain team and knowledge transfer	9.1 Plan Resource Management 9.3 Acquire Resources
Task 7	Address and remove impediments, obstacles, and blockers for the team » Determine critical impediments, obstacles, and blockers for the team » Prioritize critical impediments, obstacles, and blockers for the team » Use the network to implement solutions to remove impediments, obstacles, and blockers for the team Reassess continually to ensure impediments, obstacles, and blockers for the team are being addressed	Agile Project Management

Task 8	Negotiate project agreements » Analyze the bounds of the negotiations for an agreement » Assess priorities and determine the ultimate objective(s) » Verify objective(s) of the project agreement is/are met » Participate in agreement negotiations Determine a negotiation strategy	4.1 Develop Project Charter 5.5 Validate Scope
Task 9	Collaborate with stakeholders » Evaluate engagement needs for stakeholders » Optimize alignment between stakeholder needs, expectations, and project objectives Build trust and influence stakeholders to accomplish project objectives	13.2 Plan Stakeholder Engagement 13.3 Manage Stakeholder Engagement 13.3 Monitor Stakeholder Engagement
Task 10	Build a shared understanding » Break down situation to identify the root cause of a misunderstanding » Survey all necessary parties to reach consensus » Support outcome of parties' agreement Investigate potential misunderstandings	9.5 Manage Team 9.6 Control Resources
Task 11	Engage and support virtual teams » Examine virtual team member needs (e.g., environment, geography, culture, global, etc.) » Investigate alternatives (e.g., communication tools, colocation) for virtual team member engagement » Implement options for virtual team member engagement Continually evaluate the effectiveness of virtual team member engagement	9.5 Manage Team 9.6 Control Resources
Task 12	Define team ground rules » Communicate organizational principles with team and external stakeholders » Establish an environment that fosters adherence to the ground rules Manage and rectify ground-rule violations	9.6 Control Resources 10.1 Plan Communication Management 10.2 Manage Communications
Task 13	Mentor relevant stakeholders » Allocate the time to mentoring Recognize and act on mentoring opportunities	10.3 Monitor Stakeholders 13.3 Manage Stakeholder Engagement
Task 14	Promote team performance through the application of emotional intelligence » Assess behavior through the use of personality indicators Analyze personality indicators and adjust to the emotional needs of key project stakeholders	9.5 Manage resources 9.6 Control resources

Domain II	Process—50%	How It Maps to PMBOK 6
Task 1	Execute project with the urgency required to deliver business value » Assess opportunities to deliver value incrementally » Examine the business value throughout the project » Support the team to subdivide project tasks as necessary to find the minimum viable product	4.1 Develop Project Charter 4.3 Direct and Manage Project 5.4 Create WBS
Task 2	Manage communications » Analyze the communication needs of all stakeholders » Determine communication methods, channels, frequency, and level of detail for all stakeholders » Communicate project information and updates effectively » Confirm communication is understood and feedback is received	10.1 Plan Communication Management 10.2 Manage Communications 10.3 Monitor Communications
Task 3	Assess and manage risks » Determine risk management options » Iteratively assess and prioritize risks	11.1 Plan Risk Management 11.2 Identify Risks 11.3 Perform Qualitative Risk Analysis 11.4 Perform Quantitative Risk Analysis
Task 4	Engage stakeholders » Analyze stakeholders (e.g., power interest grid, influence, impact) » Categorize stakeholders » Engage stakeholders by category » Develop, execute, and validate a strategy for stakeholder engagement	13.1 Identify Stakeholders 13.2 Plan Stakeholder Management 13.3 Manage Stakeholders
Task 5	Plan and manage budget and resources » Estimate budgetary needs based on the scope of the project and lessons learned from past projects » Anticipate future budget challenges » Monitor budget variations and work with the governance process to adjust as necessary » Plan and manage resources	7.1 Plan Cost Management 7.2 Estimate Costs 7.3 Determine Budget
Task 6	Plan and manage schedule » Estimate project tasks (milestones, dependencies, story points) » Utilize benchmarks and historical data » Prepare schedule based on the methodology » Measure ongoing progress based on the methodology » Modify schedule as needed based on the methodology Coordinate with other projects and other operations	6.1 Plan Schedule Management 6.2 Define Activities 6.3 Sequence Activities 6.4 Estimate Activities 6.5 Develop Schedule 4.6 Perform Integrated Change Control Program/Portfolio Management/Project Management Office
Task 7	Plan and manage quality of products/deliverables » Determine quality standard required for project deliverables » Recommend options for improvement based on quality gaps Continually survey project deliverable quality	8.1 Plan Quality Management 8.2 Manage Quality 8.3 Control Quality
Task 8	Plan and manage scope » Determine and prioritize requirements » Break down scope (e.g., WBS, backlog) Monitor and validate scope	5.1 Plan Scope Management 5.2 Collect Requirements 5.3 Define Scope

Task 9	Integrate project planning activities » Consolidate the project/phase plans » Assess consolidated project plans for dependencies, gaps, and continued business value » Analyze the data collected » Collect and analyze data to make informed project decisions Determine critical information requirements	Program/Portfolio Management/Project Management Office
Task 10	Manage project changes » Anticipate and embrace the need for change (e.g., follow change management practices) » Determine a strategy to handle change » Execute change management strategy according to the methodology Determine a change response to move the project forward	4.5 Monitor and Control Project Work 4.6 Perform Integrated Change Control
Task 11	Plan and manage procurement » Define resource requirements and needs » Communicate resource requirements » Manage suppliers/contracts » Plan and manage procurement strategy Develop a delivery solution	9.1 Plan Resource Management 9.6 Control Resources 10.2 Manage Communications 13.3 Manage Stakeholder Engagement
Task 12	Manage project artifacts » Determine the requirements (what, when, where, who, etc.) for managing the project artifacts » Validate that the project information is kept up to date (i.e., version control) and accessible to all stakeholders Continually assess the effectiveness of the management of the project artifacts	4.6 Perform Integrated Change Control 5.6 Control Scope 13.3 Manage Stakeholder Engagement
Task 13	Determine appropriate project methodology/methods and practices » Assess project needs, complexity, and magnitude » Recommend project execution strategy (e.g., contracting, finance) » Recommend a project methodology/approach (i.e., predictive, agile, hybrid) Use iterative, incremental practices throughout the project life cycle (e.g., lessons learned, stakeholder engagement, risk)	4.2 Develop Project Plan 4.3 Direct and Manage Project Work
Task 14	Establish project governance structure » Determine appropriate governance for a project (e.g., replicate organizational governance) Define escalation paths and thresholds	4.1 Develop Project Charter 4.2 Develop Project Plan 9.1 Plan Resource Management
Task 15	Manage project issues » Recognize when a risk becomes an issue » Attack the issue with the optimal action to achieve project success Collaborate with relevant stakeholders on the approach to resolve the issues	11.6 Implement Risk Responses 11.7 Monitor Risks 13.3 Manage Stakeholder Engagement
Task 16	Ensure knowledge transfer for project continuity » Discuss project responsibilities within the team » Outline expectations for the working environment Confirm approach for knowledge transfers	4.3 Direct and Manage Project Work 4.4 Manage Project Knowledge
Task 17	Plan and manage project/phase closure or transitions » Determine criteria to successfully close the project or phase » Validate readiness for transition (e.g., to operations team or next phase) Conclude activities to close out project or phase (e.g., final lessons learned, retrospective, procurement, financials, resources)	4.2 Develop Project Plan 4.3 Direct and Manage Project Work 4.7 Close Project or Phase 5.5 Validate Scope

Domain III	Business Environment—8%	How It Maps to PMBOK 6
Task 1	Plan and manage project compliance » Confirm project compliance requirements (e.g., security, health, and safety, regulatory compliance) » Classify compliance categories » Determine potential threats to compliance » Use methods to support compliance » Analyze the consequences of noncompliance » Determine the necessary approach and action to address compliance needs (e.g., risk, legal) » Measure the extent to which the project is in compliance	4.1 Develop Project Charter
Task 2	Evaluate and deliver project benefits and value » Investigate that benefits are identified » Document agreement on ownership for ongoing benefit realization » Verify measurement system is in place to track benefits » Evaluate delivery options to demonstrate the value » Appraise stakeholders of value gain progress	4.1 Develop Project Charter Statement of Work Business Need Business Case
Task 3	Evaluate and address external business environment changes for impact on the scope » Survey changes to external business environment (e.g., regulations, technology, geopolitical, market) » Assess and prioritize impact on project scope/backlog based on changes in the external business environment » Recommend options for scope/backlog changes (e.g., schedule, cost changes) » Continually review the external business environment for impacts on project scope/backlog	Enterprise External Factors
Task 4	Support organizational change » Assess organizational culture » Evaluate the impact of organizational change to project and determine required actions » Evaluate the impact of the project on the organization and determine required actions	Organizational Process Assets

What Do I Need to Know About the Application Process?

Price

» Member: US $405

» Nonmember: US $555

Prerequisites

» A secondary degree (high school diploma, associate's degree, or the global equivalent)

» 7,500 hours leading and directing projects

» 35 hours of project management education

or

» Four-year degree

» 4,500 hours leading and directing projects

» 35 hours of project management education

Tips

» When filling out the application to register for the exam, your résumé should be in language PMI understands. Use key terms such as *deliverables*, *objectives*, *planning*, *initiating*, *executing*, *monitoring*, *controlling*, and *closing*. (See the sample project descriptions below.)

» PMI does not care whether you submit 1 or 100 projects if you meet the criteria.

» It is not necessary for you to have managed a project from initiation to closing.

» You must have experience in all five process groups.

» PMI only contacts you if there are issues with your application.

» Audits are entirely random. If you should get audited, the PMI team will look to verify your degree or diploma, project management experience, and 35 hours of continuing PM education.

Sample Project Description (Poor)

Darron Clark built an impressive record of:

» Achievements deploying and enhancing Oracle environments;

» Training and mentoring teams on Oracle technologies;

» Project management and administration best practices; and

» Leading the delivery of strategic projects and resolving critical issues for clients within the financial services, entertainment, manufacturing, and telecommunications industries.

Sample Project Description (Better)

This project benefited the managing director.

» In the **initiating** phase, my team determined the **stakeholders** who would be affected by this new project, which was to automate a data replication environment to be faster.

» In the **planning** phase, my team met to gather all requirements and determine **deliverables**.

» In the **executing** phase, the team members executed their roles and responsibilities.

» In the **monitoring and control** phase, I contacted team members to ascertain the status.

» In the **closing** phase, the reporting scripts were **delivered**, **accepted**, and **validated**.

			Project Management Process Groups		

	Initiating	Planning	Executing	Monitoring and Controlling	Closing
[4] Project Integration Management	4.1 Develop Project Charter	4.2 Develop Project Management Plan	4.3 Direct and Manage Project Work 4.4 Manage Project Knowledge	4.5 Monitor and Control Project Work 4.6 Perform Integrated Change Control	4.7 Close Project or Phase
[5] Project Scope Management		5.1 Plan Scope Management 5.2 Collect Requirements 5.3 Define Scope 5.4 Create WBS		5.5 Validate Scope 5.6 Control Scope	
[6] Project Schedule Management		6.1 Plan Schedule Management 6.2 Define Activities 6.3 Sequence Activities 6.4 Estimate Activity Durations 6.5 Develop Schedule		6.6 Control Schedule	
[7] Project Cost Management		7.1 Plan Cost Management 7.2 Estimate Costs 7.3 Determine Budget		7.4 Control Costs	
[8] Project Quality Management		8.1 Plan Quality Management	8.2 Manage Quality	8.3 Control Quality	
[9] Project Resource Management		9.1 Plan Resource Management 9.2 Estimate Activity Resources	9.3 Acquire Resources 9.4 Develop Team 9.5 Manage Team	9.6 Control Resources	
[10] Project Communications Management		10.1 Plan Communications Management	10.2 Manage Communications	10.3 Monitor Communications	
[11] Project Risk Management		11.1 Plan Risk Management 11.2 Identify Risks 11.3 Perform Qualitative Risk Analysis 11.4 Perform Quantitative Risk Analysis 11.5 Plan Risk Responses	11.6 Implement Risk Responses	11.7 Monitor Risks	
[12] Project Procurement Management		12.1 Plan Procurement Management	12.2 Conduct Procurements	12.3 Control Procurements	
[13] Project Stakeholder Management	13.1 Identify Stakeholders	13.2 Plan Stakeholder Engagement	13.3 Manage Stakeholder Engagement	13.4 Monitor Stakeholder Engagement	

Note: This is a typical PMP exam question. The problem has nothing to do with the answer. Focus on the "ask": for example, "All are found in the project charter except" or "As a project manager, what do you do next?"

"As a Project Manager, What Would You Do Next?" Questions

When I took the PMP exam, it seemed this wording was coming up in every question. This made the questions difficult to answer because I found no book teaching them this way, and no instructors were teaching this format. This was a question asked 80–85% of the time on the PMP exam. If you don't understand how to win this question, the exam will be more difficult to pass.

The key to answering this type of question correctly is as follows:

- Sometimes, answering an "As a project manager, what would you do next?" questions is a matter of knowing where a process comes in the five process groups and 49 processes.

- Once you know the process group you are in, the question becomes more answerable.

    a) Initiating group—For example, if a question suggests high-level requirements, high-level risks, or initial stakeholders, you are in the initial group. If the project charter has not been accepted, then the answer will be in the develop project charter or identify stakeholders process. If the project charter has been accepted, then you will need to narrow the answer from planning, executing, monitoring, and controlling and closing process groups.

    b) Planning group—all processes in the planning group are in order from develop project management plan to plan stakeholder engagement. If the question asks what comes next for define scope, the answer choices are from create WBS to plan stakeholder engagement. For example, If the question asks what comes before define scope, then the answer choices are from collect requirements to develop project management plan.

    c) Executing group—when a question is clearly in the execute group, then horizontal first, then vertical. For example, if the question asks what is next after direct and manage project work, then the answer is under monitoring and controlling, such as monitor and control project work or control costs. If there is no answer in monitoring and controlling, then the answer is vertical, such as manage project knowledge.

    d) Monitoring and controlling costs—this will depend on the question as well. If the question asks what is next, the answer could be vertical, with a process under monitoring and controlling, or horizontal, in which the project moves to closing. It depends on whether the question asks about the status of the project or suggests the project is accepting all deliverables, or the project is cancelling. Checking the status of the project is vertical from monitoring and control project work to monitor stakeholder engagement. Accepting all deliverables or cancelling immediately moves to closing the project.

e) Closing process group—if the process has all deliverables accepted or canceled, then you are in the closing process group and need to know the order of the closing process

  1. Obtain acceptance of deliverables

  2. Conduct post-project or phase-end review

  3. Record impact of tailoring any process

  4. Document lessons learned

  5. Apply appropriate updates to organizational process assets (OPA)

  6. Archive all relevant project documents

  7. Close out all procurement activities

  8. Perform team member assessments

- The PMP exam tests whether you know the difference between process groups, knowledge areas, processes, inputs, outputs, and tools and techniques.

- Other times, the PMP exam wants to know the best answer out of the choices provided.

The PMP exam is not testing if you are a project manager or if you will make a good or great project manager. The PMP exam is testing whether you can speak and understand the language of project management at this level.

Exercise to Conquer the "As a Project Manager, What Would You Do Next?" Questions

Project Management Process	Knowledge Area	Process Group	Describe the Process	What Was the Process That Came Before?	What Is the Process That Comes After?
Define Scope					
Develop Project Plan					
Sequence Activities					
Determine Budget					
Plan Procurement Management					
Direct and Manage Project Work					
Develop Team					
Implement Risk Responses					
Perform Integrated Change Control					
Control Costs					
Monitor Communications					
Close Project or Phase					
Collect Requirements					
Estimate Costs					
Perform Quantitative Risk Analysis					
Manage Quality					

Answers to "As a Project Manager, What Would You Do Next?" Questions

Project Management Process	Knowledge Area	Process Group	Describe the Process	What Was the Process That Came Before?	What Is the Process That Comes After?
Define Scope	Scope Management	Planning	What needs to be done to create the scope statement	Collect Requirements	Create WBS
Develop Project Plan	Integration Management	Planning	What needs to be done to create the project management plan	Develop Project Charter	Plan Scope Management
Sequence Activities	Schedule Management	Planning	What needs to be done to order activities	Define Activities	Estimate Activity Durations
Determine Budget	Cost Management	Planning	What needs to be done to determine the planned cost of the project	Estimate Costs	Plan Quality Management
Plan Procurement Management	Procurement Management	Planning	What needs to be done to external resources	Plan Risk Responses	Plan Stakeholder Management
Direct and Manage Project Work	Integration Management	Executing	What needs to be done to manage the project	Develop Project Management Plan	Monitor and Control Project Work
Develop Team	Resource Management	Planning	What needs to be done to train the team	Acquire Resources	Manage Team
Implement Risk Responses	Risk Management	Planning	What needs to be done to apply the risk response plan	Plan Risk Responses	Monitor Risks
Perform Integrated Change Control	Integration Management	Monitoring and Controlling	What needs to be done to manage approved project changes	Monitor and Control Project Work	Close Project and Phase
Control Costs	Cost Management	Monitoring and Controlling	What needs to be done to manage approved cost changes	Determine Budget	Direct and Manage Project Work
Monitor Communications	Communications Management	Executing	What needs to be done to track communication	Manage Communications	Close project or phase
Close Project or Phase	Integration Management	Closing	What needs to be done to end the project	Validate Scope	None
Collect Requirements	Scope Management	Planning	What needs to be done to capture requirements for the project	Plan Scope Management	Define Scope
Estimate Costs	Cost Management	Planning	What needs to be done to capture all costs related to the project	Plan Cost Management	Determine Budget
Perform Quantitative Risk Analysis	Risks Management	Planning	What needs to be done to manage and track approved changes	Perform Qualitative Risk Analysis	Plan Risk Responses
Manage Quality	Quality Management	Executing	What needs to be done to produce products within agreed-upon parameters	Plan Quality Management	Control Quality

Practice Exams

84 Questions on People

1. Abraham is a project manager on an existing project at the Best Acting Company Inc., which sells dreams. After the project kickoff, Abraham and his project team are managing the team resources process. The project plan has been approved. As a project manager, what will Abraham do next?

    a) Create WBS

    b) Control resources

    c) Perform team development

    d) Monitor stakeholder engagement

Answer: c. Performing team development is the next step for the project manager. After the project kickoff the project is in the Execute phase. Create WBS is in the planning phase. Control resources and stakeholder engagement are in the monitoring and control phase.

2. Jonathan is a project manager at a solar car company. Jonathan wants to develop a document that will give him the best chance of managing the project from start to completion. Which document does the project manager need to create next?

    a) Project management plan

    b) Project documents updates

    c) Work performance reports

    d) Team performance

Answer: a. Jonathan needs to create a project management plan which is used by the project manager to manage the project from start to completion. Project documents is not used to track project from start to completion. Work performance reports is a document that shows how well project is performing.

3. Robert is a new project manager at Use It or Lose It! Inc. Robert does not trust his employees to do their jobs, so he must monitor their every action to make sure he gets the results he wants. As a project manager, what is Robert practicing?

    a) RAM

    b) Expectancy Theory

c) McGregor's Theory X

d) McGregor's Theory Y

Answer: c. McGregor's Theory X assumes that the typical worker has little ambition, avoids responsibility, and is individual-goal oriented. McGregor's Theory Y assumes employees are internally motivated, enjoy their jobs, and work to better themselves without a direct reward in return.

4. Quasar is a project manager who wants to run an efficient project that completes on time and under budget to the client's satisfaction. When performing the develop project plan process, what will be the output document the project manager will want the most?

    a) Project management plan

    b) Project documents updates

    c) Work performance reports

    d) Team performance

Answer: a. The project management plan is the document the project manager will want most.

5. As the project manager, you have just introduced a new contractor to the project team. What is the correct order of team development according to Tuckerman's ladder?

    a) Forming, storming, norming, performing, and adjourning

    b) Performing, storming, norming, forming, and adjourning

    c) Performing, storming, adjourning, forming, and norming

    d) Forming, norming, storming, performing, and adjourning

Answer: a. Only a is in the correct order.

6. Olivia is a new project manager at World of Crowe Inc. Olivia trusts her employees to do their jobs, so she does not monitor their every action to make sure she gets the results she wants. What is the project manager practicing?

    a) RAM

    b) McGregor's Theory X

    c) Expectancy Theory

    d) McGregor's Theory Y

Answer: d. McGregor's Theory Y assumes employees are internally motivated, enjoy their jobs, and work to better themselves without a direct reward in return. McGregor's Theory X assumes that the typical worker has little ambition, avoids responsibility, and is individual-goal oriented.

7.   As a project manager, you have just introduced a new team member to the project. What are the correct elements for Tuckerman's ladder on team development?

   a) Performing, storming, norming, forming, and adjourning

   b) Starting, storming, norming, performing, and adjourning

   c) Performing, storming, adjusting, forming, and norming

   d) Forming, norming, storming, performing, and closing

Answer: a. Only a has all the correct elements. Starting, adjusting, and closing are not part of Tuckerman's ladder.

8.   David is a new project manager for New Brand Cola LLC. David wants to get off to the best start in understanding the project, people, and environment. As a project manager, David has discovered interpersonal and team skills as a tool and technique of which process?

   a) Meetings

   b) Develop project charter

   c) Organizational process assets

   d) Planning

Answer: b. Develop project charter is the only process on this list. Meetings is a tool and technique for many processes. Organizational process assets are input to many processes, and planning is a process group.

9.   Lucia is a new project manager for Razor LLC. Lucia wants to get off to the best start in understanding the project, people, and environment. Meetings are a tool and technique of which process?

   a) Meetings

   b) Develop project charter

   c) Organizational process assets

   d) Planning

Answer: b. Develop project charter is the only process on this list. Meetings is a tool and technique for many processes. Organizational process assets are input to many processes, and planning is a process group.

10. Barron is a new project manager for Best Cereal Products LLC. Barron wants to get off to the best start in understanding the project, people, and environment. All the following are inputs to the develop project charter process except

    a) SOW

    b) Enterprise environmental factors

    c) Organizational process assets

    d) Data gathering

Answer: d. Data gathering is a tool and technique, not an input.

11. Candy is a seasoned project manager at a pickle factory. The project manager needs which tool and technique to collect information?

    a) SOW

    b) Enterprise environmental factors

    c) Organizational process assets

    d) Data gathering

Answer: d. Data gathering is a tool and technique. SOW, enterprise environmental factors, and organizational process assets are inputs for develop project charter.

12. You are a new project manager for an existing project with issues. What document does the project manager need to determine the project goals, high-level risks, and high-level constraints?

    a) Communication plan

    b) Project management plan

    c) SOW

    d) Project charter

Answer: d. The communication plan is a document for planning communication of the project. The project management plan plans the overall activities of the project and contains detailed requirements of the project. The SOW is the statement of work, which includes the objectives of the project. The project charter contains the high-level requirements of the project.

13. You are a new project manager for an existing project with issues. As the project manager, what document do you need to determine how, when, and the level of authority the stakeholders communicate?

    a) Communication management plan

    b) Project management plan

    c) SOW

    d) Project charter

Answer: a. The communication management plan is a document for planning communication of the project. The project management plan plans the overall activities of the project and contains detailed requirements of the project. The SOW is the statement of work, which includes the objectives of the project. The project charter contains the high-level requirements of the project.

14. Priscilla is a project manager who transferred from another department. One of the documents Priscilla must create is vital to the success of the project in meeting its deliverables. Which document is created from the output of the develop project management plan process?

    a) Project charter

    b) Enterprise environmental factors

    c) Project management plan

    d) Organizational process assets

Answer: c. Project charter, EEF, and OPA are all inputs to the process.

15. Jonathan is the senior project manager for a High-energy company. In the beginning stages of the project, Jonathan spends much of his time conversing with the sponsor and senior management to develop a document that gives the project manager authority to commit resources to the project. What is the output of the develop project charter process?

    a) Project charter

    b) Enterprise environmental factors

    c) Project management plan

    d) Organizational process assets

Answer: a. The project management plan is the output of the process to develop the project management plan. EEF and OPA are inputs of other processes.

16. The following are tools and techniques for the develop project management plan process except

    a) Meetings

    b) Project management plan

    c) Interpersonal and team skills

    d) Expert judgments

Answer: b. The project management plan is the output of the process, not a tool and technique.

17. Ulysses is a new project manager on an existing project. The project has been in its planning stage. The process that has just been completed is collect requirements. As a project manager, what would you do next?

    a) Define scope

    b) Project management plan

    c) Plan scope management

    d) Expert judgments

Answer: a. Define scope is the planning process that would be performed next. The project management plan is an output of develop project management plan. Plan scope management would have been done previously to collect requirements. Expert judgments is a tool and technique.

18. David has been a project manager for many years. David has been communicating with the sponsor and senior management, combining SOW, assumptions, initial stakeholders, and high-level risk into one document. As the project manager, which of the following documents is he creating?

    a) Data gathering

    b) Project management plan

    c) Inspection

    d) Project charter

Answer: d. The project charter contains the objectives and other information needed to create the PMP. Data gathering and inspection are tools and techniques. The project management plan is the output of the process.

19. Danny is a new project manager on an existing project. The project has been in its planning stage. The process that has just been completed is collect requirements. As a project manager, what would you do next?

    a) Project management plan

    b) Define activities

    c) Plan scope management

    d) Expert judgments

Answer: b. Define activities is the planning process that would be performed next. The project management plan is an output of develop project management plan. Plan scope management would have been done previously to collect requirements. Expert judgments are a tool and technique.

20. Deliverables are an output of which process group?

    a) Organizational process assets

    b) Enterprise environmental factors

    c) Final report

    d) Direct and manage project work

Answer: d. Organizational process assets and enterprise environmental factors are inputs to many process groups. The final report is an output of the close project or phase process group.

21. Luke is a new project manager on an existing project. The project has been in its planning stage. The process that has just completed is define activities. As a project manager, what process did you determine was done previously to define activities?

    a) Define scope

    b) Project management plan

    c) Plan schedule management

    d) Expert judgments

Answer: c. Plan schedule management is the planning process that would have been performed prior to define activities. The project management plan is an output of develop project management plan. Plan scope management would have been done previously to collect requirements. Expert judgments is a tool and technique.

22. Which of the following is a tool and technique of direct and manage project work?

    a) Change requests

    b) PMIS

    c) Project management plan

    d) OPA updates

Answer: b. Change requests are an output of perform integrated change control process, the project management plan is an output of develop project plan process, and OPA updates are outputs of other processes. Only b is a tool and technique.

23. Shaq is a new project manager on an existing project. The project has been in its planning stage. The process that has just been completed is define activities. As a project manager, what process did he determine was done prior to define activities?

    a) Define scope

    b) Project management plan

    c) Data gathering

    d) Create WBS

Answer: d. Create WBS is the planning process that would have been performed prior to define activities. The project management plan is an output of develop project management plan. Plan scope management would have been done prior to collect requirements. Data gathering is a tool and technique.

24. Which process best exemplifies monitoring and control in project integration?

    a) Direct and manage project work

    b) Monitor and control project work

    c) Manage project knowledge

    d) Perform integrated change control

Answer: b. Choices a, c, and d are not the best exemplification of monitoring and control in project integration.

25. Glover is a new project manager on an existing project. The project has been in its execute stage. The process that has just been completed is define activities. As a project manager, which process will he do next?

    a) Define scope

    b) Validate scope

    c) Data gathering

    d) Create WBS

Answer: b. Validate scope is the process that would be performed next because the project is in the execute phase. When execute starts, then the monitor control process starts. Project management and plan scope management are planning processes. Data gathering is a tool and technique.

26. Harry is a contractor responsible for the refurbishment of an automobile showroom. The estimated refurbishment cost is $500 per square foot. The total showroom area that needs to be refurbished is 1,000 square feet. Based on Harry's experience, he knows his team can refurbish 100 square feet per week. As a project manager, how should Harry report how the project is performing?

    a) On schedule and on budget

    b) Behind schedule and over budget

    c) Ahead of schedule and over budget

    d) Behind schedule and ahead of budget

Answer: c. Harry will report the project ahead of schedule and over budget.

Cost Variance	(EV - AC) = ($25,000.00)
Schedule Variance	(EV - PV) = $25,000.00

27. Sophia is a contractor responsible for the refurbishment of an automobile showroom. The estimated refurbishment cost is $500 per square foot. The total showroom area that needs to be refurbished is 1,000 square feet. Based on Sophia's past experience, she knows her team can refurbish 100 square feet per week. As the project manager, how should Sophia report the steady-state progress of the project?

    a) $525,000

    b) $375,000

    c) $555,555.56

    d) $475,000

Answer: c. Sophia will report the steady-state as $555,555.56.

Estimate at Completion (typical, steady-state, or continuous)	(BAC / CPI) = $555,555.56

28. Jeffrey is a contractor responsible for the refurbishment of an automobile showroom. The estimated refurbishment cost is $500 per square foot. The total showroom area that needs to be refurbished is 1,000 square feet. Based on Jeffrey's experience, he knows his team can refurbish 100 square feet per week. As a project manager, how should Jeffrey report the forecast estimate at completion to senior management?

    a) $525,000

    b) $375,000

    c) $555,555.56

    d) $516,224.19

Answer: d. Jeffrey should report the estimate at completion as $516,224.19.

29. The process of defining how to estimate, acquire, manage, and utilize physical and team resources is

    a) Develop team

    b) Plan resource management

    c) Organizational theory

    d) Team charter

Answer: b. The keyword here is "how," which describes the plan—in this case, plan resource management.

30. All of the following are inputs to manage a team except

    a) Project management plan

    b) Project documents updates

    c) Work performance reports

    d) Team performance

Answer: b. Project document updates is an output.

31. Jonathan is a new project manager at Warm Hands Glove Company Inc. Jonathan does not trust his employees to do their jobs, so he must monitor their every action to make sure he gets the results he wants. Jonathan is practicing

   a) RAM

   b) McGregor's Theory X

   c) Expectancy Theory

   d) McGregor's Theory Y

Answer: b. McGregor's Theory X assumes that the typical worker has little ambition, avoids responsibility, and is individual-goal oriented. McGregor's Theory Y assumes employees are internally motivated, enjoy their jobs, and work to better themselves without a direct reward in return.

32. Antonio is a new project manager on an existing project. The project has been in its execute stage. The process that has just been completed is estimate costs. As a project manager, which process will Antonio do next?

   a) Define scope

   b) Control costs

   c) Data gathering

   d) Create WBS

Answer: b. Control costs is the process that would be performed next since the project is in the execute phase; money is being spent, so the cost must be controlled. When execute starts, then the monitor control process starts. Data gathering is a tool and technique. Define scope and create WBS are planning processes.

33. What is the correct order of team development?

   a) Performing, storming, norming, forming, and adjourning

   b) Forming, storming, norming, performing, and adjourning

   c) Forming, norming, storming, performing, and adjourning

   d) Performing, storming, adjourning, forming, and norming

Answer: b. Only b is in the correct order.

34. Sabrina is a new project manager on an existing project. The project has been canceled by senior management without cause. As a project manager, what will Sabrina do next?

    a) Negotiate with management to keep the project going

    b) Negotiate with the sponsor to keep the project going for a few more weeks because things can be turned around

    c) Begin the closing process immediately

    d) Continue the project until she has heard from the sponsor

Answer: c. Once the project manager has been notified by senior management or the sponsor that the project is being canceled, then the closing procedure must begin immediately.

35. The process of defining how to estimate, acquire, manage, and utilize physical and team resources is

    a) Develop team

    b) Team Charter Plan resource management

    c) Organizational theory

    d) Plan resource management Team charter

Answer: d. The fact that the question asks "how to" indicates the project is in the planning stage. Develop team is a process in the execute stage. Organizational theory and team charter are not processes.

36. Mark is a new project manager on an existing project. The project has moved beyond the planning stage. The vendor chosen to complete a portion of the project has started work. As a project manager, what will Mark do next?

    a) Plan what is expected of outside vendors

    b) Ask the vendor for closing reports and place in archives

    c) Control procurements

    d) Continue the project until he has heard from the sponsor

Answer: c. Once the contractor has started work, they will be monitored and tracked to make sure the results are being established according to the project plan and the vendor contract. Closing reports for archive comes in the closing phase. Planning what is expected of the vendor would have been performed in the planning stage.

37. Pepper is a new project manager for TF Banking Services. Pepper is in the process of acquiring resources. All are tools and techniques Pepper can use to aid in her search except

    a) Virtual teams

    b) Multicriteria analysis

    c) Resource management plan

    d) Negotiation

Answer: c. The resource management plan is a document and is the output of plan resource management.

38. The process of defining how to estimate, acquire, manage, and utilize physical and team resources is

    a) Develop team

    b) Plan resource management

    c) Organizational theory

    d) Team charter

Answer: b. Plan resource management is part of the planning stage and answers the question of how to estimate, acquire, manage, and utilize physical and team resources. Develop team is also a process but in the execute stage and would best fit training a resource. Choices c and d are not processes.

39. John is a new project manager on an existing project. The project is now in the execute stage. John and his project team know the plan resources they need, what the resources will do, and how long the work will take. As a project manager, what will John do next?

    a) Control resources

    b) Develop team

    c) Manage team

    d) Acquire resources

Answer: d. Since the project is now in the execute stage, the order of what occurs next is acquire resources, develop team, and manage resources.

40. What is the correct order of Tuckman's ladder?

    a) Forming, storming, norming, performing, adjourning

    b) Adjourning, forming, storming, norming, performing

c) Performing, forming, storming, norming, adjourning

d) Storming, norming, forming, performing, adjourning

Answer: a. Choices b,c, and d are not in the correct order.

41. Luther is a new project manager on an existing project. The project is now in the execute stage. Luther and his project team know the plan resources they need, what the resources will do, and how long the work will take. As a project manager, what will Luther do next?

a) Control resources

b) Develop team

c) Manage team

d) Determine stakeholders

Answer: c. Develop team will be the project manager's next task. Since the project is now in the execute stage, the order of what occurs next is acquire resources, develop team, and manage resources.

42. Robert is a new project manager at Fresh Minds, Inc. Robert does not trust his employees to do their jobs, so he must monitor their every action to make sure he gets the results he wants. Robert is practicing

a) RAM

b) McGregor's Theory X

c) Expectancy Theory

d) McGregor's Theory Y

Answer: b. McGregor's Theory X assumes that the typical worker has little ambition, avoids responsibility, and is individual-goal oriented. McGregor's Theory Y assumes employees are internally motivated, enjoy their jobs, and work to better themselves without a direct reward in return.

43. Ashley is a new project manager on an existing project. The project has now in the execute stage. Ashley and his project team know the plan resources they need, what the resources will do, and how long the work will take. As a project manager, what will Ashley do next?

a) Control resources

b) Train management

c) Lay out a grand plan for the project

d) Determine stakeholders

Answer: a. Control resources will be the project manager's next task. Since the project is now in the execute stage, the order of what occurs next is acquire resources, develop team, and manage resources. However, since none of these options are there, the choice that best answers the question is control resources.

44. Michelle is a project manager for a bookseller. One of her projects is improving the ways books can be found without assistance from the staff. Michelle needs to introduce a new member to the project team. What is the correct order of team development?

    a) Performing, storming, norming, forming, and adjourning

    b) Performing, storming, adjourning, forming, and norming

    c) Forming, norming, storming, performing, and adjourning

    d) Forming, storming, norming, performing, and adjourning

Answer: d. Only d is in the correct order.

45. The process of defining how to estimate, acquire, manage, and utilize physical and team resources is

    a) Develop team

    b) Organizational theory

    c) Plan resource management

    d) Team charter

Answer: c. Plan resource management defines how to estimate, acquire, manage, and utilize physical and team resources.

46. Pepper is a new project manager for TF Banking Services. Pepper is in the process of acquiring resources. All are tools and techniques Pepper can use to aid in her search except

    a) Virtual teams

    b) Multicriteria analysis

    c) Resource management plan

    d) Negotiation

Answer: c. The resource management plan is an output of plan resource management.

47. David is a new project manager for Monorail Enterprises. David wants to get off to the best start in understanding the project, people, and environment. Interpersonal and team skills is a tool and technique of which process?

    a) Meetings

    b) Develop project charter

    c) Organizational process assets

    d) Planning

Answer: b. Develop project charter is the only process on this list. Meetings is a tool and technique for many processes. Organizational process assets are an input to many processes, and planning is a process group.

48. All the following are inputs to the develop project charter process except

    a) SOW

    b) Enterprise environmental factors

    c) Organizational process assets

    d) Data gathering

Answer: d. Data gathering is a tool and technique, not an input.

49. You are a new project manager for an existing project with issues. What document do you need to determine the project goals, high-level risks, and high-level constraints?

    a) Communication plan

    b) Project management plan

    c) SOW

    d) Project charter

Answer: d. The communication plan is a document for planning communication of the project. The project management plan plans the overall activities of the project and contains detailed requirements of the project. The SOW is the statement of work, which includes the objectives of the project. The project charter contains the high-level requirements of the project.

50. Which is an output of the validate scope process?

    a) Work performance data

    b) Acceptable deliverables

    c) Verified deliverables

    d) Work performance information

Answer: b. The output of validate scope is acceptable deliverables. Validate scope formalizes the acceptance of the completed project deliverables. Verified deliverables are the output of the project tasks. Work performance data is raw data that is reported on change requests. Work performance information is the work performance data that has been transformed for example, number of change requests or forecast estimates.

51. Samantha is a new project manager on an existing project. After the project kickoff, Samantha and her project team have completed collection of all requirements and determined the scope. The project plan has been approved. As a project manager, what will Samantha do next?

    a) Create WBS

    b) Validate scope

    c) Lay out a grand plan for the project

    d) Negotiate with the sponsor for overtime

Answer: b. Validate scope is the best option here. Create WBS is performed in the planning process, in which the project plan has already been approved. Answer c is the approved project plan. The negotiation with a sponsor for overtime response is already answered in the project plan with the creation and approval of the schedule baseline.

52. Which answer best describes the stakeholder engagement plan?

    a) The process of developing approaches to involve project stakeholders based on their needs and expectations, addressing issues, and fostering appropriate stakeholder engagement involvement

    b) The process of monitoring project stakeholder relationships and tailoring strategies for engaging stakeholders through the modification of engagement strategies and plans

    c) The process of communicating and working with stakeholders to meet their needs and expectations

    d) The process of not communicating and working with stakeholders to meet their needs and expectations

Answer: a. If the question asks for a plan, then b is not the answer. Answer c is executing the plan. Answer d is not correct because you always want to communicate in project management. The process of developing is a "plan" type of answer.

53. William is a new project manager on an existing project. After the project kickoff, William and his project team have completed the plan procurement management process. The project plan has not been approved. As a project manager, what will William do next?

    a) Create WBS

    b) Validate scope

    c) Plan stakeholder engagement

    d) Negotiate with the sponsor for overtime

Answer: c. The next step in the planning stage after plan procurement management is to plan the stakeholder engagement process. Create WBS happens earlier in the planning stage, and validate scope is in the execute stage. Project managers will not negotiate with the sponsor.

54. Tomas is a junior project manager for a pharmaceutical company. One of Tomas's roles is to assist in the development of a project charter. What document is from the plan stakeholder engagement process?

    a) Assumption and constraint analysis

    b) Stakeholder engagement plan

    c) Project management plan

    d) Process improvement plan

Answer: b. Assumption and constraint analysis is a tool and technique. Choices c and d are outputs of other processes.

55. One of the duties of a project manager is the process of communicating and working with stakeholders to meet their needs and expectations, address issues, and foster appropriate involvement. As a project manager, what do you do next?

    a) Manage stakeholder engagement

    b) Monitor communications

    c) Manage communications

    d) Monitor stakeholder engagement

Answer: a. The difference between monitoring and managing is that monitoring is watching or observing. Managing is an action in which you are actually doing something. In this case, it is the "process of communicating and working with stakeholders."

56. Jesus is a new project manager on an existing project. After the project kickoff, Jesus and his project team have completed the plan stakeholder engagement process and are managing the stakeholder engagements. The project plan has been approved. As a project manager, what will Jesus do next?

    a) Create WBS

    b) Validate scope

    c) Plan stakeholder engagement

    d) Monitor stakeholder engagement

Answer: d. The next thing the project manager will do is monitor the stakeholder engagement as part of the project plan.

57. Kazem is a project manager with many years of experience. Kazem knows how important customer communication and satisfaction are to project management. What is the best definition of the monitor stakeholder engagement process?

    a) The process of identifying project stakeholders regularly and analyzing and documenting relevant information regarding their interests, involvement, interdependencies, influence, and impact on project success

    b) The process of communicating and working with stakeholders to meet their needs and expectations, address issues, and foster appropriate stakeholder engagement

    c) The process of providing an overview of the project stakeholder management process

    d) The process of monitoring project stakeholder relationships and tailoring strategies for engaging stakeholders through the modification of engagement strategies and plans

Answer: d. Option a is identifying stakeholders, b is manage stakeholder engagement, and c does not exist.

58. Joaquim is a very seasoned and energetic project manager. Recently, Joaquim's emails to some stakeholders have gone unanswered. When some stakeholders do respond, Joaquim must decide how to answer their concerns. Joaquim should do all the following in monitor stakeholder engagement except

    a) Managing stakeholder relationships

    b) Ignoring the stakeholders until they go away

c) Engaging with the stakeholders

d) Formulating strategies with the stakeholders

Answer: b. You would think answer b would be common sense, but it is surprising how many testers will miss a question like this on the exam. You never ignore stakeholders because communication, collaboration, and compromise are primary tools of a project manager.

59. Jeffrey is a project manager responsible for the delivery of a solar car prototype. There are many moving parts to a project on the cutting edge of technology. Resources such as people and equipment for solar technology are not as common. Jeffrey must learn the language of solar technology to deliver the project successfully. As project manager, which of the following is Jeffery not going to use as an input to manage team?

a) Project management plan

b) Project documents updates

c) Work performance reports

d) Team performance

Answer: b. Project document updates is an output. All others are inputs to one or more processes.

60. Andy is a project manager on an existing project. After the project kickoff, Andy and his project team have completed the acquire resources process. The project plan has been approved. As a project manager, what will Andy do next?

a) Create WBS

b) Develop team

c) Plan stakeholder engagement

d) Monitor stakeholder engagement

Answer: b. The next thing the project manager will do is develop a team as part of the project plan.

61. Robert is a new project manager at No Fear Inc. Robert does not trust his employees to do their jobs, so he must monitor their every action to make sure he gets the results he wants. What is Robert is practicing?

a) RAM

b) McGregor's Theory X

c) Expectancy Theory

d) McGregor's Theory Y

Answer: b. McGregor's Theory X assumes that the typical worker has little ambition, avoids responsibility, and is individual-goal oriented. McGregor's Theory Y assumes employees are internally motivated, enjoy their jobs, and work to better themselves without a direct reward in return.

62. Andy is a project manager on an existing project at the PASSMAX company, which sells passports. After the project kickoff, Andy and his project team are in the managing team resources process. The project plan has been approved. As a project manager, what will Andy do next?

   a) Create WBS

   b) Develop team

   c) Control resources

   d) Monitor stakeholder engagement

Answer: c. The next thing the project manager will do is control resources as part of the project plan. At this time, the resources have already been trained and develop. The team is producing results. As a project manager, you want to make sure the results are per the project plan.

63. As a project manager, Sandy must introduce new team members because either the previous contract did not work out, there was more work than current team members could handle, or the new team members had skills the current team members were lacking. What is the correct order of team development?

   a) Performing, storming, norming, forming, and adjourning

   b) Performing, storming, adjourning, forming, and norming

   c) Forming, norming, storming, performing, and adjourning

   d) Forming, storming, norming, performing, and adjourning

Answer: d. Only d is in the correct order.

64. Joseph is a senior project manager on an existing project for building boats. The project is currently in the execute stage. Which document will Joseph not need as an input to the manage team process?

   a) Project management plan

   b) Project documents updates

c) Work performance reports

d) Team performance

Answer: b. Project documents updates is an output.

65. Jerry is a new project manager at Cool Car Seats, Inc. Jerry does not trust his employees to do their jobs, so he must monitor their every action to make sure he gets the results he wants. Jerry is practicing

   a) RAM

   b) McGregor's Theory X

   c) Expectancy Theory

   d) McGregor's Theory Y

Answer: b. McGregor's Theory X assumes that the typical worker has little ambition, avoids responsibility, and is individual-goal oriented. McGregor's Theory Y assumes employees are internally motivated, enjoy their jobs, and work to better themselves without a direct reward in return.

66. Norman is a project manager for a ventilator company for delivery to hospitals. Norman is replacing a team member because of quality and performance issues. The new team member is getting up to speed quickly to begin producing. As the project manager, in what order will Norman perform the steps of team development?

   a) Performing, storming, norming, forming, and adjourning

   b) Performing, storming, adjourning, forming, and norming

   c) Forming, norming, storming, performing, and adjourning

   d) Forming, storming, norming, performing, and adjourning

Answer: d. Only d is in the correct order.

67. Miss Jones is a project manager on an existing project at the Best Acting Company, Inc, which sells dreams. After the project kickoff, Miss Jones and her project team are in the managing team resources process. The project plan has been approved. As a project manager, what will Miss Jones do next?

   a) Performing team development

   b) Create WBS

c) Develop team

d) Monitor stakeholder engagement

Answer: d. Develop team is the next step for the project manager.

68. Lavell is a new project manager at Prove It to Me Inc. Lavell does not trust his employees to do their jobs, so he must monitor their every action to make sure he gets the results he wants. What is Lavell practicing?

    a) RAM

    b) McGregor's Theory X

    c) Expectancy Theory

    d) McGregor's Theory Y

Answer: b. McGregor's Theory X assumes that the typical worker has little ambition, avoids responsibility, and is individual-goal oriented. McGregor's Theory Y assumes employees are internally motivated, enjoy their jobs, and work to better themselves without a direct reward in return.

69. Mr. Greene is a project manager on an existing project at the Ultimate Real Estate Company, which sells passports. After the project kickoff, Mr. Greene and his project team are in the manage team resources process. The project plan has been approved. As a project manager, what will Mr. Greene do next?

    a) Control resources

    b) Create WBS

    c) Develop team

    d) Monitor stakeholder engagement

Answer: a. The next thing the project manager will do is control resources as part of the project plan. At this time, the resources have already been trained and developed. The team is producing results. As a project manager, you want to make sure the results are per the project plan.

70. Olivia is a project manager at the corporation MAOHC. MAOHC has numerous affiliates and thousands of ongoing projects. Olivia is introducing a new team member to handle quality assurance on her project. As the project manager, in what order should Olivia perform the steps of team development?

    a) Performing, storming, norming, forming, and adjourning

b) Performing, storming, adjourning, forming, and norming

c) Forming, norming, storming, performing, and adjourning

d) Forming, storming, norming, performing, and adjourning

Answer: d. Only d is in the correct order.

71. Noah is a project manager at Emca, a producer of animated characters for worldwide distribution to children as consumers. Which tool and technique should Noah use next in the plan communications management process to create the communication management plan?

a) Change log

b) Project management plan

c) Manage quality

d) Interpersonal and team skills

Answer: d. Option a is an output, b is an input, and c is a process.

72. Emma is a project manager for Guidance Cybernetics, a maker of exoskeletons for those who have lost the use of their limbs or are paralyzed from spinal injuries. Emma's project has suffered both material and people resource setbacks. As the project manager, what should Emma choose as the best tool and technique of the plan communication management process to create the communication management plan document?

a) Change log

b) Project management plan

c) Manage quality

d) Communication technology

Answer: d. Change log and project management plan are never a tool and technique. Manage quality is a process.

73. Ava is a junior project manager learning the ropes for the company Dadcorp. Dadcorp is a company that performs the to-do list for families or single parents and other things around the home of the consumer. Conversations and meetings are part of which tool and technique?

a) Communications analysis

b) Communications technology

c) Communications model

d) Communications method

Answer: b. Communications analysis describes what is needed to maximize the value of information for project stakeholders. Communications technology includes shared portals, emails, and databases. The communications model is the encoding and decoding of messages. And the communication method is the interaction of information, such as one-way or multidirectional conversations.

74. Which best describes the manage communications process?

a) Project management plan

b) The process of ensuring timely and appropriate collection, creation, distribution, storage, retrieval, management, monitoring, and the ultimate disposition of project information

c) Work performance reports

d) Team performance

Answer: b. The project management plan describes the project, work performance reports describe the status of the project, and team performance is the evaluation of the effectiveness of the team.

75. Kazem is a project manager with many years of experience. Kazem knows how important customer communication and satisfaction are to project management. What is the best definition of the monitor stakeholder engagement process?

a) The process of identifying project stakeholders regularly and analyzing and documenting relevant information regarding their interests, involvement, interdependencies, influence, and impact on project success

b) The process of communicating and working with stakeholders to meet their needs and expectations, address issues, and foster appropriate stakeholder engagement

c) The process of providing an overview of the project stakeholder management process

d) The process of monitoring project stakeholder relationships and tailoring strategies for engaging stakeholders through the modification of engagement strategies and plans

Answer: d. Option a is identifying stakeholders, b is manage stakeholder engagement, and c does not exist.

76. The following describe monitor stakeholder engagement except

a) Managing stakeholder relationships

b) Ignoring the stakeholders until they go away

c) Engaging with the stakeholders

d) Formulating strategies with the stakeholders

Answer: b. You would think answer b would be common sense, but it is surprising how many testers will miss a question like this on the exam. You never ignore stakeholders because communication, collaboration, and compromise are primary tools of a project manager.

77. The process of communicating and working with stakeholders to meet their needs and expectations, address issues, and foster appropriate involvement is

   a) Manage stakeholder engagement

   b) Monitor communications

   c) Manage communications

   d) Monitor stakeholder engagement

Answer: a. The difference between monitoring and managing is that monitoring is watching or observing. Managing is an action in which you are actually doing something. In this case, it is the "process of communicating and working with stakeholders."

78. Elijah is a project manager at Poor Man's Industries, a maker of economical products that look expensive. As the project manager, Elijah will supply all the inputs to manage a team except

   a) Project management plan

   b) Project documents updates

   c) Work performance reports

   d) Team performance

Answer: b. Project document updates is an output.

79. Robert is a new project manager at MAX Testosterone Support, Inc. Robert does not trust his employees to do their jobs, so he must monitor their every action to make sure he gets the results he wants. Robert is practicing

   a) RAM

   b) McGregor's Theory X

   c) Expectancy Theory

   d) McGregor's Theory Y

Answer: b. McGregor's Theory X assumes that the typical worker has little ambition, avoids responsibility, and is individual-goal oriented. McGregor's Theory Y assumes employees are internally motivated, enjoy their jobs, and work to better themselves without a direct reward in return.

80. What is the correct order of team development?

    a) Forming, storming, norming, performing, and adjourning

    b) Performing, storming, adjourning, forming, and norming

    c) Forming, norming, storming, performing, and adjourning

    d) Performing, storming, norming, forming, and adjourning

Answer: a. Only a is in the correct order.

81. David is a project manager on an existing project at the Boat Makers Company, which sells passports. After the project kickoff, David and his project team are in the managing team resources process. The project plan has been approved. As a project manager, what will David do next?

    a) Create WBS

    b) Control resources

    c) Develop team

    d) Monitor stakeholder engagement

Answer: b. The next thing the project manager will do is control resources as part of the project plan. At this time, the resources have already been trained and developed. The team is producing results. As a project manager, you want to make sure the results are per the project plan.

82. Daryl is a project manager on an existing project at the Best Acting Company Inc., which sells dreams. Before the project kickoff, Daryl and her project team are planning to perform qualitative risk analysis. The project plan has not been approved. As a project manager, what will Daryl do next?

    a) Plan risk management

    b) Create WBS

    c) Control resources

    d) Monitor stakeholder engagement

Answer: a. Plan risk management is the next step for the project manager.

83. Daryl is a project manager on an existing project at the Best Acting Company Inc., which sells dreams. Before the project kickoff, Daryl and her project team are planning to perform qualitative risk analysis. The project plan has not been approved. As a project manager, what does Daryl do prior to performing qualitative risk analysis?

    a) Implement risk responses

    b) Plan risk responses

    c) Control resources

    d) Plan communication management

Answer: b. Plan communication management is the step that comes before planning to perform qualitative risk analysis.

84. Daryl is a project manager on an existing project at the Best Acting Company, Inc, which sells dreams. Before the project kickoff, Daryl and her project team are planning to perform qualitative risk analysis. The project plan has not been approved. As a project manager, what will Daryl do next?

    a) Create WBS

    b) Control resources

    c) Monitor stakeholder engagement

    d) Plan risk management

Answer: d. Plan risk management is the next step for the project manager.

16 Questions on Business

1. Daniel is a new project manager for IT Providers LLC. Daniel wants to get off to the best start understanding the project, people, and environment. Interpersonal and team skills are a tool and technique of which process?

    a) Meetings

    b) Develop project charter

    c) OPA

    d) Planning

Answer: a. Meetings are the only tool and technique on this list. Develop project charter is a process. OPA is input, and planning alone is a word, not a tool and technique.

2. Mia is a new project manager for Warbuck LLC. Mia and her team inherited a project with many assumptions and constraints. All the requirements are not available, and the deliverables do not match up with client expectations. Mia wants to get off to the best start understanding the project, people, and environment. All the following are inputs to develop project charter except

    a) SOW

    b) Assumptions and constraints

    c) OPA

    d) Data analysis

Answer: d. SOW, assumptions, and constraints and OPA are all inputs to the project charter. Data analysis is a tool and technique.

3. Lucas is a new project manager for a computer company. As a new project manager who documents the develop project charter process, which documents does Lucas needs to examine?

    a) Project management plan and requirements plan

    b) Project charter and assumptions log

    c) Quality management plan and change management plan

    d) Stakeholder management plan

Answer: b. The output when developing a charter is a project charter and assumptions log.

48

4. David is a new project manager for Unique Homes Corp. David wants to get off to the best start in understanding the project, people, and environment. Interpersonal and team skills are a tool and technique of which process?

   a) Meetings

   b) Develop project charter

   c) Organizational process assets

   d) Planning

Answer: b. Develop project charter is the only process on this list. Meetings is a tool and technique for many processes. Organizational process assets are an input to many processes, and planning is a process group.

5. All the following are inputs to the develop project charter process except

   a) SOW

   b) Enterprise environmental factors

   c) Organizational process assets

   d) Data gathering

Answer: d. Data gathering is a tool and technique, not an input.

6. Priscilla is a project manager for an existing project with issues. What document does the project manager need to determine the project goals, high-level risks, and high-level constraints?

   a) Communication plan

   b) Project management plan

   c) SOW

   d) Project charter

Answer: d. The communication plan is a document for planning communication of the project. The project management plan plans the overall activities of the project and contains detailed requirements of the project. The SOW is the statement of work, which includes the objectives of the project. The project charter contains the high-level requirements of the project.

7. Daryl is a senior project manager for a book publishing company. Daryl wants to identify all current stakeholders for the project. All the documents below are inputs to the identify stakeholders process except

   a) Project charter

   b) EEF

   c) Expert judgments

   d) Organizational process assets

Answer: c. Expert judgments is a tool and technique.

8. Asheem is a project manager working remotely, so some of his team is in different locations performing their work. As project manager, Asheem determines the output of the develop project management plan process is

   a) Project charter

   b) Enterprise environmental factors

   c) Project management plan

   d) Organizational process assets

Answer: c. Project charter, EEF, and OPA are all inputs to the process.

9. Thomas has been working as a project manager for over 20 years. He has recently acquired his project management professional certificate. Which document does Thomas need to examine that maps the project deliverables to its requirements?

   a) OPA

   b) Requirements traceability matrix

   c) Project management plan

   d) Data analysis

Answer: b. The requirements traceability matrix maps the project deliverables to its requirements. The OPA and project management plan are inputs. Data analysis is a tool and technique.

10. Adrianne is a transferred project manager on loan from another department. Adrianne's first task is to develop a schedule management plan. Which order will Adrianne use for inputs to the plan schedule management process?

   a) Project charter, project management plan, scope management plan, development approach, EEF, and OPA

   b) Perform qualitative risk analysis, perform quantitative risk analysis, and plan risk responses

   c) Project management plan, project documents, approved change requests, EEF, and OPA

   d) Project charter, project management plan, quality management plan, project life cycle development, EEF, and OPA

Answer: a. Choice b describes plan risk management, and c describes direct and manage projects. As stated earlier, knowing the sequences of the planning group in all knowledge areas is crucial to passing the PMP exam.

11. Isabella is a project manager for Soylent Purple Corporation. As the project manager, which of the following will she use as an output of the process implement risk response plan?

   a) Change requests

   b) Data analysis

   c) Approved changes

   d) OPA

Answer: a. Data analysis is a tool and technique of most processes. Approved changes are an output of performed integrated change control and an input to direct and manage project work. OPA is an input to most processes.

12. Oliver is a project manager for the Very Tough Corporation of America. As project manager, he will use all the following as inputs to develop project charter except

   a) SOW

   b) Assumptions and constraints

   c) OPA

   d) Data analysis

Answer: d. Data analysis is a tool and technique. Statement of work, assumptions and constraints, and organizational process assets are inputs to the project charter.

13. Megan is a new project manager for an existing project with issues. What document does Megan need to determine the project goals, high-level risks, and high-level constraints?

    a) Communication plan

    b) Project management plan

    c) SOW

    d) Project charter

Answer: d. The project management plan has the overall activities of the project and contains detailed requirements of the project. The SOW is the statement of work, which contains the objectives of the project. The project charter contains the high-level requirements of the project.

14. Mason is a new project manager for Tube Socks LLC. Mason wants to get off to the best start understanding the project, people, and environment. As the project manager, Mason would choose all as inputs to the identify stakeholders process except

    a) Project charter

    b) EEF

    c) Expert judgments

    d) Organizational process assets

Answer: c. Expert judgments is always a tool and technique.

15. Jamis is a new project manager for the World-Eaters Corp. World-Eaters Corp is a company that terraforms planets so humans can live there comfortably. As a project manager, Jamis will use all tools and techniques to determine budget except

    a) Expert judgments

    b) Historical information review

    c) Funding limit reconciliation

    d) Business case

Answer: d. Expert judgments, historical information review, and funding limit reconciliation are all tools and techniques that can be used to determine the budget.

16. Sophia is a new project manager for Flatliners Inc., a company that makes and sells defibrillators to the medical industry. Sophia wants to get off to the best start understanding the company environment. As the project manager, which output would she choose for the determine budget process?

    a) Cost baseline

    b) Alternative analysis

    c) Business need

    d) Voting

Answer: a. Options b, c, and d are not outputs.

100 Questions on Process

1. Patrick is a new project manager for NoTouchTV LLC. Patrick wants to get off to the best start understanding the project, people, and environment. As a project manager, what process will Patrick perform that contains the project's objectives, assumptions, constraints, and high-level requirements?

    a) Meetings

    b) Develop project charter

    c) OPA

    d) Planning

Answer: b. Develop project charter is the process that creates the project charter document, which contains the project's objectives, assumptions, constraints, and high-level requirements. Meetings is a tool and technique. OPA is the organization policies, procedures, and practices, and planning is not a process. Develop project plan is a process.

2. Promise is a project manager at MoreBooks Inc. Promise wants to get off to the best start on her project. Promise will accept all the following as inputs to develop project charter except

    a) SOW

    b) Assumptions and constraints

    c) OPA

    d) Data analysis

Answer: d. Data analysis is a tool and technique. SOW, OPA, and assumptions and constraints are used in the develop project charter process.

3. Paul is a project manager with many years of experience in developing projects, managing personnel, document distribution, and bringing projects in on time and under budget. Paul needs to get started on this project and come up to speed immediately because senior management and the sponsor are getting anxious. As a project manager, what does Paul determine are the outputs of the develop project charter process?

    a) Project management plan and requirements plan

    b) Project charter and assumptions log

c) Quality management plan and change management plan

d) Stakeholder management plan

Answer: b. The project charter and assumptions log are the outputs of the develop charter process.

4. Zoey is a new project manager for HoverMobiles. Zoey wants to get off to the best start understanding the project, people, and environment. All are inputs to the identify stakeholder group except

a) Project charter

b) EEF

c) Expert judgment

d) OPA

Answer: c. Expert judgment is a tool and technique. Project charter, EEF, and OPA are inputs to most identify stakeholder processes.

5. Logan is a new project manager for iClassified LLC, an internet newspaper company that specializes in online advertisements. Logan wants to understand his new project, so he must secure the right documents and have meetings with the right people. As the project manager, Logan would ask for all documents that pertain to the project charter except those that

a) Formally authorize the existence of a project

b) Provide the project manager the authority to apply organizational resources to the project

c) State the high-level constraints and assumptions of the project

d) State the details of project deliverables

Answer: d. The project charter does not have detailed information. Options a, b, and c all describe the project charter.

6. Amelia is a new project manager for Tyronn Toys LLC. Amelia wants to get off to the best start understanding the project, people, and environment. Which best describes the develop project charter process?

a) The process of developing a document that formally authorizes the existence of a project and provides the project manager with the authority to apply organizational resources to project activities

b) The process of documenting how the project and product scope will be defined, validated, and controlled throughout the project

c) The process of developing detailed descriptions of the project and products, which is what the project includes and excludes

d) The process of estimating the number of work periods needed to complete activities with the estimated resources

Answer: a. Choice b better describes plan scope management. Choice c, develop charter, does process detailed information. Choices b, c, and d are performed in the planning stage of the project.

7. Frances is starting a new project that involves infrastructure and database migration. Frances needs to create documents for the best plan of communication for the team. Deliverables are an output of which process group?

   a) OPA

   b) EEF

   c) Final report

   d) Direct and manage project work

Answer: d. OPA and EEF are inputs to other processes, and the final report is an output of close process.

8. Samuel is a new project manager with good experience in change management to do the necessary work. All the following are inputs to process direct and manage project work except

   a) Approved changes

   b) Project management plan

   c) Deliverables

   d) OPA

Answer: c. Deliverables is an output of direct and manage the project work process. Options a, b and c are inputs to direct and manage project work.

9. Charlotte is a senior project manager for Grayson Enterprises. Charlotte wants to avoid scope creep and gold plating on this project. Which choice best describes the direct and manage project work process?

   a) The process of leading and performing the work defined in the project plan and implementing the approved changes to achieve the project objectives

b) The process of improving the competencies of team members and the overall team environment to enhance project performance

c) The process of obtaining seller responses, selecting sellers, and awarding a contract

d) The process of documenting project decisions, specifying the approach, and identifying potential sellers

Answer: a. Choice b is the develop team process, and c and d involve procurements.

10. The output of create WBS is

a) Decomposition

b) Scope baseline

c) Project management plan

d) Product scope statement

Answer: b. Decomposition is a tool and technique. The project management plan is an output of develop project plan process

11. James is a fresh project manager hired from a competitor. James has a friend who wants to be chosen as a contractor for this project. The bidding for the project does not start until next spring. Which best describes the create WBS process??

a) The process of developing a detailed description of the project and product

b) The process of creating a scope management plan that documents how the project and product scope will be defined, validated, and controlled

c) The process of subdividing project deliverables and project work into smaller, more manageable components

d) The process of monitoring the status of the project and product scope and managing changes in the scope baseline

Answer: c. Option b describes plan scope management and d describes monitor and control project work.

12. Harper is a new project manager hired from a competitor. Harper wants to get off to the best start understanding the project, people, and environment. Which are number systems in the WBS dictionary and WBS, respectively?

a) Code of account identifier and (1.0, 1.1, 1.1.1)

b) Chart of accounts and (a, ab, abc)

c) Control chart and $(1, 2, 3)$

d) All of the above

Answer: a. Code of account identifier and $(1.0, 1.1, 1.1.1)$ are the correct number systems.

13. Henri is a new project manager for the ElitePens Company. Henri wants to get off to the best start understanding the project, people, and environment. What is the output of plan communication management?

a) Project management plan

b) Project documents

c) Communications management plan

d) Communication baseline

Answer: c. The project management plan is the output of develop project plan. Communication baseline does not exist in PMBOK.

14. Charles is a seasoned project manager and is a wizard at communication management. Which answer below best fits the tools and technique of plan communication management?

a) Change log

b) Project management plan

c) Manage quality

d) Interpersonal and team skills

Answer: d. Interpersonal and team skills are the only tools and techniques in the list. The project management plan is an output of the develop project plan. Manage quality is a process. The change log is an output of perform integrated change control.

15. Ethan is a new project manager for VirtuNext, a maker of virtual games play systems. Ethan wants to get off to the best start understanding the project, people, and environment. What tool and technique of plan communication management would Ethan use next?

a) Change log

b) Project management plan

c) Manage quality

d) Communication technology

Answer: d. Communication technology is the only tool and technique on the list. The project management plan is an output of the develop project plan. Manage quality is a process. The change log is an output of perform integrated change control.

16. Ella is a new project manager for the PlanetEx Corporation. Ella wants to avoid team conflicts in meetings by setting up ground rules. As the project manager, which tool and technique would Ella choose next for the manage communications process?

     a) Change log

     b) Project management plan

     c) Manage quality

     d) Interpersonal and team skills

Answer: d. Interpersonal and team skills are only tool and technique on the list. The project management plan is an output of develop project plan. Manage quality is a process. The change log is an output of perform integrated change control.

17. Mateo is a new project manager for the Canopy Corp. Mateo, like all project managers, wants to manage the perfect project: on time, under budget, great quality to the customers' satisfaction. Manage communication is a process of which knowledge area?

     a) Plan communications management

     b) Project quality management

     c) Manage tools and techniques

     d) Project communications management

Answer: d. There are ten knowledge areas in the *PMBOK* 6th edition. You can get a quick glance at all ten knowledge areas in *PMBOK*, page 25.

18. Luna is a new project manager for Clark Enterprises. Luna wants to avoid quality issues that cause defects and require rework. Luna and his team carefully design and monitor quality into the project plan. Which best describes the manage communications process?

     a) Project management plan

     b) The process of ensuring timely and appropriate collection, creation, distribution, storage, retrieval, management, monitoring, and the ultimate disposition of project information

     c) Work performance reports

     d) Team performance

Answer: b. Manage communications is the process of ensuring timely and appropriate collection, creation, distribution, storage, retrieval, management, monitoring, and the ultimate disposition of project information.

19. Sebastian is a new project manager for Prince International. Sebastian wants to build team cohesiveness, so he schedules team company parties so that the team can bond with games and be better together as workers. Which process would Sebastian use next to communicate and work with stakeholders to meet their needs and expectations, address issues, and foster appropriate involvement?

    a) Manage stakeholder engagement

    b) Monitor communications

    c) Manage communications

    d) Monitor stakeholder engagement

Answer: a. Manage stakeholder engagement is the correct response. Revisit glossary for definitions.

20. Jack is a new project manager for the Stonewall Corp. Jack's team is tasked with improving a business process within the organization. Which answer best describes the manage communications process?

    a) The process of developing an appropriate approach and plan for project communication activities based on the information needs of each stakeholder, the available organizational assets, and the needs of the project

    b) The document that includes information on staff acquisition and release, resource calendars, recognition and rewards, compliance, and safety

    c) The process of ensuring timely and appropriate collection, creation, distribution, storage, retrieval, management, monitoring, and the ultimate disposition of project information

    d) The process of ensuring the information needs of the project and its stakeholders

Answer: c. Manage communications is the process of ensuring timely and appropriate collection, creation, distribution, storage, retrieval, management, monitoring, and the ultimate disposition of project information.

21. Camila is a new project manager for the Oneil Oil Company. Camila wants to get off to the best start understanding the project, people, and environment. The process of communicating and working with stakeholders to meet their needs and expectations, address issues, and foster appropriate involvement is

    a) Monitor communications

    b) Manage stakeholder engagement

c) Manage communications

d) Monitor stakeholder engagement

Answer: b. The process described is manage stakeholder engagement.

22. Jackson is a new project manager for the Atlanta Airlines Corporation. Jackson wants to get off to the best start understanding the project, people, and environment. Which answer best describes monitor communications?

   a) The process of developing an appropriate approach and plan for project communication activities based on the information needs of each stakeholder, the available organizational assets, and the needs of the project

   b) The document that includes information on staff acquisition and release, resource calendars, recognition and rewards, and compliance and safety

   c) The process of monitoring communications and the process of ensuring the information needs of the project and its stakeholders are met

   d) The process of ensuring the information needs of the project and its stakeholders are met

Answer: c. This choice best describes monitor communications.

23. Aria is a new project manager for Yoda Propulsion Systems. Aria wants to avoid equipment delays and improve worker performance, so Aria registers with a company application that monitors all facets of scheduling from order to delivery. Aria also has daily stand up meetings to make sure there is always progress in the project. As the project manager, what description of the resource management plan should best suit Aria?

   a) The process of developing an appropriate approach and plan for project communication activities based on the information needs of each stakeholder, the available organizational assets, and the needs of the project

   b) The document that includes information on staff acquisition and release, resource calendars, recognition and rewards, and compliance and safety

   c) The process of monitoring communications and the process of ensuring the information needs of the project and its stakeholders are met

   d) The process of ensuring the information needs of the project and its stakeholders are met

Answer: b. Option b best describes the resource management plan.

24. Linda is a new project manager with some experience in risk analysis to do the necessary work. What is the output of plan risk management?

   a) Communication management plan

   b) Configuration management plan

   c) Home improvement plan

   d) Risk management plan

Answer: d. The risk management plan is the output of plan risk management.

25. Elizabeth is starting a new project that involves infrastructure and database upgrades. What description best identifies plan risk management?

   a) The process of defining how to conduct risk management activities

   b) The process of using existing knowledge and creating new knowledge to achieve the project's objectives and contribute to organizational learning

   c) The process of translating the quality management plan into executable project activities that incorporate the organization's quality policies

   d) Risk baseline

Answer: a. Option a best describes plan risk management. Option c is plan quality management, and d does not exist in PMBOK.

26. Mila is a new project manager for the CyberWorld Corp. Mila wants to impress the managers who hired her by performing well on day one on a massive project that will take a year to complete. As the project manager, which document will Mila create from the plan risk management process?

   a) Cost management plan

   b) Risk management plan

   c) Scope baseline

   d) Risk baseline

Answer: b. Answer a is the output of plan cost management. Answer c is the output of define scope, and d does not exist in PMBOK.

27. Benjamin is a new project manager for Anaconda Copper. Benjamin wants to get off to the best start understanding the project, people, and environment. Which process best describes identify risk?

   a) The process of identifying individual risks as well as sources of overall project risks and documenting their characteristics

   b) Data analysis and interpersonal skills

   c) Project management plan

   d) The process of defining how to estimate, acquire, manage, and utilize physical and team resources

Answer: a. Option b is a tool and technique, c is a document, and d is plan resource management.

28. Kenneth is a new project manager with minimal experience in acquiring proper resources to do the necessary work. Which description best fits perform qualitative risk analysis?

   a) The process of prioritizing individual project risks for further analysis by assessing their probability of occurrence and impact

   b) The process of numerically analyzing the effects of identified risks on overall project objects

   c) Identify risks, perform a qualitative risk analysis, perform a quantitative risk analysis, and plan risk responses

   d) Plan schedule management, define activities, sequence activities, and develop schedules

Answer: a. Answer b is perform quantitative risk analysis. Answer c is project risk management, and d is project schedule management.

29. Aurora is a new project manager for Kool Klothes LLC. Aurora wants to get off to the best start understanding the project, people, and environment. Which answer is the best description of perform quantitative risk analysis?

   a) The process of numerically analyzing the effects of identified risks on overall project objects

   b) Identify risks, perform a qualitative risk analysis, perform a quantitative risk analysis, and plan risk responses

   c) Plan schedule management, define activities, sequence activities, estimate activity resources, estimate activity costs, and develop schedules

   d) Estimate costs and determine budget

Answer: a. Option a best describes perform quantitative risk analysis.

30. Kenneth is a new project manager with minimal experience in acquiring proper resources to do the necessary work. Which description best describes perform qualitative risk analysis?

    a) The process of numerically analyzing the effects of identified risks on overall project objects

    b) Identify risks, perform qualitative risk analysis, perform quantitative risk analysis, and plan risk responses

    c) The process of prioritizing individual project risks for further analysis by assessing their probability of occurrence and impact

    d) Plan schedule management, define activities, sequence activities, estimate activity resources, estimate activity costs, and develop schedule

Answer: c. Choice c best describes perform qualitative risk analysis.

31. Ellie is a new project manager for TinHooks LLC. Ellie's team is tasked with acquiring and installing a new computer and hardware system for use in the organization. Which answer is the best description of perform quantitative risk analysis?

    a) The process of numerically analyzing the effects of identified risks on overall project objects

    b) Identify risks, perform qualitative risk analysis, perform quantitative risk analysis, and plan risk responses

    c) Plan schedule management, define activities, sequence activities, estimate activity resources, estimate activity costs, and develop schedule

    d) Estimate costs and determine budget

Answer: a. Option a best describes perform quantitative risk analysis.

32. Carter is a new project manager for Blazed Enterprises. He is managing a project that develops a new pharmaceutical compound to bring to market. As a project manager, which input would Carter choose for the perform qualitative risk analysis process?

    a) Project management plan

    b) Alternative analysis

    c) OPA updates

    d) EEF updates

Answer: a. Choice b is a tool and technique. Choices c and d are outputs to other processes.

33. Robert is one of the best project managers the company has. Lately, Robert has seen a switch in management style. SMEs are being switched from one project to another without explanation or permission. Which answer is the best description of perform quantitative risk analysis?

   a) It is the process of numerically analyzing the effects of identified risks on overall project objects.

   b) It is the process by which we identify risks, perform qualitative risk analysis, perform quantitative risk analysis, and plan risk responses.

   c) It is the process by which we plan schedule management, define activities, sequence activities, estimate activity resources, estimate activity costs, and develop schedules.

   d) It involves estimating costs and determining the budget.

Answer: a. Choice a is the best description for perform quantitative risk analysis.

34. The project management plan plans the overall activities of the project and contains detailed requirements of the project. The SOW is the statement of work, which contains the objectives of the project. The project charter contains the high-level requirements of the project. All are inputs to the identify stakeholders process except

   a) Project charter

   b) EEF

   c) Expert judgments

   d) Organizational process assets

Answer: c. Expert judgments is a tool and technique.

35. Alysia is a new project manager for Headgear Inc. Alysia wants to show the company they have made the correct decision by asking for the right documents to get up to speed and asking the right questions in meetings. What is the output of plan stakeholder management?

   a) Stakeholder management plan

   b) Stakeholder baseline

   c) Risk register

   d) RBS

Answer: a. Answer b does not exist in PMBOK. Answer c is an output of identify risks. Answer d could be either a risk breakdown structure or resource breakdown structure, neither of which is the answer.

36. The process of communicating and working with stakeholders to meet their needs and expectations, address issues, and foster appropriate involvement describes which process?

    a) Manage stakeholder engagement

    b) Monitor communications

    c) Manage communications

    d) Monitor stakeholder engagement

Answer: a. The difference between monitoring and managing is that monitoring is watching or observing. Managing is an action in which you are actually doing something. In this case, it is the "process of communicating and working with stakeholders."

37. Kazem is a project manager with many years of experience. Kazem knows how important customer communication and satisfaction are to project management. What is the best definition of the monitor stakeholder engagement process?

    a) The process of identifying project stakeholders regularly and analyzing and documenting relevant information regarding their interests, involvement, interdependencies, influence, and impact on project success

    b) The process of communicating and working with stakeholders to meet their needs and expectations, address issues, and foster appropriate stakeholder engagement

    c) The process of providing an overview of the project stakeholder management process

    d) The process of monitoring project stakeholder relationships and tailoring strategies for engaging stakeholders through the modification of engagement strategies and plans

Answer: d. Option a is identifying stakeholders, b is managing stakeholder engagement, and c does not exist.

38. Avery is a project manager newly hired from a competitor. Avery wants to show the company they have made the correct decision by asking for the right documents to get up to speed and asking the right questions in meetings. The following describe monitor stakeholder engagement except

    a) Managing stakeholder relationships

    b) Ignoring the stakeholders until they go away

    c) Engaging with the stakeholders

    d) Formulating strategies with the stakeholders

Answer: b. You would think answer b would be common sense, but it is surprising how many testers will miss a question like this on the exam. You never ignore stakeholders because communication, collaboration, and compromise are primary tools of a project manager.

39. Grayson is a senior project manager for Nearlight Enterprises. Grayson's team is tasked with modifying a computer software program used in the organization. As the project manager, which definition would Grayson choose as the best description of plan cost management?

    a) The process of defining how the project cost will be estimated, budgeted, managed, monitored, and controlled

    b) The process of defining how to estimate, acquire, manage, and utilize physical and team resources

    c) The process of defining how to conduct risk management activities

    d) The process of identifying the relationships among project activities

Answer: a. Option b is plan resource management. Option c is manage risks.

40. Abigail is a project manager for a new underwater concept company. Abigail's team is tasked with conducting research to develop a new manufacturing process for the organization. As the project manager, which output of the plan cost management process would Abigail choose?

    a) Risk management plan

    b) Cost baseline

    c) Cost management plan

    d) Schedule baseline

Answer: c. Option b is an output of plan risk management. Option c is an output of plan cost management. Option d is an output of define scope.

41. Leo is a new project manager for a security software company that protects against hackers and credit card scams. Leo team is tasked with building a complete enterprise system to meet the sponsor's vision. Which is the best description of estimate costs?

    a) The process of analyzing sequences, durations, resource requirements, and schedule constraints to create a project model for project executions, monitoring, and controlling

    b) The process of developing an approximation of the monetary resources needed to complete the work

c) The process of developing an approach and plan for project communications activities based on the information needs of each stakeholder and the project

d) The process of defining how to estimate, acquire, manage, and utilize physical and team resources

Answer: b. Option a is plan schedule management. Option d is plan resource management.

42. Sofia is a new project manager for a computer animation company. Sofia's team has the task of acquiring resources and computer equipment and installing and configuring software so developers can program. Which of the following depicts the order of activities in project cost management?

a) Collect requirements, define scope, and create WBS

b) Identify risks, perform qualitative risk analysis, perform quantitative risk analysis, and plan risk responses

c) Plan schedule management, define activities, sequence activities, estimate activity durations, and develop schedule

d) Estimate costs and determine budget

Answer: d. The order is plan cost management, estimate costs, and determine budget.

43. As a project manager, you are planning the activities in the project schedule. Which of the following depicts the order of activities in plan cost management?

a) Collect requirements, define scope, and create WBS

b) Identify risks, perform qualitative risk analysis, perform quantitative risk analysis, and plan risk responses

c) Plan schedule management, define activities, sequence activities, estimate activity resources, estimate activity costs, and develop schedule

d) Estimate costs and determine budget

Answer: d. Option a describes scope management, b defines risk management, and c is schedule management.

44. Which is not a tool and technique used in the estimate activity durations process?

a) Analogous estimating

b) Bottom-up estimating

c) Three-point estimating

d) Duration estimates

Answer: d. Analogous, bottom-up, and three-point estimating are tools and techniques for the estimate activity durations process.

45. Mary is a project manager for a real estate company. Using the PERT beta distribution formula, how long will it take Mary to complete the project if most likely = 32, optimistic = 20, and pessimistic = 50?

a) 44

b) 33

c) 34

d) 32

Answer: b. (20 + 32(4) + 50) / 6 = 33

46. The project manager continues to put numbers together for cost and schedule. Using the triangular distribution method, how long will it take the project manager to complete the project if most likely = 32, optimistic = 20, and pessimistic = 50?

a) 44

b) 33

c) 34

d) 32

Answer: c. (32 + 20 + 50) / 3 = 34

47. The following are all tools and techniques that can be used to determine budget except

a) Expert judgments

b) Historical information review

c) Funding limit reconciliation

d) Business documents

Answer: d. Expert judgments, historical information review, and funding limit reconciliation are all tools and techniques that can be used to determine the budget.

48. Which is an output of the determine budget process?

    a) Cost baseline

    b) Alternative analysis

    c) Project management plan

    d) Voting

Answer: a. Options b, c, and d are not outputs.

49. As a project manager, you are planning the activities in the project schedule. What is the output of plan schedule management?

    a) Collect requirements, define scope, and create WBS

    b) Identify risks, perform qualitative risk analysis, perform quantitative risk analysis, and plan risk responses

    c) Create the schedule management plan

    d) Estimate costs and determine the budget

Answer: c. Option a describes scope management, b describes defining risk management, and d is cost management.

50. As the project manager, which inputs would you choose for the plan schedule management process?

    a) Project charter, project management plan, scope management plan, development approach, EEF, and OPA

    b) Perform qualitative risk analysis, perform quantitative risk analysis, and plan risk responses

    c) Project management plan, project documents, approved change requests, EEF, and OPA

    d) Project charter, project management plan, quality management plan, project life cycle development, EEF, and OPA

Answer: a. Choice b describes plan risk management, and c describes direct and manage projects. As stated earlier, knowing the sequences of the planning group in all knowledge areas is crucial to passing the PMP exam.

51. Which of the following depicts the order of activities in schedule management?

   a) Collect requirements, define scope, and create the WBS

   b) Identify risks, perform qualitative risk analysis, perform quantitative risk analysis, and plan risk responses

   c) Plan schedule management, define activities, sequence activities, estimate activity durations, and develop schedules

   d) Estimate costs and determine budget

Answer: c. Option a describes scope management, b defines risk management, and d is cost management.

52. As the project manager in the define activities process, work is decomposed into which of the following?

   a) Work packages

   b) WBS

   c) Activities

   d) WBS and activities

Answer: c. Decomposition into activities occurs in the define activities process. Decomposition into work packages occurs in the create WBS process. Answer d is a typical PMP exam trick to trip you up because it combines processes like WBS and activities.

53. Jason is a new project manager who is currently in the planning phase of a project. Jason has defined the activities—what should he do next?

   a) Sequence activities

   b) Estimate costs

   c) Collect requirements

   d) Identify risks

Answer: a. The question clearly states that Jason is still in the planning process, so what process occurs after the sequence that is in the list of choices and part of the planning process group? Define activities, sequence activities, estimate activity duration, et cetera. Knowing the order of processes in the planning process group is crucial to passing the exam. ***Memorize the order of processes in the planning process group!***

54. Jason is a new project manager who is currently in the planning phase of a project. Jason has defined the activities. As a project manager, what did Jason do before defining the activities?

    a) Sequence activities

    b) Estimate costs

    c) Plan schedule management

    d) Identify risks

Answer: c. See the order of processes in the planning process group.

55. As the project manager, which of the four types of PDM relationships will you use least often?

    a) Finish to Start (FS)

    b) Finish to Finish (FF)

    c) Start to Finish (SF)

    d) Start to Start (SS)

Answer: c. Start to Finish (SF) is very rarely used.

56. As the project manager, which of the four types of PDM relationships will you use most often?

    a) Finish to Start (FS)

    b) Finish to Finish (FF)

    c) Start to Finish (SF)

    d) Start to Start (SS)

Answer: a. Finish to Start (FS) is the most commonly used.

57. As a project manager, you are planning the activities in the project schedule. Which of the following depicts the order of activities in cost management?

    a) Collect requirements, define scope, and create WBS

    b) Identify risks, perform qualitative risk analysis, perform quantitative risk analysis, and plan risk responses

    c) Plan schedule management, define activities, sequence activities, estimate activity resources, estimate activity costs, and develop schedule

d) Estimate costs and determine budget

Answer: d. Option a describes scope management, b defines risk management, and c is schedule management.

58. Which is not a tool and technique used in the estimate activity durations process?

    a) Analogous estimating

    b) Bottom-up estimating

    c) Three-point estimating

    d) Duration estimates

Answer: d. Analogous, bottom-up, and three-point estimating are tools and techniques for the estimate activity durations process.

59. As the project manager, when using the PERT beta distribution formula, how long will it take Mary to complete the project if most likely = 32, optimistic = 20, and pessimistic = 50?

    a) 44

    b) 33

    c) 34

    d) 32

Answer: b. (20 + 32(4) + 50) / 6 = 33

60. Mary is a project manager for a biochemical firm. By using the triangular distribution method, how long will it take Mary to complete the project if most likely = 32, optimistic = 20, and pessimistic = 50?

    a) 44

    b) 33

    c) 34

    d) 32

Answer: c. (32 + 20 + 50) / 3 = 34

61. Which of the following depicts the order of activities in schedule management?

   a) Collect requirements, define scope, and create WBS

   b) Identify risks, perform qualitative risk analysis, perform quantitative risk analysis, and plan risk responses

   c) Plan schedule management, define activities, sequence activities, estimate activity durations and develop schedule

   d) Estimate costs and determine budget

Answer: c. Choice a is plan scope management, b is plan risk management, and d is plan cost management.

62. All are tools and techniques of the develop schedule process except

   a) Schedule compression

   b) Data analysis

   c) Project documents

   d) Critical path method

Answer: c. Project documents are inputs.

63. Judy is a superb project manager at her firm. She is currently working on a project in which a fix is necessary. As a project manager, what should Judy do next?

   a) Check the release documents

   b) Notify the sponsor

   c) Evaluate the impact of the change

   d) Implement the risk response plan

Answer: c. She should evaluate the impact of the change.

64. Judy is a top project manager at her firm. She is currently working on a project in which a fix *might be* necessary. As a project manager, what should Judy do next?

   a) Prevent changes from occurring

   b) Notify the sponsor

   c) Evaluate the impact of the change

   d) Implement the risk response plan

Answer: a. She should prevent changes from occurring.

65. Mitchell is a project manager for a solar car company on a new project that has not started. He wants to know where he can get information about projects like the one he is about to start. Where would Mitchell go first to get this information?

   a) Program manager

   b) PMO

   c) Portfolio office

   d) Sponsor

Answer: b. Answer b is the best choice. Answer a is an option as the **project manager** can go to the program manager; however, the program manager will go to the PMO and then give the information to the PM. There is no portfolio office. The sponsor would not be an option.

66. Jeffrey is a new project manager for Apocrypha Inc., a producer of religious books and artifacts. As the new project manager, he must have a plan in which many criteria are met for the condition of the books and artifacts. As a project manager, what document must Jeffrey create to set guidelines in criteria?

   a) Project management plan

   b) Project documents

   c) Risk management plan

   d) Quality management plan

Answer: d. Option a is the output of develop project plan, b is not the output of the plan quality management process, and c is the output of plan risk management.

67. Marshall is a project manager for the Action Solar Company, a maker of sun car parts. Quality is important in the company. Which best describes the plan quality management process?

   a) The process of identifying quality requirements and standards for the project and its deliverables and documenting how the project will demonstrate compliance with quality requirements and standards

   b) The process of monitoring and recording the results of executing the quality management activities to assess performance and ensure the project outputs are complete, correct, and meet customer requirements

   c) The process of translating the quality management plan into executable quality activities that incorporate the organization's quality policies into the project

   d) None of the above

Answer: a. Option b is monitoring quality. Option c is managing quality, and d is not the answer.

68. Which of the following is an input to the manage quality process?

    a) Quality reports

    b) Quality metrics

    c) Data gathering

    d) Enterprise environmental factors

Answer: b. Quality reports are an output; enterprise environmental factors are not input in this process, and data gathering is a tool and technique.

69. Terri is a new project manager at a manufacturing firm. She has completed the planning stage. Her team has begun implementing the work according to the project plan. One of Terri's team members has noticed a problem with her task but has not yet found a fix. What tools can be used to determine the cause of the problem?

    a) Prototypes

    b) An oscilloscope

    c) Fishbone

    d) Bottom-up estimating

Answer: c. An oscilloscope is outside the scope of PMP. Prototypes are used to find problems in the design, and bottom-up estimating is used to estimate the time and cost of a project.

70. David is a new project manager for Voice Activated Systems Enterprises. He wants to get off to the best start understanding ways to deliver a quality product. David and his team are planning for accuracy in quality. Which of the following tools is one of the seven rules of quality control?

    a) Analysis technique

    b) Cause-and-effect diagram

    c) Data representation

    d) Manage quality

Answer: b. Only the cause-and-effect diagram is one of the seven rules of quality control.

71. Emma is a project manager at a paper factory. Before the project starts, she requests information about political influence and public opinion. Which of these are influences out of the project manager's control?

    a) Enterprise environmental factors

    b) Organizational process assets

    c) Evolution environmental factors

    d) Extreme environmental factors

Answer: a. Enterprise environmental factors are influences outside the project manager's control. Organizational process assets are factors within the organization's and project team's control. And c and d are not part of the project management plan.

72. Susan is a project manager with many years of experience. Her current project is especially difficult because of problems with the timeline getting extended many times. This could be because the scope is not well defined, and the delays are causing increases in cost because of increased hours of work on the project for fixes. Susan can find all of the following in the project charter except

    a) Project purpose

    b) High-level requirements

    c) Detailed requirements

    d) Key stakeholder list

Answer: c. The project charter does not contain detailed information of any type. Detailed information is found in the project management plan.

73. Bradford is the new project manager at Green Thumb Nursery. His current project has constantly run into delays because of new deliverables that must be added for the project to be a success. As a project manager, which documents should Bradford check first to determine deliverables?

    a) Scope management plan and requirements management plan

    b) Project charter and project management plan

    c) Quality management plan and process improvement plan

    d) Risk management plan and risk response plan

Answer: b. The project charter will contain the vision of what is expected from the project. The project management plan will include the WBS, which will include project deliverables.

74. Jamerson is the project manager of Aqua Rooms, which are short-term underwater apartments. The project Jamerson is managing is consistently encountering incomplete requirements. As a project manager, he would use all tools and techniques to collect requirements except

a) Data analysis

b) Decision-making

c) Organizational process assets

d) Interpersonal skills and team skills

Answer: c. Organizational process assets are inputs. But a, b, and d are all tools and techniques.

75. Jamal is a senior project manager at a major pharmaceutical company. The project involves the testing of a new drug to halt aging. The project data is currently being collected. As a senior project manager, which requirement will Jamal not capture as an input to collect requirements?

a) Project management plan

b) Communication management plan

c) Project documents

d) EEF

Answer: b. The communication management plan is not an input to collect requirements. The communication management plan is a guide on how the project team will send, receive, distribute, store, and dispose of communication material.

76. Maria is a newly hired contract project manager who wants all documents related to the current project. Which document will Maria most want to map deliverables to their respective requirements?

a) OPA

b) Requirements traceability matrix

c) Project management plan

d) Data analysis

Answer: b. The requirements traceability matrix maps deliverables to their respective requirements. The OPA and project management plan are inputs. Data analysis is a tool and technique.

77. Which answer best describes the define scope process?

a) The process of developing a detailed description of the project and product

b) The process of creating a scope management plan that documents how the project and product scope will be defined, validated, and controlled

c) The process of subdividing project deliverables and project work into smaller, more manageable components

d) The process of monitoring the status of the project and product scope and managing changes in the scope baseline

Answer: a. Answer b describes the plan scope management process. Answer c describes the create WBS process. Answer d best describes monitoring and controlling a process.

78. Work that is outside the scope of the project is demanded by a sponsor, senior management, or stakeholders other than the project team. Which answer best describes this scenario?

a) Gold plating

b) Work that is necessary

c) Work that is unnecessary

d) Scope creep

Answer: d. Gold plating is work outside the scope of the project but deemed necessary by the project team. Answers b and c are general concepts that help narrow down the scope of the project.

79. There is work performed outside the scope of the project and suggested by the project team. Which answer best describes this action?

a) Gold plating

b) Work that is necessary

c) Work that is unnecessary

d) Scope creep

Answer: a. Gold plating occurs when project team members make unnecessary and unwanted changes to the project.

80. Which process best exemplifies monitoring and control in project integration?

   a) Direct and manage project work

   b) Monitor and control project work

   c) Manage project knowledge

   d) Perform integrated change control

Answer: b. Direct and manage project work is in the execute process groups and describe the performance of work. Manage project knowledge manages documents found, generated, compiled, or created because of the work. Perform integrated change control is a process that occurs when the original work plan must deviate with an approved change.

81. Harry is a contractor responsible for the refurbishment of an automobile showroom. The estimated refurbishment cost is $500 per square foot. The total showroom area that needs to be refurbished is 1,000 square feet. Based on his past experience, he knows his team can refurbish 100 square feet per week. As a project manager, how would Harry report how the project is performing?

   a) On schedule and on budget

   b) Behind schedule and over budget

   c) Ahead of schedule and over budget

   d) Behind schedule and ahead of budget

Answer: c. As a project manager, you report the fact at the time and not what you know or assume will happen later. Harry would report the project as ahead of schedule and over budget.

Cost Variance	(EV - AC) = $25,000.00
Schedule Variance	(EV - PV) = $25,000.00

82. Harry is a contractor responsible for the refurbishment of an automobile showroom. The estimated refurbishment cost is $500 per square foot. The total showroom area that needs to be refurbished is 1,000 square feet. Based on his past experience, he knows his team can refurbish 100 square feet per week. As the project manager, Harry will report the steady-state value of the project as

   a) $525,000

   b) $375,000

   c) $555,555.56

   d) $475,000

Answer: c. The steady-state value of the project is computed with the formula below.

Estimate at Completion (typical, steady-state, or continuous)	(BAC / CPI) = $555,555.56

83. Jacob is a contractor responsible for the refurbishment of an automobile showroom. The estimated refurbishment cost is $500 per square foot. The total showroom area that needs to be refurbished is 1,000 square feet. Based on his past experience, he knows his team can refurbish 100 square feet per week. As a project manager, what does Jacob compute the estimate at completion to be?

    a) $525,000

    b) $375,000

    c) $555,555.56

    d) $516,224.19

Answer: d. The estimate at completion formula is (AC + (BAC-EV)) / (CPI * SPI). (AC + (BAC-EV)) / (CPI * SPI) = $516,224.19

Complete table solutions below:

Estimated refurbishment cost $500.00 per square foot

Total showroom area   1,000.00 square feet

Refurbishment pace   100.00 square feet per week

Term	Value
Budget at Completion	($500 x 1,000) = $500,000.00
Planned Value	(4 / 10 x BAC) = $200,000.00
Earned Value	(45% x BAC) = $225,000.00
Actual Cost	$250,000.00
Cost Variance	(EV - AC) = $25,000.00
Schedule Variance	(EV - PV) = $25,000.00
Cost Performance Index	(EV / AC) = 0.90
Schedule Performance Index	(EV / PV) = 1.13
Estimate at Completion (atypical)	(AC + (BAC - EV)) = 525,000
Estimate at Completion (forecast)	(AC+ (BAC - EV)) / (CPI * SPI) = 516,224.19
Estimate at Completion (typical, steady-state or continuous)	(BAC / CPI) = $555,555.56
Estimate to Complete	(EAC - AC) = $305,555.56
Variance at Completion	(BAC - EAC) = $55,555.56

Total duration (1,000 / 100) = 10.00 weeks

Duration Elapsed = 4.00 weeks

Percentage completion = 45%

84. Judy is a superb project manager at her firm. She is currently working on a project in which a fix is necessary. As a project manager, what should Judy do next?

   a) Check the release documents

   b) Notify the sponsor

   c) Evaluate the impact of the change

   d) Implement the risk response plan

Answer: c. If the fix is necessary, then checking release documents has already occurred. Implementing the risk response plan would occur if a risk previously planned had occurred. Notifying sponsor might occur if a fix was not previously planned for, and the issue that necessitated the fix would impact the project adversely either in cost, schedule, or quality.

85. Patricia is a top project manager at her firm. She is currently working on a project in which a fix *might be* necessary. As a project manager, what should Patricia do next?

   a) Prevent changes from occurring

   b) Notify the sponsor

   c) Evaluate the impact of the change

   d) Implement the risk response plan

Answer: a. The project manager would want to prevent the change from occurring and seek alternative solutions. However, if the change must occur, then evaluate the impact of the change. Implement the risk response plan would occur if a risk previously planned had occurred. Notify sponsor might occur if the fix was not previously planned for, and the issue that necessitated the fix would impact the project adversely, either in cost, schedule, or quality.

86. Jeffrey is a project manager and wants to define how to estimate, acquire, manage, and utilize physical and team resources. Which process fits the definition for Jeffrey?

   a) Develop team

   b) Plan resource management

   c) Organizational theory

   d) Team charter

Answer: b. The keyword here is "how," which describes the plan—in this case, plan resource management. Develop team is in the execute process group, and you would see terms such as "manager," "administer," "train," and "translate." Organization theory and team charter describe the organization and the team, respectively, and would not utilize "how."

87. Robert is a new project manager at Use It or Lose It! Inc. Robert does not trust his employees to do their jobs, so he must monitor their every action to make sure he gets the results he wants. As a project manager, what management type is Robert practicing?

    a) RAM

    b) McGregor's Theory X

    c) Expectancy Theory

    d) McGregor's Theory Y

Answer: b. McGregor's Theory X assumes that the typical worker has little ambition, avoids responsibility, and is individual-goal oriented. McGregor's Theory Y assumes employees are internally motivated, enjoy their jobs, and work to better themselves without a direct reward in return.

88. Carmen is a new project manager who wants to impress everyone with how good her skills and knowledge are. When a new contractor is added to the team, she wants to use the correct order of team development. Which is the correct order of team development, according to Tuckerman's Ladder?

    a) Performing, storming, norming, forming, and adjourning

    b) Performing, storming, adjourning, forming, and norming

    c) Forming, norming, storming, performing, and adjourning

    d) Forming, storming, norming, performing, and adjourning

Answer: d. Only d is in the correct order. All others are not in the correct order, according to Tuckerman's ladder.

89. Which answer best describes the process to manage communications?

    a) Project management plan

    b) The process of ensuring timely and appropriate collection, creation, distribution, storage, retrieval, management, monitoring, and the ultimate disposition of project information

    c) Work performance reports

    d) Team performance

Answer: b. The project management plan describes the project, work performance reports describe the status of the project, and team performance is the evaluation of the effectiveness of the team.

90. The process of communicating and working with stakeholders to meet their needs and expectations, address issues, and foster appropriate involvement is

   a) Manage stakeholder engagement

   b) Monitor communications

   c) Manage communications

   d) Monitor stakeholder engagement

Answer: a. The difference between monitoring and managing is that monitoring is watching or observing. Managing is an action in which you are actually doing something. In this case, it is the "process of communicating and working with stakeholders."

91. Frank is a project manager with Carmon Lip Balm LLC. He and his project team meticulously put together a project plan that captured and strategized for many risks. One of the risks has just materialized. As a project manager, what should Frank do next?

   a) Plan risk management

   b) Monitor risks

   c) Use his interpersonal and team management skills

   d) Implement risk responses

Answer: d. Plan risk management is a process to first create the risk management plan document. Interpersonal skills is a tool and technique. Risks are being monitored to see if any occur. If a risk does occur, the next step as a project manager is to implement the risk response strategy.

92. Debbie is a project manager at Cool Socks Inc. She is in the planning process for a new project and has completed the sequence activities process. The kickoff of the project occurred three months ago. The project team is currently managing the project. As a project manager, what would Debbie do next?

   a) Estimate activity durations

   b) Close the project

   c) Control schedule

   d) Identify stakeholders

Answer: c. We are clearly in the execute phase of the project. We have already estimated durations because we have entered the execute phase. There is no mention of project close or cancellation. Identifying stakeholders is going on throughout the life cycle of the project. The best answer is control schedule.

93. Which of the following is an output of the process implement risk response plan?

    a) Change requests

    b) Data analysis

    c) Approved changes

    d) OPA

Answer: a. Data analysis is a tool and technique of most processes. Approved changes are outputs of performed integrated change control and inputs to direct and manage project work. OPA is an input to most processes.

94. Joseph is a project manager with Carmon Lip Balm LLC. He and his project team meticulously put together a project plan that captured and strategized for many risks. One of the risks has just materialized. As a project manager, what should Joseph do next?

    a) Plan risk management

    b) Monitor risks

    c) Use his interpersonal and team management skills

    d) Implement risk responses

Answer: d. Plan risk management is a process to first create the risk management plan document. Interpersonal skills is a tool and technique. Risks are being monitored to see if any occur. If a risk does occur, the next step as a project manager is to implement the risk response strategy.

95. Mila is a project manager at Cool Socks Inc. She is in the planning process for a new project and has completed the sequence activities process. The kickoff of the project occurred three months ago. The project team is currently managing the project. As a project manager, what would Mila do next?

    a) Estimate activity durations

    b) Close the project

    c) Control schedule

    d) Identify stakeholders

Answer: c. We are clearly in the execute phase of the project. We have already estimated durations because we have entered the execute phase. There is no mention of project close or cancellation. Identifying stakeholders is going on throughout the life cycle of the project. The best answer is control schedule.

96. Which of the following is an output of the process implement risk response plan?

    a) Change requests

    b) Data analysis

    c) Approved changes

    d) OPA

Answer: a. Data analysis is a tool and technique of most processes. Approved changes are outputs of performed integrated change control and inputs to direct and manage project work. OPA is an input to most processes.

97. All are components of tools and techniques in the manage project knowledge process except

    a) Knowledge management

    b) Information management

    c) Interpersonal and team skills

    d) Lessons learned register

Answer: d. The lessons learned register is an input.

98. Which of the following is an input to the manage project knowledge process?

    a) Alternative analysis

    b) Deliverables

    c) OPA updates

    d) Project management plan updates

Answer: b. Choice a is a tool and technique of another process; c and d are outputs to other processes.

99. What is the output of the validate scope process?

   a) Work performance data

   b) Acceptable deliverables

   c) Verified deliverables

   d) Work performance information

Answer: b. Acceptable deliverables is the output of the validate scope process.

100. Susan is a first-time project manager; however, she is excited to make a good impression. Halfway through her project, Susan gets an email from the client that the project will be canceled because of a funding issue. What should Susan do next?

   a) Try to negotiate with the client and suggest where to find additional funding

   b) Prepare the final project report

   c) Tell the team this is only a temporary setback; it happened before on a similar project, but the problem was cleared shortly

   d) Ask senior management to talk to the client

Answer: b. Susan should immediately begin the closing process. Prepare the final report is the only answer that is part of the closing process.

Mock Exam—Concentration Simplified

1. Ali is a new project manager for Remote Lawnmowers LLC. Ali wants to get off to the best start understanding the project, people, and environment. Interpersonal and team skills is a tool and technique of which process?

    a) Meetings

    b) Develop project charter

    c) OPA

    d) Planning

2. All the following are inputs to develop project charter except

    a) SOW

    b) Assumptions and constraints

    c) OPA

    d) Data analysis

3. The outputs to develop project charter are

    a) Project management plan and requirements plan

    b) Project charter and assumptions log

    c) Quality management plan and change management plan

    d) Stakeholder management plan

4. All are inputs to identify stakeholder group except

    a) Project charter

    b) EEF

    c) Expert judgment

    d) OPA

5. All describe a project charter except

   a) Formally authorizes the existence of a project

   b) Provides project manager the authority to apply organizational resources to the project

   c) States the high-level constraints and assumptions of the project

   d) States the details of project deliverables

6. Which best describes the develop project charter process?

   a) The process of developing a document that formally authorizes the existence of a project and provides the project manager with the authority to apply organizational resources to project activities

   b) The process of documenting how the project and product scope will be defined, validated, and controlled throughout the project

   c) The process of developing detailed descriptions of the project and products, which is what the project includes and excludes

   d) The process of estimating the number of work periods needed to complete activities with the estimated resources

7. Which tool and technique would a project manager use to collect information about a potential project during project integration management?

   a) Data analysis

   b) Data representation

   c) Manage quality

   d) Data gathering

8. All are tools and techniques in the identify stakeholders process except

   a) Brainstorming

   b) Data analysis

   c) Change requests

   d) Data representation

9. What is the output of the identify stakeholders process?

   a) Project management plan

   b) Stakeholder register

   c) Quality management plan

   d) Requirements management plan

10. The output of the develop project management plan is

   a) Change management plan

   b) Configuration management plan

   c) Project management plan

   d) Stakeholder baseline

11. Which is the correct definition of the develop project management plan?

   a) The process of developing a document that formally authorizes the existence of a project and provides the project manager with the authority to apply organizational resources to project activities

   b) The process of documenting how the project and product scope will be defined, validated, and controlled throughout the project

   c) The process of developing detailed descriptions of the project and products, which is what the project includes and excludes

   d) The process of what needs to be done to define, prepare, and coordinate all subsidiary activities to produce a document that defines the project

12. All are part of develop project management plan except

   a) Define all subsidiary activities

   b) State high-level requirements

   c) Prepare all subsidiary activities

   d) Coordinate all subsidiary activities

13. All are part of a project management plan except

   a) How work will be executed

   b) How work will be monitored

   c) Implementing project work

   d) How work will be closed

14. Which is the best definition of the project management plan?

   a) The process of developing a document that formally authorizes the existence of a project and provides the project manager with the authority to apply organizational resources to project activities

   b) The document that describes how work will be executed, monitored, and controlled, and closed

   c) The process of developing detailed descriptions of the project and products, which is what the project includes and excludes

   d) The process of what needs to be done to define, prepare, and coordinate all subsidiary activities to produce a document that defines the project

15. All are contained in plan scope management except

   a) How the project and product scope will be defined

   b) Implementing change requests

   c) How the project and product scope will be validated

   d) How the project and product scope will be controlled throughout the project

16. Which best describes the plan scope management process?

   a) The process of developing a document that formally authorizes the existence of a project and provides the project manager with the authority to apply organizational resources to project activities

   b) The process of documenting how the project and product scope will be defined, validated, and controlled throughout the project

   c) The process of developing detailed descriptions of the project and products which is what the project includes and excludes

   d) The process of estimating the number of work periods needed to complete activities with the estimated resources

17. All are contained in the define scope process except

    a) What the project includes and excludes

    b) The output of the project scope statement

    c) A detailed description of the project and products

    d) How the project and product scope will be validated

18. Which best describes the define scope process?

    a) The process of developing a document that formally authorizes the existence of a project and provides the project manager with the authority to apply organizational resources to project activities

    b) The process of documenting how the project and product scope will be defined, validated, and controlled throughout the project

    c) The process of developing detailed descriptions of the project and products, which is what the project includes and excludes

    d) The process of estimating the number of work periods needed to complete activities with the estimated resources

19. All the following describe estimate activity durations except

    a) Determine risks

    b) The process of estimating work periods

    c) The work periods to complete activities

    d) Estimated resources to complete activities

20. Which best describes the estimate activity durations process?

    a) The process of developing a document that formally authorizes the existence of a project and provides the project manager with the authority to apply organizational resources to project activities

    b) The process of documenting how the project and product scope will be defined, validated, and controlled throughout the project

    c) The process of developing detailed descriptions of the project and products, which is what the project includes and excludes

    d) The process of estimating the number of work periods needed to complete activities with the estimated resources

21. The output of develop project management plan is

    a) Project charter

    b) EEF

    c) Project management plan

    d) OPA

22. The outputs of plan scope management are

    a) Scope management plan and requirements management plan

    b) Quality management plan and process improvement plan

    c) Resource management plan and resource breakdown structure

    d) Risk management plan and risk improvement plan

23. The _____ are influences out of the project manager's control.

    a) Enterprise environmental factors

    b) OPA

    c) Evolution environmental factors

    d) Extreme environmental factors

24. _____ are factors internal to the organization that affect the project.

    a) Optimal process assets

    b) Omni process assets

    c) Organization process assets

    d) Optical process assets

25. Ahmal is a project manager with many years of experience. His current project is especially difficult because of problems with the timeline getting extended many times. This could be because the scope is not well defined, causing increases in cost because of increased hours of work on the project for fixes. All may be found in the project charter except

    a) Project purpose

    b) High-level requirements

c) Detail requirements

d) Key stakeholder list

26. Susan is a project manager with many years of experience. Susan's current project is especially difficult because of problems with the timeline getting extended many times. This could be because the scope is not well defined, causing increases in cost because of increased hours of work on the project for fixes. Which best describes the collect requirements process?

    a) Project purpose

    b) The process to determine, document, and manage stakeholder needs and requirements to meet project objectives

    c) Detail requirements

    d) Key stakeholder list

27. Susan is a project manager with many years of experience. Susan's current project is especially difficult because of problems with the timeline getting extended many times. This could be because the scope is not well defined, causing increases in cost because of increased hours of work on the project for fixes. Which tool and technique links product requirements from their origins to the deliverables that satisfy them?

    a) Project purpose

    b) Requirements traceability matrix

    c) Detail requirements

    d) Key stakeholder list

28. The output of define scope is

    a) Project documents

    b) Data analysis

    c) Project scope statement

    d) Risk management plan

29. David is a project manager with many years of experience. David's current project is especially difficult because of problems with the timeline getting extended many times. This could be because the scope is not well defined, causing increases in cost because of increased hours of work on the project for fixes. Which best describes the define scope process?

    a) Project purpose

    b) The process to determine, document, and manage stakeholder needs and requirements to meet project objectives

    c) Detail requirements

    d) The process of developing detailed descriptions of the project and products

30. Susan is a project manager with many years of experience. Susan's current project is especially difficult because of problems with the timeline getting extended many times. This could be because the scope is not well defined, causing increases in cost because of increased hours of work on the project for fixes. What is the output of define scope?

    a) Project scope statement and project document updates

    b) The process of determining, documenting, and managing stakeholder needs and requirements to meet project objectives

    c) Detail requirements

    d) The process of developing detailed descriptions of the project and products

31. Which best describes the define scope process?

    a) The process of developing a detailed description of the project and product

    b) The process of creating a scope management plan that documents how the project and product scope will be defined, validated, and controlled

    c) The process of subdividing project deliverables and project work into smaller, more manageable components

    d) The process of monitoring the status of the project and product scope and managing changes in the scope baseline

32. The output of create WBS is

    a) Decomposition

    b) Scope baseline

c) Project management plan

d) Product scope statement

33. Which process best describes create WBS?

   a) The process of developing a detailed description of the project and product

   b) The process of creating a scope management plan that documents how the project and product scope will be defined, validated, and controlled

   c) The process of subdividing project deliverables and project work into smaller, more manageable components

   d) The process of monitoring the status of the project and product scope and managing changes in the scope baseline

34. Which are number systems in the WBS dictionary and WBS, respectively?

   a) Code of account identifier and (1.0, 1.1, 1.1.1)

   b) Chart of accounts and (a, ab, abc)

   c) Control chart and (1, 2, 3)

   d) All of the above

35. The scope baseline consists of

   a) The process of developing a detailed description of the project and product

   b) The project scope statement, WBS, WBS dictionary, and planning package

   c) The process of subdividing project deliverables and project work into smaller, more manageable components

   d) The process of monitoring the status of the project and product scope and managing changes in the scope baseline

36. The output of plan schedule management is

   a) Cost baseline

   b) Scope baseline

   c) Schedule baseline

   d) Schedule management plan

37. All describe project schedule management except

   a) Define activities

   b) Sequence activities

   c) Change requests

   d) Estimate activity durations

38. As a project manager, James is planning the activities in the project schedule management. Which of the following depicts the order of activities in schedule management?

   a) Collect requirements, define scope, create WBS

   b) Identify risks, perform qualitative risk analysis, perform quantitative risk analysis, and plan risk responses

   c) Plan schedule management, define activities, sequence activities, estimate activity durations, and develop schedule

   d) Estimate costs and determine budget

39. Jason is a new project manager currently in the planning phase of a project. He has defined the activities. As a project manager, what should Jason do next?

   a) Sequence activities

   b) Estimate costs

   c) Plan schedule management

   d) Identify risks

40. Peter is a new project manager currently in the planning phase of a project. He has defined the activities. As a project manager, what did Peter do prior to defining activities?

   a) Sequence activities

   b) Estimate costs

   c) Plan schedule management

   d) Identify risks

41. As a senior project manager, you are planning the activities in the project schedule. What is the output of plan schedule management?

    a) Collect requirements, define scope, create WBS

    b) Identify risks, perform qualitative risk analysis, perform quantitative risk analysis, plan risk responses

    c) Schedule management plan

    d) Estimate costs, determine budget

42. The output of define activities is

    a) Activity list, milestone list, activity attributes, and change requests

    b) Identify risks, perform qualitative risk analysis, perform quantitative risk analysis, and plan risk responses

    c) Plan schedule management, define activities, sequence activities, estimate activity resources, estimate activity costs, and develop schedule

    d) Estimate costs and determine budget

43. As a junior project manager, you are planning the activities in the project schedule. Which of the following depicts the order of activities in schedule management?

    a) Collect requirements, define scope, and create WBS

    b) Identify risks, perform qualitative risk analysis, perform quantitative risk analysis, and plan risk responses

    c) Plan schedule management, define activities, sequence activities, estimate activity durations, and develop schedule

    d) Estimate costs and determine budget

44. The output of define activity consists of all except

    a) Activity list

    b) Milestone list

    c) Rolling wave

    d) Activity attributes

45. The output of sequence activities is

    a) Change request

    b) Project management plan

    c) Project schedule network diagram

    d) Data analysis

46. Jason is a new project manager currently in the planning phase of a project. He has defined the activities. As a project manager, what should Jason do next?

    a) Sequence activities

    b) Estimate costs

    c) Collect requirements

    d) Identify risks

47. John is one of the top project managers in the company. He is concerned about the order of some of the sequenced activities. Of the four types of PDM relationships, which are used most often?

    a) Finish to Start (FS)

    b) Finish to Finish (FF)

    c) Start to Finish (SF)

    d) Start to Start (SS)

48. Robert is a junior project manager at a consulting firm. He has been signed to a high-profile project and needs to be sure the sequence of activities is accurate. Of the four types of PDM relationships, which is used least often?

    a) Finish to Start (FS)

    b) Finish to Finish (FF)

    c) Start to Finish (SF)

    d) Start to Start (SS)

49. Which is one of the tools and techniques for estimating activity duration?

    a) Parametric analogous

    b) Schedule compression

    c) Critical path method

    d) EEF

50. The best description of estimate activity duration is

    a) The process of estimating the number of work periods needed to complete activities with the estimated resources

    b) The process of defining how the project cost will be estimated, budgeted, managed, monitored, and controlled

    c) The process of identifying quality requirements and standards for the project and its deliverables and documenting how the project will demonstrate compliance with quality requirements

    d) The process of estimating team resources and quantity of materials, equipment, and supplies necessary to perform project work

51. What is the output of estimate activity duration?

    a) Duration estimates

    b) Change requests

    c) Project management plan

    d) Data analysis

52. Which process best describes develop schedule?

    a) The process of analyzing sequences, durations, resource requirements, and schedule constraints to create a project model for project executions, monitoring, and controlling

    b) Critical path method

    c) Project documents

    d) Schedule baseline

53. All are tools and techniques for develop schedule except

    a) Critical path

    b) Resource optimization

    c) Schedule data

    d) Schedule compression

54. What is the critical path in days of a project in which the following activities are defined as follows: activity A has a duration of 5 days and starts the project; activities B and C have durations of 3 and 4 days, respectively, and follow A; activity E has a duration of 2 days and follows activity B; activity F has a duration of 2 days and follows activity E; activity D has a duration of 2 days and follows activity C; and activity G has a duration of 5 days and follows F and D.

    a) 17 days

    b) 16 days

    c) 18 days

    d) 14 days

55. Now, what is the critical path of a project in which the following activities are defined as follows: activity A has a duration of 5 days and starts the project; activities B and C have durations of 3 and 4 days, respectively, and follow A; activity E has a duration of 2 days and follows activity B; activity F has a duration of 2 days and follows activity E; activity D has a duration of 2 days and follows activity C; and activity G has a duration of 5 days and follows F and D.

    a) ABEFG

    b) ACDG

    c) There is no critical path.

    d) The critical path can be reduced or changed.

56. What is the float in days of project activities E and C, respectively, where activities are defined as follows : activity A has a duration of 5 days and starts the project; activities B and C have durations of 3 and 4 days, respectively, and follow A; activity E has a duration of 2 days and follows activity B; activity F has a duration of 2 days and follows activity E; activity D has a duration of 2 days and follows activity C; and activity G has a duration of 5 days and follows F and D.

a) 0, 1

b) 1, 0

c) Float is negative, so the project is ahead of schedule.

d) Float is negative, so activity is ahead of schedule.

57. The best description of plan cost management is

a) The process of defining how the project cost will be estimated, budgeted, managed, monitored, and controlled

b) The process of defining how to estimate, acquire, manage, and utilize physical and team resources

c) The process of defining how to conduct risk management activities

d) The process of identifying the relationships among project activities

58. The output of plan cost management is

a) Risk management plan

b) Cost baseline

c) Cost management plan

d) Schedule baseline

59. Which is not a tool and technique used in estimate activity duration?

a) Analogous estimating

b) Bottom-up estimating

c) Three-point estimating (PERT)

d) Duration estimates

60. The best description of estimate costs is

a) The process of analyzing sequences, durations, resource requirements, and schedule constraints to create a project model for project executions, monitoring, and controlling

b) The process of developing an approximation of the monetary resources needed to complete the work

c) The process of developing an approach and plan for project communications activities based on the information needs of each stakeholder and the project

d) The process of defining how to estimate, acquire, manage, and utilize physical and team resources

61. The best description of determine budget process is

a) The process of aggregating the estimated costs of individual activities or work packages to establish an authorized cost baseline

b) The process of developing an approximation of the monetary resources needed to complete the work

c) The process of developing options, selecting strategies, and agreeing on actions to address project risk exposure

d) The process of documenting project decisions, specifying the approach, and identifying potential sellers

62. All are outputs of determine budget except

a) Cost baseline

b) Project funding

c) Data analysis

d) Cost estimates

63. As a project manager III, Michael is planning the activities in the project schedule. Which of the following depicts the order of activities in plan cost management?

a) Collect requirements, define scope, and create WBS

b) Identify risks, perform qualitative risk analysis, perform quantitative risk analysis, and plan risk responses

c) Plan schedule management, define activities, sequence activities, estimate activity resources, estimate activity costs, and develop schedule

d) Estimate costs and determine budget

64. Which best describes plan quality management?

   a) The process of identifying quality requirements and standards for the project and its deliverables and documenting how the project will demonstrate compliance with quality requirements and/or standards

   b) The process of monitoring and recording the results of executing the quality management activities to assess performance and ensure the project outputs are complete and correct and meet customer requirements

   c) The process of translating the quality management plan into executable quality activities that incorporate the organization's quality policies into the project

   d) None of the above

65. There has been a concern about too many issues after each completed activity in the project. William is a project manager and wants to fix this problem. Which is a part of the cost of conformance?

   a) Rework

   b) Testing

   c) Internal failure costs

   d) Liabilities

66. David is a project manager for a top-five IT consulting firm. David believes issues of activities failing can be averted. Which is a part of the cost of nonconformance?

   a) Training

   b) Destructive testing loss

   c) Inspections

   d) Lost business

67. Richard is excited about his first full-time project manager role. He is assigned to multiple projects. Nonconformance issues continue to be a problem on one of Richard's projects. All are a part of preventive costs except

   a) Time to do it right

   b) Training

   c) Inspections

   d) Document processes

68. As a project manager, it is a good practice to have as many tools as possible to track whether the quality is occurring at a high level on a project. Which of the following is not one of the seven basic quality tools?

    a) Flowcharts

    b) Control charts

    c) Risk management

    d) Check sheets

69. Joseph has been a project manager for 12 years. The process of defining how to estimate, acquire, manage, and utilize physical and team resources is

    a) Develop team

    b) Plan resource management

    c) Organizational theory

    d) Team charter

70. Which tool and technique of plan resource management identifies responsible, accountable, consult, and inform parties of tasks/activities?

    a) RBS

    b) RACI charts

    c) Responsibility assignment matrix

    d) Organizational theory

71. The following resources necessary to perform work could be represented in estimate activity resource except

    a) Team resources and quantity of materials

    b) Equipment

    c) Supplies necessary

    d) Analogous estimating

72. Which answer represents the best definition of an estimate activity resource?

   a) The process of developing approaches to involve project stakeholders based on their needs, expectations, interests, and potential impact on the project

   b) The process of estimating team resources and the quantity of materials, equipment, and supplies necessary to perform project work

   c) The process of translating the quality management plan into executable project activities that incorporate the organization's quality policies

   d) The process of numerically analyzing the combined effects of identified individual project risks

73. Thomas is a new project manager with minimal experience in acquiring proper resources to do the necessary work. The following tools and techniques can assist Thomas in estimating resources except

   a) Bottom-up estimating

   b) Analogous estimating

   c) Parametric estimating

   d) Resource breakdown structure (RBS)

74. Which process best describes estimate activity resources?

   a) The process of estimating team resources and the quantity of materials, equipment, and supplies necessary to perform project work

   b) The process of defining how to estimate, acquire, manage, and utilize physical and team resources

   c) The process of identifying quality requirements and standards for the project and its deliverables and documenting how the project will demonstrate compliance with quality requirements

   d) The process of defining how to conduct risk management activities

75. Charles is a seasoned project manager and a wizard at communication management. Which answer below best fits the tool and technique of plan communication management?

   a) Change log

   b) Project management plan

   c) Manage quality

   d) Interpersonal and team skills

76. Patricia is starting a new project that involves infrastructure and database migration. She needs to create documents for the best plan of communication for the team. Which answer best describes a communications management plan?

   a) The process of developing an appropriate approach and plan for project communication activities based on the information needs of each stakeholder, available organizational assets, and the needs of the project

   b) The document that includes information on staff acquisition and release, resource calendars, recognition and rewards, compliance, and safety

   c) The process of ensuring timely and appropriate collection, creation, distribution, storage, retrieval, management, monitoring, and ultimate disposition of project information

   d) The process of ensuring the information needs of the project and its stakeholders

77. What is the output of plan communication management?

   a) Project management plan

   b) Project documents

   c) Communications management plan

   d) Communication baseline

78. Jennifer is an IT project manager at an airline's electronics company. The project is behind schedule, and additional people will need to be brought onto the project to get it back on schedule. What tools and techniques can the project manager use to determine the number of communication channels?

   a) EV - AC

   b) PERT

   c) AC + (BAC - EV)

   d) N(n+1) / 2

79. As a project manager, you are planning the activities in the project schedule. Which of the following depicts the order of activities in risk management?

   a) Collect requirements, define scope, and create WBS

   b) Identify risks, perform qualitative risk analysis, perform quantitative risk analysis, and plan risk responses

c) Plan schedule management, define activities, sequence activities, estimate activity resources, estimate activity costs, and develop schedule

d) Estimate costs and determine budget

80. Linda is a new project manager with some experience in risk analysis to do the necessary work. What is the output of plan risk management?

a) Communication management plan

b) Configuration management plan

c) Home improvement plan

d) Risk management plan

81. Elizabeth is starting a new project that involves infrastructure and database upgrades. What description best identifies plan risk management?

a) The process of defining how to conduct risk management activities

b) The process of using existing knowledge and creating new knowledge to achieve the project's objectives and contribute to organizational learning

c) The process of translating the quality management plan into executable project activities that incorporate the organization's quality policies

d) Risk baseline

82. Which process best describes plan communications management?

a) The process of numerically analyzing the combined effect of identified individual project risks

b) The process of developing an approach and plan for project communications activities based on the information needs of each stakeholder and the project

c) Plan-Do-Check-Act

d) The process of prioritizing individual project risks for further analysis by assessing their probability of occurrence and impact

83. Which process best describes project risk management?

a) The process of prioritizing individual project risks for further analysis by assessing their probability of occurrence and impact

b) The process of defining how to estimate, acquire, manage, and utilize physical and team resources

c) The process of defining how to conduct risk management activities

d) The process of identifying individual risks as well as sources of overall project risks and documenting their characteristics

84. The output of plan risk management is

a) Cost management plan

b) Risk management plan

c) Scope baseline

d) Risk baseline

85. Which process best describes identify risk?

a) The process of identifying individual risks as well as sources of overall project risks and documenting their characteristics

b) Data analysis and interpersonal skills

c) Project management plan

d) The process of defining how to estimate, acquire, manage, and utilize physical and team resources

86. Barbara is starting a new project that involves application and database migration. A tool and technique that can be used in assessing risk impact is

a) Project management plan

b) Project document updates

c) Risk probability and impact assessment

d) Risk register

87. Kenneth is a new project manager with minimal experience in acquiring proper resources to do the necessary work. Which description best describes perform qualitative risk analysis?

a) The process of prioritizing individual project risks for further analysis by assessing their probability of occurrence and impact

b) The process of numerically analyzing the effect of identified risks on overall project objects

c) Identify risks, perform qualitative risk analysis, perform quantitative risk analysis, and plan risk responses

d) Plan schedule management, define activities, sequence activities, estimate activity resources, estimate activity costs, and develop schedule

88. Which answer is the best description of perform quantitative risk analysis?

    a) The process of numerically analyzing the effect of identified risks on overall project objects

    b) Identify risks, perform qualitative risk analysis, perform quantitative risk analysis, and plan risk responses

    c) Plan schedule management, define activities, sequence activities, estimate activity resources, estimate activity costs, and develop schedule

    d) Estimate costs and determine budget

89. The following are tools and techniques to perform quantitative risk analysis except

    a) Simulations

    b) EEF

    c) Tornado diagram

    d) Facilitation

90. Sandra is a senior project manager at a solar auto electronics company. This new role brings many new challenges she has rarely faced before. The following are strategies for negative risks/threats except

    a) Avoid

    b) Mitigate

    c) Share

    d) Transfer

91. llowing are strategies for positive risks/threats except

    a) Exploit

    b) Mitigate

    c) Share

    d) Enhance

92. Dorothy is a project manager at a local marketing firm. Dorothy needs to perform a risk analysis, which includes quantitative and qualitative risk analysis. All are tools and techniques to plan risk responses except

    a) Expert judgment

    b) Interpersonal and team skills

    c) Contingency response strategy

    d) Change requests

93. Which best describes the plan procurement management process?

    a) The process of documenting project decisions, specifying the approach, and identifying potential sellers

    b) The process of using existing knowledge and creating new knowledge to achieve the project's objectives and contribute to organizational learning

    c) The process of obtaining team members, facilities, equipment, materials, supplies, and other resources necessary to complete the project work

    d) The process of developing an approach and plan for project communications activities based on the information needs of each stakeholder and the project

94. Andrew is a seasoned project manager and a wizard at an electric automobile company. The process of documenting project procurement decisions, specifying the approach, and identifying potential sellers is

    a) Data analysis

    b) Procurement management plan

    c) OPA

    d) Plan procurement management

95. The following are contract types in plan procurement management except

    a) Fixed-priced contracts

    b) Time and material contracts

    c) Standard contracts

    d) Cost-reimbursable contracts

96. Which answer best describes plan stakeholder engagement?

   a) The process of developing approaches to involve project stakeholders based on their needs and expectations, addressing issues, and fostering appropriate stakeholder engagement

   b) The process of monitoring project stakeholder relationships and tailoring strategies for engaging stakeholders through the modification of engagement strategies and plans

   c) The process of communicating and working with stakeholders to meet their needs and expectations

   d) The process of not communicating and working with stakeholders to meet their needs and expectations

97. What is the output of plan stakeholder management?

   a) Stakeholder management plan

   b) Stakeholder baseline

   c) Risk register

   d) RBS

98. Bill is an experienced project manager who wants to be sure his team collects all the necessary requirements. Which best describes plan scope management?

   a) The process of developing a detailed description of the project and product

   b) The process of creating a scope management plan that documents how the project and product scope will be defined, validated, and controlled

   c) The process of subdividing project deliverables and project work into smaller, more manageable components

   d) The process of monitoring the status of the project and product scope and managing changes in the scope baseline

99. The output of the plan scope management process is

   a) Scope baseline

   b) Requirements plan

   c) Scope management plan

   d) EEF

100. Bill is an experienced project manager who wants to be sure his team collects all the necessary requirements. Which best describes WBS?

    a) The process of developing a detailed description of the project and product

    b) The process of creating a scope management plan that documents how the project and product scope will be defined, validated, and controlled

    c) The process of subdividing project deliverables and project work into smaller, more manageable components

    d) The process of monitoring the status of the project and product scope and managing changes in the scope baseline

101. Bill is an experienced project manager who wants to be sure his team collects all the necessary requirements. Which best describes controlling scope?

    a) The process of developing a detailed description of the project and product

    b) The process of creating a scope management plan that documents how the project and product scope will be defined, validated, and controlled

    c) The process of subdividing project deliverables and project work into smaller, more manageable components

    d) The process of monitoring the status of the project and product scope and managing changes in the scope baseline

102. Bill is an experienced project manager who wants to be sure his team collects all the necessary requirements. What are the outputs to plan scope management?

    a) Accepted deliverables and change requests

    b) Requirements documentation and requirements traceability matrix

    c) The process of subdividing project deliverables and project work into smaller, more manageable components

    d) Scope management plan and requirements management plan

103. What are the tools and techniques to collect requirements?

    a) Prototypes

    b) Project documents

    c) Requirements documentation

    d) Project management plan

104. The output of the collect requirements process is

    a) OPA

    b) Data analysis

    c) Requirements documentation

    d) Subject matter expert

105. Bill is an experienced project manager who wants to be sure his team collects all the necessary requirements. All are ways to collect requirements during project planning except

    a) Prototypes

    b) Data analysis

    c) Project documents

    d) Expert judgments

106. Which of the following best defines collect requirements?

    a) The process to determine, document, and manage stakeholder needs and requirements to meet project objectives

    b) Requirements baseline

    c) The process of identifying the relationships among project activities

    d) Decompose into lower-level components

107. Steven is a new project manager with minimal experience in project management to do the necessary work. Which best describes the define scope process?

    a) The process of developing a detailed description of the project and product

    b) The process of creating a scope management plan that documents how the project and product scope will be defined, validated, and controlled

    c) The process of subdividing project deliverables and project work into smaller, more manageable components

    d) The process of monitoring the status of the project and product scope and managing changes in the scope baseline

108. Kimberly is a project manager responsible for adding a new structure to a building. Which process best describes create WBS?

    a) The process of developing a detailed description of the project and product

    b) The process of creating a scope management plan that documents how the project and product scope will be defined, validated, and controlled

    c) The process of subdividing project deliverables and project work into smaller, more manageable components

    d) The process of monitoring the status of the project and product scope and managing changes in the scope baseline

109. Senior management called the project manager, Emily, into a meeting to talk about cost concerns. Senior management wants Emily to take as much time as needed. However, they do want the most accurate estimate of the current cost. Which cost management tool and technique will provide the most accurate cost estimates?

    a) Bottom-up estimating

    b) Analogous estimating

    c) Parametric estimating

    d) EVM

110. Amanda is a new project manager at a manufacturing firm. Senior management wants the most accurate information from Amanda to determine what the project will cost and how long the project will take. Amanda has been instructed to take as long as she needs. What tool and technique would Amanda use to satisfy this requirement from senior management?

    a) Prototypes

    b) An oscilloscope

    c) Fishbone

    d) Bottom-up estimating

111. Raymond is a top-level project manager at a construction company. During the implementation phase of a project, there was an atypical issue that caused a minor setback for Raymond and his team. Then BAC = 120, EV = 10, PV = 12, AC = 11. What is the EAC of the project?

    a) 132

    b) 120

    c) 121

    d) 156.2

112. Joyce is a top-level project manager at a construction company. During the implementation phase of a project, there was a typical issue that caused a minor setback for Joyce and her team. Then BAC = 120, EV = 10, PV = 12, AC = 11. What is the EAC of the project?

    a) 132

    b) 120

    c) 144

    d) 156.2

113. Nathan is a top-level project manager as a construction company. Then BAC = 120, EV = 10, PV = 12, AC = 11. What is the EAC forecast earning of the project?

    a) 132

    b) 120

    c) 121

    d) 156.2

114. Lauren is a seasoned project manager and is very good at solving projects that are not in conformance. Which is a part of the cost of conformance?

    a) Rework

    b) Testing

    c) Internal failure costs

    d) Liabilities

115. Douglas is a project manager with some experience in quality project management to do the necessary work. Which is a part of the cost of nonconformance?

    a) Training

    b) Destructive testing loss

    c) Inspections

    d) Lost business

116. Jeremy is a project manager at a local marketing firm. Jeremy needs to perform a quality audit. All are a part of preventive costs except

    a) Time to do it right

    b) Training

    c) Inspections

    d) Document processes

117. Gerald is a project manager responsible for adding a new structure to a building. The process of defining how to estimate, acquire, manage, and utilize physical and team is

    a) Develop team

    b) Plan resource management

    c) Organizational theory

    d) Team charter

118. Which answer below best fits the tools and techniques of manage communications?

    a) Change log

    b) Project management plan

    c) Manage quality

    d) Interpersonal and team skills

119. As a project manager, Jacob is planning the activities in risk management. Which of the following depicts the order of activities in risk management?

    a) Collect requirements, define scope, and create WBS

    b) Identify risks, perform qualitative risk analysis, perform quantitative risk analysis, and plan risk responses

    c) Plan schedule management, define activities, sequence activities, estimate activity resources, estimate activity costs, and develop schedule

    d) Estimate costs and determine budget

120. The process of documenting project procurement decisions, specifying the approach, and identifying potential sellers is

    a) Data analysis

    b) Procurement management plan

    c) OPA

    d) Plan procurement management

121. Janine is a longtime project manager at Aspire LLC. Janine needs to work with the procurement department to secure people with sufficient skills. Which answer best describes plan stakeholder engagement?

    a) The process of developing approaches to involve project stakeholders based on their needs and expectations, address issues, and foster appropriate stakeholder engagement

    b) Templates for the risk management plan, risk register, and risk report

    c) The process of managing procurement relationships, monitoring contract performance, making changes and corrections as appropriate, and closing out contracts

    d) The process of obtaining seller responses, selecting a seller, and awarding a contract

122. Frances is starting a new project that involves infrastructure and database migration. Frances needs to create documents for the best plan of communication for the team. Deliverables are an output of which process group?

    a) OPA

    b) EEF

    c) Final report

    d) Direct and manage project work

123. Samuel is a new project manager with good experience in change management to do the necessary work. The following are inputs to the direct and manage project work process except

   a) Approved changes

   b) Project management plan

   c) Deliverables

   d) OPA

124. Which of the following best describes the process direct and manage project work?

   a) The process of leading and performing the work defined in the project plan and implementing the approved changes to achieve the project objectives

   b) The process of improving the competencies of team members and the overall team environment to enhance project performance

   c) The process of obtaining seller responses, selecting sellers, and awarding a contract

   d) The process of documenting project decisions, specifying the approach, and identifying potential sellers

125. Jose is a project manager with great people skills. Interpersonal and team skills involve all of the following except

   a) Active listening

   b) Expert judgment

   c) Networking

   d) Political awareness

126. The following are a part of tools and techniques in manage project knowledge except

   a) Knowledge management

   b) Information management

   c) Interpersonal and team skills

   d) Lessons learned register

127. Which process best describes manage project knowledge?

    a) The process of using existing knowledge and creating new knowledge to achieve the project's objectives and contribute to organizational learning

    b) The process of communicating and working with stakeholders to meet their needs, expectations, interests, and potential impact on the project

    c) The process of developing a document that formally authorizes the existence of a project and provides the project manager with authority to apply organizational resources to project activities

    d) The process of what needs to be done to define, prepare, and coordinate all subsidiary activities to produce a document that defines the project

128. All are tools and techniques to manage project knowledge except

    a) Information management

    b) Active listening

    c) Deliverables

    d) Knowledge management

129. The following are inputs of the manage quality process except

    a) Project documents

    b) Project management plan

    c) EEF

    d) OPA

130. Which of the following is an input to the manage quality process?

    a) Quality reports

    b) Quality metrics

    c) Data gathering

    d) EEF

131. Which description best identifies the manage quality process?

    a) The process of obtaining seller responses, selecting sellers, and awarding a contract

    b) The process of translating the quality management plan into executable project activities that incorporate the organization's quality policies

    c) The process of communicating and working with stakeholders to meet their needs, expectations, interests, and potential impact on the project

    d) The process of leading and performing the work defined in the project plan and implementing the approved changes to achieve the project objectives

132. All are quality management styles except

    a) Philip Crosby

    b) Kaizen

    c) Deming

    d) Maslow

133. Pepper is a new project manager for TF Banking Services. Pepper is in the process of acquiring resources. All are tools and techniques Pepper can use to aid in her search except

    a) Virtual teams

    b) Multicriteria analysis

    c) Resource management plan

    d) Negotiation

134. Which process best describes acquire resources?

    a) The process of improving the competencies of team members and the overall team environment to enhance project performance

    b) The process of obtaining team members, facilities, equipment, materials, supplies, and other resources necessary to complete the project work

    c) The process of tracking team member performance, providing feedback, resolving issues, and managing team changes to optimize project performance

    d) The process of defining how to estimate, acquire, manage, and utilize physical and team resources

135. What is the correct order of Tuckman's ladder?

    a) Forming, storming, norming, performing, adjourning

    b) Adjourning, forming, storming, norming, performing

    c) Performing, forming, storming, norming, adjourning

    d) Storming, norming, forming, performing, adjourning

136. When developing teams, what is the most desired location of team members?

    a) Virtual teams

    b) Colocation

    c) Meetings

    d) Team performance assessments

137. When developing teams, what is the most desired location of team members?

    a) Virtual teams

    b) Colocation

    c) Meetings

    d) Team performance assessments

138. All the following are inputs to manage team except

    a) PMP

    b) Project documents updates

    c) Work performance reports

    d) Team performance

139. Which description best defines develop team?

    a) The process of tracking team member performance, providing feedback, resolving issues, and managing team changes to optimize project performance

    b) The process of ensuring timely and appropriate collection, creation, distribution, storage, retrieval, management, monitoring, and ultimate disposition of project information

c) The process of leading and performing the work defined in the project plan and implementing the approved changes to achieve the project objectives

d) The process of improving the competencies of team members and the overall team environment to enhance project performance

140. Of the four types of conflict management, which is considered the best outcome?

a) Avoid

b) Force

c) Compromise

d) Collaborate

141. Which best describes the manage resources process?

a) The process of reviewing all change requests; approving changes; managing changes to deliverables, project documents, and the project management plan; and communicating decisions

b) The process of tracking team member performance, providing feedback, resolving issues, and managing team changes to optimize project performance

c) The process of obtaining team members, facilities, equipment, materials, supplies, and other resources necessary to complete the project work

d) The process of translating the quality management plan into executable project activities that incorporate the organization's quality policies

142. Of the four types of conflict management, which is considered the worst outcome?

a) Avoid

b) Force

c) Compromise

d) Collaborate

143. Manage communication is a process of which knowledge area?

a) Plan communications management

b) Project quality management

c) Manage communications is not a process.

d) Project communications management

144. Which best describes the manage communications process?

    a) PMP

    b) The process of ensuring timely and appropriate collection, creation, distribution, storage, retrieval, management, monitoring, and the ultimate disposition of project information

    c) Work performance reports

    d) Team performance

145. All are traits of interpersonal and team skills except

    a) Active listening

    b) Conflict management

    c) Political awareness

    d) Change requests

146. Frank is a project manager with Carmon Lip Balm LLC. He and his project team meticulously put together a project plan which captured and strategized for many risks. One of them has just materialized. As a project manager, what should Frank do next?

    a) Plan risk management

    b) Monitor risks

    c) Use his interpersonal skills and team management

    d) Implement risk responses

147. Which definition correctly defines implement risk responses?

    a) The process of implementing the agreed-upon risk response

    b) The process of obtaining seller responses, selecting sellers, and awarding a contract

    c) The process of monitoring the status of the project and product scope and managing changes to the scope baseline

    d) The process of improving the competencies of team members and the overall team environment to enhance project performance

148. Which of the following is an output of implement risk response?

   a) Expert judgment

   b) Risk management plan

   c) Interpersonal skills

   d) Change requests

149. The process of obtaining seller responses, selecting a seller, and awarding a contract is

   a) Plan procurement management

   b) Conduct procurements

   c) Control procurements

   d) Project procurement management

150. All are tools and techniques to select a seller except

   a) Advertising

   b) Bidder conference

   c) Proposal evaluation

   d) Asking your best friend

151. Which definition accurately describes the conduct procurements process?

   a) The process of obtaining seller responses, selecting sellers, and awarding a contract

   b) The process of formalizing acceptance of the completed project deliverables

   c) The process of performing integrated change control

   d) The process of monitoring and recording the results of executing the quality management plan activities to assess performance and ensure project outputs are complete, correct, and meet customer expectations

152. The process of communicating and working with stakeholders to meet their needs and expectations, address issues, and foster appropriate involvement is

   a) Manage stakeholder engagement

   b) Monitor communications

c) Manage communications

d) Monitor stakeholder engagement

153. All are tools and techniques of manage stakeholder engagement except

a) Feedback

b) Negotiation

c) Ground rules

d) Change request

154. The output of manage stakeholder engagement is

a) EEF

b) Expert judgment

c) Change request

d) Change log

155. Which process best exemplifies monitoring and control in project integration?

a) Direct and manage project work

b) Monitor and control project work

c) Manage project knowledge

d) Perform integrated change control

156. What is the best definition of monitoring and control?

a) The process of tracking, reviewing, and reporting the overall progress to meet performance objectives defined in the project management plan

b) The process of reviewing all change requests; approving changes; managing changes to deliverables, project documents, and the project management plan; and communicating decisions

c) The process of formalizing acceptance of the completed project deliverables

d) The process of monitoring the status of the project and product scope and managing changes to the scope baseline

157. Judy is a top project manager at her firm. She is currently working on a project in which a fix is necessary. As a project manager, what should Judy do next?

   a) Check the release documents

   b) Notify the sponsor

   c) Evaluate the impact of the change

   d) Implement the risk response plan

158. What is the best definition of perform integrated change control?

   a) The process of tracking, reviewing, and reporting the overall progress to meet performance objectives defined in the project management plan

   b) The process of reviewing all change requests; approving changes; managing changes to deliverables, project documents, and the project management plan; and communicating decisions

   c) The process of formalizing acceptance of the completed project deliverables

   d) The process of monitoring the status of the project and product scope and managing changes to the scope baseline

159. All are tools and techniques of the perform integrated change control process except

   a) Meetings

   b) Expert judgment

   c) Project management updates

   d) Multicriteria decision analysis

160. What is the best definition of validate scope?

   a) The process of tracking, reviewing, and reporting the overall progress to meet performance objectives defined in the project management plan

   b) The process of reviewing all change requests; approving changes; managing changes to deliverables, project documents, and the project management plan; and communicating decisions

   c) The process of formalizing acceptance of the completed project deliverables

   d) The process of monitoring the status of the project and product scope and managing changes to the scope baseline

161. Which is the output of validate scope?

 a) Work performance data

 b) Acceptable deliverables

 c) Verified deliverables

 d) Work performance information

162. Which is an input to validate scope?

 a) Verified deliverables

 b) Acceptable deliverables

 c) Inspection

 d) Scope baseline

163. What is the best definition of perform integrated change control?

 a) The process of tracking, reviewing, and reporting the overall progress to meet performance objectives defined in the project management plan

 b) The process of reviewing all change requests; approving changes; managing changes to deliverables, project documents, and the project management plan; and communicating decisions

 c) The process of formalizing acceptance of the completed project deliverables

 d) The process of monitoring the status of the project and product scope and managing changes to the scope baseline

164. All are inputs to control scope except

 a) Scope management plan

 b) Change management plan

 c) Change requests

 d) Scope baseline

165. Which is a tool and technique for control scope?

    a) Trend analysis

    b) EEF

    c) Work performance information

    d) Project document updates

166. What is the best definition of control schedule?

    a) The process of monitoring the status of the project and product scope and managing changes to the scope baseline

    b) The process of monitoring project costs to the cost baseline

    c) The process of monitoring and recording the results of executing the quality management plan activities to assess performance and ensure project outputs are complete, correct, and meet customer expectations

    d) The process of ensuring the physical resources assigned and allocated to the project are available as planned versus actual utilization of resources and taking corrective actions as necessary

167. The following are tools and techniques used in control schedule except

    a) Critical path method

    b) PMIS

    c) Resource optimization

    d) Change requests

168. All are outputs for the control schedule process except

    a) Schedule forecasts

    b) Change requests

    c) Work performance information

    d) PMIS

169. What is the best definition of control costs?

    a) The process of monitoring the status of the project and product scope and managing changes to the scope baseline

    b) The process of monitoring project costs to the cost baseline

    c) The process of monitoring and recording the results of executing the quality management plan activities to assess performance and ensure project outputs are complete, correct, and meet customer expectations

    d) The process of ensuring the physical resources assigned and allocated to the project are available as planned versus actual utilization of resources and taking corrective actions as necessary

170. All are tools and techniques of control costs except

    a) Earned value analysis

    b) Trend analysis

    c) TCPI

    d) PERT

171. Which of the following is an output of control costs?

    a) Cost forecasts

    b) PMIS

    c) Cost management plan

    d) OPA

172. What is the best definition of control quality?

    a) The process of monitoring the status of the project and product scope and managing changes to the scope baseline

    b) The process of monitoring the status of the project to update the project schedule and manage changes to the schedule baseline

    c) The process of monitoring and recording the results of executing the quality management plan activities to assess performance and ensure project outputs are complete, correct, and meet customer expectations

d) The process of ensuring the physical resources assigned and allocated to the project are available as planned versus actual utilization of resources and taking corrective actions as necessary

173. Which description best describes control quality?

   a) The process of monitoring and recording the results of executing the quality management plan activities to assess performance and ensure project outputs are complete, correct, and meet customer expectations

   b) EVM

   c) PERT

   d) The process of finalizing all activities for the project, phase, or contract

174. Terri is a new project manager at a manufacturing firm. She has currently completed the planning stage. Her team has begun implementing the work according to the project plan. One of Terri's team members has noticed a problem with her task but has not yet found a fix. What tools can be used to determine the cause of the problem?

   a) Prototypes

   b) An oscilloscope

   c) Fishbone

   d) Bottom-up estimating

175. David is a new project manager for Hydro-Autos Enterprises. He wants to get off to the best start understanding ways to deliver a quality product. David and his team are planning for accuracy in quality. Which of the following tools is one of the seven rules of quality control?

   a) Analysis technique

   b) Cause-and-effect diagram

   c) Data representation

   d) Quality audit

176. Susan is a new project manager for Bikes Incorporated. She wants to get off to the best start understanding ways to deliver a quality product. She and her team are planning for accuracy in quality. They can check for quality using each of these rules of quality control except

   a) Control chart

   b) Quality audit

   c) Pareto chart

   d) Scatter diagram

177. Aaron is the project manager at a communication company that builds precision devices. His team has produced a device that is consistently measured with the same output value with little scattering, but the output is not close to the true value. This is an example of what?

   a) Accuracy

   b) Cost of quality

   c) Prevention over inspection

   d) Precision

178. What is the best definition of control resources?

   a) The process of monitoring the status of the project and product scope and managing changes to the scope baseline

   b) The process of monitoring project costs to the cost baseline

   c) The process of monitoring and recording the results of executing the quality management plan activities to assess performance and ensure project outputs are complete, correct, and meet customer expectations

   d) The process of ensuring the physical resources assigned and allocated to the project are available as planned versus actual utilization of resources and taking corrective actions as necessary

179. Robert is a new project manager at Use It or Lose It! Inc. Robert does not trust his employees to do their jobs, so he must monitor their every action to make sure he gets the results he wants. Robert is practicing

   a) RAM

   b) McGregor's Theory X

   c) Expectancy Theory

   d) McGregor's Theory Y

180. What is the correct order of team development?

   a) Performing, storming, norming, forming, and adjourning

   b) Performing, storming, adjourning, forming, and norming

   c) Forming, norming, storming, performing, and adjourning

   d) Forming, storming, norming, performing, and adjourning

181. What are the least and most desired methods of conflict resolution?

   a) Avoidance and collaboration

   b) Compromise and smoothing

   c) Force and avoidance

   d) Compromise and collaboration

182. The document that includes information on staff acquisition and release, resource calendars, recognition and rewards, compliance, and safety is

   a) Resource plan

   b) Project management plan

   c) Staffing management plan

   d) Project resource plan

183. Which answer best describes the manage communications process?

   a) The process of developing an appropriate approach and plan for project communication activities based on the information needs of each stakeholder, the available organizational assets, and the needs of the project

   b) The document that includes information on staff acquisition and release, resource calendars, recognition and rewards, compliance, and safety

   c) The process of ensuring timely and appropriate collection, creation, distribution, storage, retrieval, management, monitoring, and the ultimate disposition of project information

   d) The process of ensuring the information needs of the project and its stakeholders

184. Which answer best describes monitor communications?

    a) The process of developing an appropriate approach and plan for project communication activities based on the information needs of each stakeholder, the available organizational assets, and the needs of the project

    b) The document that includes information on staff acquisition and release, resource calendars, recognition and rewards, compliance, and safety

    c) The process of ensuring timely and appropriate collection, creation, distribution, storage, retrieval, management, monitoring, and the ultimate disposition of project information

    d) The process of ensuring the information needs of the project and its stakeholders are met

185. Tom is a new project manager for World Force Inc. Tom's team consisted of 6 members, including Tom; 2 new members have just been added. What is the number of channels of communication?

    a) 13

    b) 12

    c) 15

    d) 28

186. Tom is a new project manager for World Force Inc. Tom's team consisted of 6 members, including Tom; 2 new members have just been added. How many more channels of communication are there now?

    a) 13

    b) 12

    c) 15

    d) 28

187. Which best identifies the monitor risks process?

    a) The process of monitoring the implementation of the agreed-upon risk response plan, tracking identified risks, analyzing new risks, and evaluating the risk process

    b) The process of formalizing acceptance of the completed project deliverables

    c) The process of tracking, reviewing, and reporting the overall progress to meet performance objectives defined in the project management plan

    d) Data analysis

188. Joe is a project manager who has a sponsor who does not like risk, so Joe must identify the risks and list the probability of occurrence. What answer best describes the risk management plan?

   a) It is all the requirements of the project.

   b) It is the process of defining how to conduct risk management activities for a project.

   c) It is not a desirable choice when managing large projects.

   d) It is a grid for mapping the probability of each risk occurrence and the impact on project objectives if the risk occurs.

189. Joe is a project manager who has a sponsor who does not like risk, so Joe must identify the risks and list the probability of occurrence. Which answer best describes the probability impact matrix?

   a) It is all the requirements of the project.

   b) It is the process of defining how to conduct risk management activities for a project.

   c) It is not a desirable choice when managing large projects.

   d) It is a grid for mapping the probability of each risk occurrence and the impact on project objectives if the risk occurs.

190. Janine is a longtime project manager at Aspire LLC. Janine needs to work with the procurement department to secure people with sufficient skills. Which answer best describes control procurements management?

   a) The process of documenting project decisions, specifying the approach, and identifying potential sellers

   b) Templates for the risk management plan, risk register, and risk report

   c) The process of managing procurement relationships, monitoring contract performance, making changes and corrections as appropriate, and closing out contracts

   d) The process of obtaining seller responses, selecting a seller, and awarding a contract

191. Which process best describes conduct procurements?

   a) The process of documenting project decisions, specifying the approach, and identifying potential sellers

   b) The process of communicating and working with stakeholders to meet their needs and expectations, address issues, and foster appropriate stakeholder engagement

   c) The process of obtaining seller responses, selecting sellers, and awarding a contract

   d) Templates for the risk management plan, risk register, and risk report

192. Which statement best describes the control procurements process?

   a) The process of documenting project decisions, specifying the approach, and identifying potential sellers

   b) Templates for the risk management plan, risk register, and risk report

   c) The process of managing procurement relationships, monitoring contract performance, making changes and corrections as appropriate, and closing out contracts

   d) The process of communicating and working with stakeholders to meet their needs and expectations, address issues, and foster appropriate stakeholder engagement

193. Kazem is a project manager with many years of experience. Kazem knows how important customer communication and satisfaction are to how a project is managed. What is the best definition of monitor stakeholder engagement?

   a) The process of identifying project stakeholders regularly and analyzing and documenting relevant information regarding their interests, involvement, interdependencies, influence, and impact on project success

   b) The process of communicating and working with stakeholders to meet their needs and expectations, address issues, and foster appropriate stakeholder engagement

   c) The process of providing an overview of the project stakeholder management process

   d) The process of monitoring project stakeholder relationships and tailoring strategies for engaging stakeholders through the modification of engagement strategies and plans

194. The following describe monitor stakeholder engagement except

   a) Managing stakeholder relationships

   b) Ignoring the stakeholders until they go away

   c) Engaging with the stakeholders

   d) Formulating strategies with the stakeholders

195. The sponsor is not very happy with the progress of the project. The sponsor says to stop all efforts on the project immediately. As a project manager, what would you do next?

   a) Start the closing process

   b) Gain formal acceptance

   c) Release the team

   d) Close the project

196. What is the best definition of the close process?

   a) The process of finalizing all activities for the project, phase, or contract

   b) The process of monitoring project costs to the cost baseline

   c) The process of monitoring the status of the project and product scope and managing changes to the scope baseline

   d) The process of ensuring the information needs of the project and its stakeholders are met

197. The sponsor has accepted all deliverables of the project. As a project manager, what would you do next?

   a) Close the project

   b) Gain formal acceptance

   c) Document lessons learned

   d) Release the team

198. All are part of the closing process except

   a) Obtain stakeholder satisfaction

   b) Release the team

   c) EEF

   d) Prepare final project report

199. The sponsor has accepted all deliverables of the project. As a project manager, what would you do next?

   a) Release the team

   b) Gain formal acceptance

   c) Document lessons learned

   d) Close the project

200. The following are part of the closing process except

   a) Obtain stakeholder satisfaction

   b) Release the team

   c) EEF updates

   d) Prepare final project report

Mock Exam—Concentration Solutions

1.	b	**2.**	d	**3.**	b	**4.**	c
5.	d	**6.**	a	**7.**	d	**8.**	c
9.	b	**10.**	c	**11.**	d	**12.**	b
13.	c	**14.**	b	**15.**	b	**16.**	b
17.	d	**18.**	c	**19.**	a	**20.**	d
21.	c	**22.**	a	**23.**	a	**24.**	c
25.	c	**26.**	b	**27.**	b	**28.**	c
29.	d	**30.**	a	**31.**	a	**32.**	b
33.	c	**34.**	a	**35.**	b	**36.**	d
37.	c	**38.**	c	**39.**	a	**40.**	c
41.	c	**42.**	a	**43.**	c	**44.**	b
45.	c	**46.**	a	**47.**	a	**48.**	c
49.	a	**50.**	a	**51.**	a	**52.**	a
53.	a	**54.**	a	**55.**	a	**56.**	a
57.	a	**58.**	c	**59.**	d	**60.**	b
61.	a	**62.**	c	**63.**	d	**64.**	a
65.	b	**66.**	d	**67.**	c	**68.**	c
69.	b	**70.**	b	**71.**	d	**72.**	b
73.	d	**74.**	a	**75.**	d	**76.**	a
77.	c	**78.**	b	**79.**	d	**80.**	a
81.	b	**82.**	b	**83.**	c	**84.**	b
85.	a	**86.**	c	**87.**	b	**88.**	a
89.	b	**90.**	c	**91.**	b	**92.**	d
93.	a	**94.**	d	**95.**	c	**96.**	a
97.	a	**98.**	b	**99.**	c	**100.**	c
101.	d	**102.**	d	**103.**	a	**104.**	c
105.	c	**106.**	a	**107.**	a	**108.**	c

109. a	110. d	111. c	112. a
113. d	114. b	115. d	116. c
117. b	118. d	119. b	120. d
121. a	122. d	123. c	124. a
125. b	126. d	127. a	128. c
129. c	130. b	131. b	132. d
133. c	134. b	135. a	136. b
137. b	138. b	139. d	140. d
141. b	142. a	143. d	144. b
145. d	146. d	147. a	148. d
149. b	150. d	151. a	152. a
153. d	154. c	155. b	156. a
157. c	158. b	159. c	160. c
161. b	162. a	163. b	164. c
165. a	166. a	167. d	168. d
169. b	170. d	171. a	172. c
173. a	174. c	175. b	176. b
177. d	178. d	179. b	180. d
181. a	182. c	183. c	184. d
185. d	186. a	187. a	188. b
189. d	190. c	191. c	192. c
193. d	194. b	195. a	196. a
197. c	198. c	199. c	200. a

Mock Exam Two

200 Questions—4 Hours

1. Assume a project costs $10,000 today and will return $2,500 per year for 5 years. Your required return on investments is 10%. As a project manager, should you do the project?

    a) No, because the project will make a great profit.

    b) No, because the payback period is four years.

    c) No, because "the required return on investments is 10%."

    d) Yes, because the project meets the organization's strategic goals.

2. Lauren is a contractor responsible for the refurbishment of an automobile showroom. The estimated refurbishment cost is $500 per square foot. The total showroom area that needs to be refurbished is 1,000 square feet. Based on Lauren's past experience, she knows the project team can refurbish 100 square feet per week. What is the steady-state value?

    a) $525,000

    b) $375,000

    c) $555,555.56

    d) $475,000

3. Walter is a new project manager for SelectMates LLC. He wants to get off to the best start in understanding the project, people, and environment. Interpersonal and team skills is a tool and technique of which process?

    a) Meetings

    b) Develop project charter

    c) Organizational process assets

    d) Planning

4. Megan is a new project manager for an existing project with issues. What document does she need to determine the project goals, high-level risks, and high-level constraints?

   a) Communication plan

   b) Project management plan

   c) SOW

   d) Project charter

5. If a stakeholder has high interest but low power, what is the best way to manage the stakeholder?

   a) Keep satisfied

   b) Manage closely

   c) Keep informed

   d) Monitor

6. The output of the develop project management plan process is

   a) Project charter

   b) Enterprise environmental factors

   c) Project management plan

   d) Organizational process assets

7. The following are tools and techniques for the develop project management plan process except

   a) Meetings

   b) Project management plan

   c) Interpersonal and team skills

   d) Expert judgments

8. Which of the following is an input to develop the project management plan?

   a) Data gathering

   b) Project management plan

   c) Inspection

   d) Project charter

9. The _____ are influences out of the project manager's control.

    a) Enterprise environmental factors

    b) Organizational process assets

    c) Evolution environmental factors

    d) Extreme environmental factors

10. Susan is a project manager with many years of experience. Her current project is especially difficult because of problems with the timeline getting extended many times. This could be because the scope is not well defined, and the delays are causing increases in cost because of increased hours of work on the project for fixes. All are found in the project charter except

    a) Project purpose

    b) High-level requirements

    c) Detailed requirements

    d) Key stakeholder list

11. Which of the following are outputs to the plan scope management process?

    a) Scope management plan and requirements management plan

    b) Project charter and project management plan

    c) Quality management plan and process improvement plan

    d) Risk management plan and risk response plan

12. Which document would the project manager use to achieve the plan benefits of timeline, tools, and resources to ensure benefits are fully realized?

    a) Project management plan

    b) Benefits management plan

    c) Projects documents

    d) OPA

13. Which of the following is an output of the collect requirements process?

   a) OPA

   b) Requirements traceability matrix

   c) Project management plan

   d) Data analysis

14. Which best describes the define scope process?

   a) The process of developing a detailed description of the project and product

   b) The process of creating a scope management plan that documents how the project and product scope will be defined, validated, and controlled

   c) The process of subdividing project deliverables and project work into smaller, more manageable components

   d) The process of monitoring the status of the project and product scope and managing changes in the scope baseline

15. Work that is performed that is outside the scope of the project but is demanded by a sponsor, senior management, or stakeholders other than the project team is called

   a) Gold plating

   b) Work that is necessary

   c) Work that is unnecessary

   d) Scope creep

16. Which are number systems in the WBS dictionary and WBS, respectively?

   a) Code of account identifier and (1.0, 1.1, 1.1.1)

   b) Chart of accounts and (a, ab, abc)

   c) Control chart and (1, 2, 3)

   d) All of the above

17. The following are tools and techniques used to collect requirements except

   a) Data analysis

   b) Decision-making

   c) Organizational process assets

   d) Interpersonal skills and team skills

18. The scope baseline consists of

   a) The process of developing a detailed description of the project and product

   b) The project scope statement, WBS, WBS dictionary, and planning package

   c) The process of subdividing project deliverables and project work into smaller, more manageable components

   d) The process of monitoring the status of the project and product scope and managing changes in the scope baseline

19. As a project manager, you are planning the activities in the project schedule. What is the output of plan schedule management?

   a) Collect requirements, define scope, and create WBS

   b) Identify risks, perform qualitative risk analysis, perform quantitative risk analysis, and plan risk responses

   c) Create the schedule management plan

   d) Estimate costs and determine the budget

20. The inputs to the plan schedule management process are

   a) Project charter, project management plan, scope management plan, development approach, EEF, and OPA

   b) Perform qualitative risk analysis, perform quantitative risk analysis, and plan risk responses

   c) Project management plan, project documents, approved change requests, EEF, and OPA

   d) Project charter, project management plan, quality management plan, project life cycle, development, EEF, and OPA

21. Susan is a first-time project manager; however, she is excited to make a good impression. Halfway through her project, Susan gets an email from the client that the project will be canceled because of a funding issue. What should she do next?

    a) Try to negotiate with the client and suggest where to find additional funding

    b) Prepare the final project report

    c) Tell the team this is only a temporary setback; it happened before on a similar project, but the problem was cleared shortly.

    d) Ask senior management to talk to the client

22. Which of the following depicts the order of activities in schedule management?

    a) Collect requirements, define scope, and create the WBS

    b) Identify risks, perform qualitative risk analysis, perform quantitative risk analysis, and plan risk responses

    c) Plan schedule management, define activities, sequence activities, estimate activity durations, and develop schedules

    d) Estimate costs and determine budget

23. In the define activities process, work is decomposed into which of the following?

    a) Work packages

    b) WBS

    c) Activities

    d) WBS and activities

24. Carl is a new project manager who is currently in the planning phase of a project. He has defined the activities—what should he do next?

    a) Sequence activities

    b) Estimate costs

    c) Collect requirements

    d) Identify risks

25. The work performed outside of scope and suggested by the project team is called

    a) Gold plating

    b) Work that is necessary

    c) Work that is unnecessary

    d) Scope creep

26. The following are inputs to collect requirements except

    a) Project management plan

    b) Communication management plan

    c) Project documents

    d) EEF

27. Jesse is a new project manager who is currently in the planning phase of a project. He has defined the activities. As a project manager, what did Jesse do before defining the activities?

    a) Sequence activities

    b) Estimate costs

    c) Plan schedule management

    d) Identify risks

28. Madison is a project manager responsible for adding a new structure to a building. Of the four types of PDM relationships, which are used most often?

    a) Finish to Start (FS)

    b) Finish to Finish (FF)

    c) Start to Finish (SF)

    d) Start to Start (SS)

29. Jacqueline is a project manager at a local marketing firm. She needs to perform a sequence of activities. Which of the following depicts the order of activities in schedule management?

    a) Collect requirements, define scope, and create WBS

    b) Identify risks, perform qualitative risk analysis, perform quantitative risk analysis, and plan risk responses

c) Plan schedule management, define activities, sequence activities, estimate activity durations, and develop schedule

d) Estimate costs and determine budget

30. Which answer best represents the order of plan scope management?

   a) Identify risks, perform qualitative risk analysis, perform quantitative risk analysis, and plan risk responses

   b) Collect requirements, define scope, and create WBS

   c) Plan schedule management, define activities, sequence activities, estimate activity durations, and develop schedule

   d) Estimate costs and determine budget

31. The following are tools and techniques of the develop schedule process except

   a) Schedule compression

   b) Data analysis

   c) Project documents

   d) Critical path method

32. Which is a tool and technique of the plan cost management process?

   a) Alternative analysis

   b) Project documents

   c) Project plan updates

   d) Rolling wave technique

33. Mary is a new project manager. How much will it cost for Mary to complete the project if most likely = $2,000, optimistic = $1,000, and pessimistic = $3,000, using three-point estimation?

   a) $44

   b) $2,000

   c) $2,167

   d) $32

34. The following are tools and techniques that can be used to determine budget except

    a) Expert judgments

    b) Historical information review

    c) Funding limit reconciliation

    d) Business documents

35. Which is an output of the determine budget process?

    a) Cost baseline

    b) Alternative analysis

    c) Project management plan

    d) Voting

36. What is the output of the plan quality management process?

    a) Project management plan

    b) Project documents

    c) Risk management plan

    d) Quality management plan

37. Which best describes the plan quality management process?

    a) The process of identifying quality requirements and standards for the project and its deliverables and documenting how the project will demonstrate compliance with quality requirements and standards

    b) The process of monitoring and recording the results of executing the quality management activities to assess performance and ensure the project outputs are complete, correct, and meet customer requirements

    c) The process of translating the quality management plan into executable quality activities that incorporate the organization's quality policies into the project

    d) None of the above

38. Terry is a new project manager at a telecommunication company. She has a lot of experience in project management to do the necessary work. The process of defining how to estimate, acquire, manage, and utilize physical and team resources is

    a) Develop team

    b) Plan resource management

    c) Organizational theory

    d) Team charter

39. Theodore is a new project manager with minimal experience in acquiring proper resources to do the necessary work. The following tools and techniques can assist Theodore in estimating resources except

    a) Bottom-up estimating

    b) Analogous estimating

    c) Parametric estimating

    d) Resource breakdown structure (RBS)

40. Christian is a project manager at a local marketing firm. He needs to manage the project team to prevent scope creep and gold plating. All the following are inputs to manage a team except

    a) Project management plan

    b) Project documents updates

    c) Work performance reports

    d) Team performance

41. Which is a tool and technique of plan communications management?

    a) Change log

    b) Project management plan

    c) Manage quality

    d) Interpersonal and team skills

42. Which answer below best fits the tools and techniques of plan communication management?

    a) Change log

    b) Project management plan

    c) Manage quality

    d) Communication technology

43. Conversations and meetings are part of which tool and technique?

    a) Communications analysis

    b) Communications technology

    c) Communications model

    d) Communications method

44. Of the four types of PDM relationships, which is used least often?

    a) Finish to Start (FS)

    b) Finish to Finish (FF)

    c) Start to Finish (SF)

    d) Start to Start (SS)

45. Which of the following depicts the order of activities in estimate costs?

    a) Collect requirements, define scope, and create WBS

    b) Identify risks, perform qualitative risk analysis, perform quantitative risk analysis, and plan risk responses

    c) Plan schedule management, define activities, sequence activities, estimate activity durations, and develop schedule

    d) Estimate costs and determine budget

46. Which of the following depicts the order of activities in plan risk management?

    a) Collect requirements, define scope, and create WBS

    b) Identify risks, perform qualitative risk analysis, perform quantitative risk analysis, and plan risk responses

c) Plan schedule management, define activities, sequence activities, estimate activity resources, estimate activity costs, and develop schedule

d) Estimate costs and determine budget

47. Which is a tool and technique of plan risk management?

a) Stakeholder analysis

b) Project documents

c) Decomposition

d) Project management plan updates

48. The output of identify risk is

a) Project management plan

b) Procurement plan

c) Project documents

d) Risk register

49. Which is an output of the plan risk management process?

a) Project management plan

b) Communications management plan

c) Data analysis

d) Risk management plan

50. A tool and technique that can be used in assessing risk impact is

a) Project management plan

b) Project document updates

c) Risk probability and impact assessment

d) Risk register

51. Which is an input to the perform qualitative risk analysis process?

   a) Project management plan

   b) Alternative analysis

   c) OPA updates

   d) EEF updates

52. Which answer is the best description of perform quantitative risk analysis?

   a) It is the process of numerically analyzing the effect of identified risks on overall project objects.

   b) It is the process by which we identify risks, perform qualitative risk analysis, perform quantitative risk analysis, and plan risk responses.

   c) It is the process by which we plan schedule management, define activities, sequence activities, estimate activity resources, estimate activity costs, and develop schedules.

   d) It involves estimating costs and determining budget.

53. Which is both an input and output of the process perform quantitative risk analysis?

   a) Risk report

   b) Analysis report

   c) Rolling wave

   d) Decomposition

54. All are tools and techniques of the plan risk responses process except

   a) Expert judgments

   b) Interpersonal and team skills

   c) Contingency response strategy

   d) Change requests

55. Which is a tool or technique of the plan risk response process?

   a) Interpersonal and team skills

   b) Process improvement plan

c) Project management plan

d) Quality management plan

56. The process of documenting project procurement decisions, specifying the approach, and identifying potential sellers is

   a) Data analysis

   b) Procurement management plan

   c) Organizational process assets

   d) Plan procurement management

57. The output of the plan procurement management process is

   a) Procurement management plan

   b) Project management plan

   c) Conduct procurement

   d) Control procurement

58. Which answer best describes the plan stakeholder engagement process?

   a) The process of developing approaches to involve project stakeholders based on their needs and expectations, addressing issues, and fostering appropriate stakeholder involvement

   b) The process of monitoring project stakeholder relationships and tailoring strategies for engaging stakeholders through the modification of engagement strategies and plans

   c) The process of communicating and working with stakeholders to meet their needs and expectations

   d) The process of not communicating and working with stakeholders to meet their needs and expectations

59. The output of plan stakeholder engagement is

   a) Assumption and constraint analysis

   b) Stakeholder engagement plan

   c) Project management plan

   d) Process improvement plan

60. Deliverables are an output of which process group?

    a) Organizational process assets

    b) Enterprise environmental factors

    c) Final report

    d) Direct and manage project work

61. The following are components of tools and techniques in the manage project knowledge process except

    a) Knowledge management

    b) Information management

    c) Interpersonal and team skills

    d) Lessons learned register

62. Which of the following is an input to the manage project knowledge process?

    a) Alternative analysis

    b) Deliverables

    c) OPA updates

    d) Project management plan updates

63. Which of the following is an input to the manage quality process?

    a) Quality reports

    b) Quality metrics

    c) Data gathering

    d) Enterprise environmental factors

64. Pepper is a new project manager for TF Banking Services. She is in the process of acquiring resources. All are tools and techniques Pepper can use to aid in her search except

    a) Virtual teams

    b) Multicriteria analysis

    c) Resource management plan

    d) Negotiation

65. What is the correct order of Tuckman's ladder?

    a) Forming, storming, norming, performing, adjourning

    b) Adjourning, forming, storming, norming, performing

    c) Performing, forming, storming, norming, adjourning

    d) Storming, norming, forming, performing, adjourning

66. All of the following are inputs to manage a team except

    a) Project management plan

    b) Project documents updates

    c) Work performance reports

    d) Team performance

67. Which best describes the process to manage communications?

    a) Project management plan

    b) The process of ensuring timely and appropriate collection, creation, distribution, storage, retrieval, management, monitoring, and the ultimate disposition of project information

    c) Work performance reports

    d) Team performance

68. Frank is a project manager with Carmon Lip Balm LLC. He and his project team meticulously put together a project plan which captured and strategized for many risks. One of the risks has just materialized. As a project manager, what should Frank do next?

    a) Plan risk management

    b) Monitor risks

    c) Use his interpersonal and team management skills

    d) Implement risk responses

69. Debbie is a project manager at Cool Socks Inc. She is in the planning process for a new project and has completed the sequence activities process. The kickoff of the project occurred three months ago. The project team is currently managing the project. As a project manager, what should she do next?

    a) Estimate activity durations

    b) Close the project

    c) Control schedule

    d) Identify stakeholders

70. Which of the following is an output of the implement risk response plan process?

    a) Change requests

    b) Data analysis

    c) Approved changes

    d) OPA

71. The process of obtaining seller responses, selecting a seller, and awarding a contract is

    a) Plan procurement management

    b) Conduct procurements

    c) Control procurements

    d) Project procurement management

72. All are tools and techniques to select a seller except

    a) Advertising

    b) Bidder conference

    c) Proposal evaluation

    d) Asking your best friend

73. The process of communicating and working with stakeholders to meet their needs and expectations, address issues, and foster appropriate involvement is

    a) Manage stakeholder engagement

    b) Monitor communications

    c) Manage communications

    d) Monitor stakeholder engagement

74. Which process best exemplifies monitoring and controlling in project integration?

    a) Direct and manage project work

    b) Monitor and control project work

    c) Manage project knowledge

    d) Perform integrated change control

75. Harry is a contractor responsible for the refurbishment of an automobile showroom. The estimated refurbishment cost is $500 per square foot. The total showroom area that needs to be refurbished is 1,000 square feet. Based on his past experience, he knows his team can refurbish 100 square feet per week. How is the project performing?

    a) On schedule and on budget

    b) Behind schedule and over budget

    c) Ahead of schedule and over budget

    d) Behind schedule and ahead of budget

76. Which of the following is a tool and technique of direct and manage project work?

    a) Change requests

    b) PMIS

    c) Project management plan

    d) OPA updates

77. Judy is a superb project manager at her firm. She is currently working on a project in which a fix is necessary. As a project manager, what should Judy do next?

    a) Check the release documents

    b) Notify the sponsor

    c) Evaluate the impact of the change

    d) Implement the risk response plan

78. Judy is a top project manager at her firm. She is currently working on a project in which a fix *might be* necessary. As a project manager, what should Judy do next?

    a) Prevent changes from occurring

    b) Notify the sponsor

    c) Evaluate the impact of the change

    d) Implement the risk response plan

79. What is the output of the validate scope process?

    a) Work performance data

    b) Acceptable deliverables

    c) Verified deliverables

    d) Work performance information

80. All are inputs to control scope except

    a) Scope management plan

    b) Change management plan

    c) Change requests

    d) Scope baseline

81. All are tools and techniques used in the control schedule process except

    a) Critical path method

    b) PMIS

c) Resource optimization

d) Change requests

82. Which tool/technique is best for controlling cost and schedule?

   a) EVM

   b) PERT

   c) PMIS

   d) Cost forecast

83. Which tool/technique is best for planning cost and schedule?

   a) EVM

   b) PERT

   c) PMIS

   d) Cost forecast

84. Terri is a new project manager at a manufacturing firm. She currently has completed the planning stage. Her team has begun implementing the work according to the project plan. One of Terri's team members has noticed a problem with her task but has not yet found a fix. What tools can be used to determine the cause of the problem?

   a) Prototypes

   b) An oscilloscope

   c) Fishbone

   d) Bottom-up estimating

85. David is a new project manager for Combo-Wash/Dry Services. He wants to get off to the best start understanding ways to deliver a quality product. David and his team are planning for accuracy in quality. Which of the following tools is one of the seven rules of quality control?

   a) Analysis technique

   b) Cause-and-effect diagram

   c) Data representation

   d) Quality audit

86. Robert is a new project manager at Use It or Lose It! Inc. Robert does not trust his employees to do their jobs, so he must monitor their every action to make sure he gets the results he wants. Robert is practicing

   a) RAM

   b) McGregor's Theory X

   c) Expectancy Theory

   d) McGregor's Theory Y

87. What is the correct order of team development?

   a) Performing, storming, norming, forming, and adjourning

   b) Performing, storming, adjourning, forming, and norming

   c) Forming, norming, storming, performing, and adjourning

   d) Forming, storming, norming, performing, and adjourning

88. Which answer best describes monitor communications?

   a) The process of developing an appropriate approach and plan for project communication activities based on the information needs of each stakeholder, the available organizational assets, and the needs of the project

   b) The document that includes information on staff acquisition and release, resource calendars, recognition and rewards, and compliance and safety

   c) The process of monitoring communications and the process of ensuring the information needs of the project and its stakeholders are met

   d) The process of ensuring the information needs of the project and its stakeholders are met

89. Tom is a new project manager for World Force Inc. His team consisted of 6 members, including Tom; 2 new members have just been added. What is the number of channels of communication?

   a) 13

   b) 12

   c) 15

   d) 28

90. Tom is a new project manager for World Force Inc. Tom's team consisted of 6 members, including Tom; 2 new members have just been added. How many more channels of communication are there now?

   a) 13
   b) 12
   c) 15
   d) 28

91. Which answer best describes the risk management plan?

   a) It contains all the requirements of the project.
   b) It is the process of defining how to conduct risk management activities for a project.
   c) It is not a desirable choice when managing large projects.
   d) It is used for mapping the probability of each risk occurrence and the impact on project objectives if the risk occurs.

92. Joe is a project manager and has a sponsor who does not like risk, so Joe must identify the risks and list the probability of occurrence. Which answer best describes the probability and impact matrix?

   a) It contains all the requirements of the project.
   b) It is the process of defining how to conduct risk management activities for a project.
   c) It is not a desirable choice when managing large projects.
   d) It is used for mapping the probability of each risk occurrence and the impact on project objectives if the risk occurs.

93. Janine is a longtime project manager at Aspire LLC. She needs to work with the procurement department to secure people with sufficient skills. Which answer best describes the control procurements process?

   a) The process of documenting project decisions, specifying the approach, and identifying potential sellers
   b) The process of creating templates for the risk management plan, risk register, and risk report
   c) The process of managing procurement relationships, monitoring contract performance, making changes and corrections as appropriate, and closing out contracts
   d) The process of obtaining seller responses, selecting a seller and awarding a contract

94. Which is a tool or technique of the control procurements process?

   a) Project management plan

   b) Communication management plan

   c) Change requests

   d) Claims administration

95. Kazem is a project manager with many years of experience. He knows how important customer communication and satisfaction are to how a project is managed. What is the best definition of the monitor stakeholder engagement process?

   a) The process of identifying project stakeholders regularly and analyzing and documenting relevant information regarding their interests, involvement, interdependencies, influence, and impact on project success

   b) The process of communicating and working with stakeholders to meet their needs and expectations, address issues, and foster appropriate stakeholder engagement

   c) The process of providing an overview of the project stakeholder management process

   d) The process of monitoring project stakeholder relationships and tailoring strategies for engaging stakeholders through the modification of engagement strategies and plans

96. The following describe monitor stakeholder engagement except

   a) Managing stakeholder relationships

   b) Ignoring the stakeholders until they go away

   c) Engaging with the stakeholders

   d) Formulating strategies with the stakeholders

97. Susan is a first-time project manager; however, she is excited to make a good impression. Halfway through her project, Susan gets an email from the client that the project will be canceled because of a funding issue. What should she do next?

   a) Try to negotiate with the client and suggest where to find additional funding

   b) Prepare the final project report

   c) Tell the team this is only a temporary setback; it happened before on a similar project, but the problem was cleared shortly.

   d) Ask senior management to talk to the client

98. Which is a tool and technique of the close project or phase process?

   a) Regression analysis

   b) OPA

   c) EEF

   d) Deliverables

99. Judy is a superb project manager at her firm. She is currently working on a project in which a fix is necessary. As a project manager, what should Judy do next?

   a) Check the release documents

   b) Notify the sponsor

   c) Evaluate the impact of the change

   d) Implement the risk response plan

100. Judy is a top project manager at her firm. She is currently working on a project in which a fix *might be* necessary. As a project manager, what should Judy do next?

   a) Prevent changes from occurring

   b) Notify the sponsor

   c) Evaluate the impact of the change

   d) Implement the risk response plan

101. What is the output of the validate scope process?

   a) Work performance data

   b) Acceptable deliverables

   c) Verified deliverables

   d) Work performance information

102. All are inputs to control scope except

   a) Scope management plan

   b) Change management plan

   c) Change requests

   d) Scope baseline

103. All tools and techniques used in the control schedule process except

   a) Critical path method

   b) PMIS

   c) Resource optimization

   d) Change requests

104. Which tool/technique is best for controlling cost and schedule?

   a) EVM

   b) PERT

   c) PMIS

   d) Cost forecast

105. Which tool/technique is best for planning cost and schedule?

   a) EVM

   b) PERT

   c) PMIS

   d) Cost forecast

106. Terri is a new project manager at a manufacturing firm. She currently has completed the planning stage. Her team has begun implementing the work according to the project plan. One of Terri's team members has noticed a problem with her task but has not yet found a fix. What tools can be used to determine the cause of the problem?

   a) Prototypes

   b) An oscilloscope

   c) Fishbone

   d) Bottom-up estimating

107. David is a new project manager for Dog Dispenser Corp. He wants to get off to the best start understanding ways to deliver a quality product. David and his team are planning for accuracy in quality. Which of the following tools is one of the seven rules of quality control?

   a) Analysis technique

   b) Cause-and-effect diagram

   c) Data representation

   d) Quality audit

108. Robert is a new project manager at Use It or Lose It! Inc. He does not trust his employees to do their jobs, so he must monitor their every action to make sure he gets the results he wants. Robert is practicing

   a) RAM

   b) McGregor's Theory X

   c) Expectancy Theory

   d) McGregor's Theory Y

109. What is the correct order of team development?

   a) Performing, storming, norming, forming, and adjourning

   b) Performing, storming, adjourning, forming, and norming

   c) Forming, norming, storming, performing, and adjourning

   d) Forming, storming, norming, performing, and adjourning

110. Which answer best describes monitor communications?

   a) The process of developing an appropriate approach and plan for project communication activities based on the information needs of each stakeholder, the available organizational assets, and the needs of the project

   b) The document that includes information on staff acquisition and release, resource calendars, recognition and rewards, and compliance and safety

   c) The process of monitoring communications and the process of ensuring the information needs of the project and its stakeholders are met

   d) The process of ensuring the information needs of the project and its stakeholders are met

111. Tom is a new project manager for World Force Inc. Tom's team consisted of 6 members, including Tom; 2 new members have just been added. What is the number of channels of communications now?

    a) 13

    b) 12

    c) 15

    d) 28

112. Tom is a new project manager for World Force Inc. Tom's team consisted of 6 members, including Tom; 2 new members have just been added. How many more channels of communication are there now?

    a) 13

    b) 12

    c) 15

    d) 28

113. Which of the following depicts the order of activities in cost management?

    a) Collect requirements, define scope, and create WBS

    b) Identify risks, perform qualitative risk analysis, perform quantitative risk analysis, and plan risk responses

    c) Plan schedule management, define activities, sequence activities, estimate activity resources, estimate activity costs, and develop schedule

    d) Estimate costs and determine budget

114. Joe is a project manager and has a sponsor who does not like risk, so Joe must identify the risks and list the probability of occurrence. Which answer best describes the probability and impact matrix?

    a) It contains all the requirements of the project.

    b) It is the process of defining how to conduct risk management activities for a project.

    c) It is not a desirable choice when managing large projects.

    d) It is used for mapping the probability of each risk occurrence and the impact on project objectives if the risk occurs.

115. Janine is a longtime project manager at Aspire LLC. She needs to work with the procurement department to secure people with sufficient skills. Which answer best describes the control procurements process?

   a) The process of documenting project decisions, specifying the approach, and identifying potential sellers

   b) The process of creating templates for the risk management plan, risk register, and risk report

   c) The process of managing procurement relationships, monitoring contract performance, making changes and corrections as appropriate, and closing out contracts

   d) The process of obtaining seller responses, selecting a seller, and awarding a contract

116. The project management plan plans the overall activities of the project and contains detailed requirements of the project. The SOW is the statement of work, which contains the objects of the project. The project charter contains the high-level requirements of the project. All are inputs to the identify stakeholders process except

   a) Project charter

   b) EEF

   c) Expert judgments

   d) Organizational process assets

117. Which is a tool or technique of the control procurements process?

   a) Project management plan

   b) Communication management plan

   c) Change requests

   d) Claims administration

118. Kazem is a project manager with many years of experience. He knows how important customer communication and satisfaction are to how a project is managed. What is the best definition of the monitor stakeholder engagement process?

   a) The process of identifying project stakeholders regularly and analyzing and documenting relevant information regarding their interests, involvement, interdependencies, influence, and impact on project success

   b) The process of communicating and working with stakeholders to meet their needs and expectations, address issues, and foster appropriate stakeholder engagement

c) The process of providing an overview of the project stakeholder management process

d) The process of monitoring project stakeholder relationships and tailoring strategies for engaging stakeholders through the modification of engagement strategies and plans

119. The following describe monitor stakeholder engagement except

   a) Managing stakeholder relationships

   b) Ignoring the stakeholder until they go away

   c) Engaging with the stakeholders

   d) Formulating strategies with the stakeholders

120. Which is a tool and technique of the close project or phase process?

   a) Regression analysis

   b) OPA

   c) EEF

   d) Deliverables

121. Senior management is attempting to decide on which project to invest. Which one would you recommend?

   a) It has a present value of $1,157.00.

   b) The payback period is four years.

   c) The net present value will be -$523.03.

   d) IRR will be 7.93%.

122. All the following are inputs to the develop project charter process except

   a) SOW

   b) Enterprise environmental factors

   c) Organizational process assets

   d) Data gathering

123. The following are part of the closing process except

    a) Obtain stakeholder satisfaction

    b) Release the team

    c) EEF

    d) Prepare the final project report

124. The sponsor has accepted all deliverables of the project. As a project manager, what would you do next?

    a) Release the team

    b) Gain formal acceptance

    c) Document lessons learned

    d) Close the project

125. The following are part of the closing process except

    a) Obtain stakeholder satisfaction

    b) Release the team

    c) EEF updates

    d) Prepare final project report

126. The outputs to develop project charter are

    a) Project management plan and requirements plan

    b) Project charter and assumptions log

    c) Quality management plan and change management plan

    d) Stakeholder management plan

127. All are inputs to identify stakeholder group except

    a) Project charter

    b) EEF

    c) Expert judgment

    d) OPA

128. All describe a project charter except

    a) Formally authorizes the existence of a project

    b) Provides project manager the authority to apply organizational resources to the project

    c) States the deliverables of the project

    d) States the details of project deliverables

129. Which best identifies the monitor risks process?

    a) The process of monitoring the implementation of the agreed-upon risk response plan, tracking identified risks, analyzing new risks, and evaluating the risk process

    b) The process of formalizing acceptance of the completed project deliverables

    c) The process of tracking, reviewing, and reporting the overall progress to meet performance objectives defined in the project management plan

    d) Data analysis

130. Joe is a project manager who has a sponsor who does not like risk, so Joe must identify the risk and list the probability of occurrence. Which answer best describes the risk management plan?

    a) It is all the requirements of the project.

    b) It is the process of defining how to conduct risk management activities for a project.

    c) It is not a desirable choice when managing large projects.

    d) It is a grid for mapping the probability of each risk occurrence and the impact on project objectives if the risk occurs.

131. Which best describes the process plan scope management?

    a) The process of developing a document that formally authorizes the existence of a project and provides the project manager with the authority to apply organizational resources to project activities.

    b) The process of how the project and product scope will be defined, validated and controlled throughout the project.

    c) The process of developing detailed descriptions of the project and products. This is what the project includes and excludes.

    d) The process of estimating the number of work periods needed to complete activities with the estimated resources.

132. All are contained in the define scope process except

    a) What the project includes and excludes

    b) The output is the project scope statement

    c) A detailed description of the project and products

    d) How the project and product scope will be validated

133. Joe is a project manager who has a sponsor who does not like risk, so Joe must identify the risk and list the probability of occurrence. Which answer best describes the probability impact matrix?

    a) It is all the requirements of the project.

    b) It is the process of defining how to conduct risk management activities for a project.

    c) It is not a desirable choice when managing large projects.

    d) It is a grid for mapping the probability of each risk occurrence and the impact on project objectives if the risk occurs.

134. Which best describes the define scope process?

    a) The process of developing a document that formally authorizes the existence of a project and provides the project manager with authority to apply organizational resources to project activities

    b) The process of how the project and product scope will be defined, validated, and controlled throughout the project

    c) The process of developing detailed descriptions of the project and products, which is what the project includes and excludes

    d) The process of estimating the number of work periods needed to complete activities with the estimated resources

135. All the following describe estimate activity durations except

    a) Determine risks

    b) The process of estimating work periods

    c) The work periods to complete activities

    d) Estimated resources to complete activities

136. Which answer best describes the manage communications process?

   a) The process of developing an appropriate approach and plan for project communication activities based on the information needs of each stakeholder, the available organizational assets, and the needs of the project

   b) The document that includes information on staff acquisition and release, resource calendars, recognition, rewards, compliance, and safety

   c) The process of ensuring timely and appropriate collection, creation, distribution, storage, retrieval, management, monitoring, and the ultimate disposition of project information

   d) The process of ensuring the information needs of the project and its stakeholders

137. Which answer best describes monitor communications?

   a) The process of developing an appropriate approach and plan for project communication activities based on the information needs of each stakeholder, the available organizational assets, and the needs of the project

   b) The document that includes information on staff acquisition and release, resource calendars, recognition, rewards, compliance, and safety

   c) The process of ensuring timely and appropriate collection, creation, distribution, storage, retrieval, management, monitoring, and the ultimate disposition of project information

   d) The process of ensuring the information needs of the project and its stakeholders are met

138. Tom is a new project manager for World Force Inc. His team consisted of 6 members, including Tom; 2 new members have just been added. What is the number of channels of communication?

   a) 13

   b) 12

   c) 15

   d) 28

139. Tom is a new project manager for World Force Inc. Tom's team consisted of 6 members, including Tom; 2 new members have just been added. How many more channels of communication are there now?

   a) 13

   b) 12

   c) 15

   d) 28

140. Which best describes the estimate activity durations process?

   a) The process of developing a document that formally authorizes the existence of a project and provides the project manager with authority to apply organizational resources to project activities

   b) The process of how the project and product scope will be defined, validated, and controlled throughout the project

   c) The process of developing detailed descriptions of the project and products. This is what the project includes and excludes

   d) The process of estimating the number of work periods needed to complete activities with the estimated resources

141. The output of develop project management plan is

   a) Project charter

   b) EEF

   c) Project management plan

   d) OPA

142. The outputs of plan scope management are

   a) Scope management plan and requirements management plan

   b) Quality management plan and process improvement plan

   c) Resource management plan and resource breakdown structure

   d) Risk management plan and risk improvement plan

143. The _____ are influences out of the project manager's control.

   a) Enterprise environmental factors

   b) OPA

   c) Evolution environmental factors

   d) Extreme environmental factors

144. _____ are factors internal to the organization that affect the project.

   a) Optimal process assets

   b) Omni process assets

   c) Organization process assets

   d) Optical process assets

145. Susan is a new project manager for Bikes Incorporated. She wants to get off to the best start understanding ways to deliver a quality product. Susan and her team are planning for accuracy in quality. They can check for quality using each of these rules of quality control except

   a) Control chart

   b) Quality audit

   c) Pareto chart

   d) Scatter diagram

146. Aaron is the project manager at a communication company that builds precision devices. His team has produced a device that is consistently measured with the same output value with little scattering, but the output is not close to the true value. This is an example of what?

   a) Accuracy

   b) Cost of quality

   c) Prevention over inspection

   d) Precision

147. What is the best definition of control resources?

   a) The process of monitoring the status of the project and product scope and managing changes to the scope baseline

   b) The process of monitoring project costs to the cost baseline

   c) The process of monitoring and recording the results of executing the quality management plan activities to assess performance and ensure project outputs are complete, correct, and meet customer expectations

   d) The process of ensuring the physical resources assigned and allocated to the project are available as planned versus actual utilization of resources and taking corrective actions as necessary

148. Robert is a new project manager at Use It or Lose It! Inc. Robert does not trust his employees to do their jobs, so he must monitor their every action to make sure he gets the results he wants. Robert is practicing

   a) RAM

   b) McGregor's Theory X

   c) Expectancy Theory

   d) McGregor's Theory Y

149. What is the correct order of team development?

   a) Performing, storming, norming, forming, and adjourning

   b) Performing, storming, adjourning, forming, and norming

   c) Forming, norming, storming, performing, and adjourning

   d) Forming, storming, norming, performing, and adjourning

150. What are the least and most desired methods of conflict resolution?

   a) Avoidance and collaboration

   b) Compromise and smoothing

   c) Force and avoidance

   d) Compromise and collaboration

151. The document that includes information on staff acquisition and release, resource calendars, recognition, rewards, compliance, and safety is

   a) Resource plan

   b) Project management plan

   c) Staffing management plan

   d) Project resource plan

152. Deliverables are an output of which process group?

a) OPA

b) EEF

c) Final report

d) Direct and manage project work

153. The following are inputs to the direct and manage project work process except

a) Approved changes

b) Project management plan

c) Deliverables

d) OPA

154. Which of the following best describes the direct and manage project work process?

a) The process of leading and performing the work defined in the project plan and implementing the approved changes to achieve the project objectives

b) The process of improving the competencies of team members and the overall team environment to enhance project performance

c) The process of obtaining seller responses, selecting sellers, and awarding a contract

d) The process of documenting project decisions, specifying the approach, and identifying potential sellers

155. Interpersonal and team skills involve all except

a) Active listening

b) Expert judgment

c) Networking

d) Political awareness

156. The following are a part of tools and techniques in manage project knowledge except

a) Knowledge management

b) Information management

c) Interpersonal and team skills

d) Lessons learned register

157. Which process best exemplifies monitoring and control in project integration?

a) Direct and manage project work

b) Monitor and control project work

c) Manage project knowledge

d) Perform integrated change control

158. What is the best definition of monitoring and control?

a) The process of tracking, reviewing, and reporting the overall progress to meet performance objectives defined in the project management plan

b) The process of reviewing all change requests; approving changes; managing changes to deliverables, project documents and the project management plan; and communicating decisions

c) The process of formalizing acceptance of the completed project deliverables

d) The process of monitoring the status of the project and product scope and managing changes to the scope baseline

159. Judy is a top project manager at her firm. She is currently working on a project in which a fix is necessary. As a project manager, what should Judy do next?

a) Check the release documents

b) Notify the sponsor

c) Evaluate the impact of the change

d) Implement the risk response plan

160. What is the best definition of perform integrated change control?

a) The process of tracking, reviewing, and reporting the overall progress to meet performance objectives defined in the project management plan

b) The process of reviewing all change requests; approving changes; managing changes to deliverables, project documents, and the project management plan; and communicating decisions

c) The process of formalizing acceptance of the completed project deliverables

d) The process of monitoring the status of the project and product scope and managing changes to the scope baseline

161. All are tools and techniques of the perform integrated change control process except

   a) Meetings

   b) Expert judgment

   c) Project management updates

   d) Multicriteria decision analysis

162. Of the four types of conflict management, which is considered the worst outcome?

   a) Avoid

   b) Force

   c) Compromise

   d) Collaborate

163. Manage communication is a process of which knowledge area?

   a) Plan communications management

   b) Project quality management

   c) Manage communications is not a process

   d) Project communications management

164. Which best describes the manage communications process?

   a) PMP

   b) The process of ensuring timely and appropriate collection, creation, distribution, storage, retrieval, management, monitoring, and the ultimate disposition of project information

   c) Work performance reports

   d) Team performance

165. All are traits of interpersonal and team skills except

   a) Active listening

   b) Conflict management

c) Political awareness

d) Change requests

166. Frank is a project manager with Carmon Lip Balm LLC. He and his project team meticulously put together a project plan that captured and strategized for many risks. One of them has just materialized. As a project manager, what should Frank do next?

a) Plan risk management

b) Monitor risks

c) Use his interpersonal skills and team management

d) Implement risk responses

167. Which of the following correctly defines implement risk responses?

a) The process of implementing the agreed-upon risk response

b) The process of obtaining seller responses, selecting sellers, and awarding a contract

c) The process of monitoring the status of the project and product scope and managing changes to the scope baseline

d) The process of improving the competencies of team members and the overall team environment to enhance project performance

168. Which of the following is an output of implement risk response?

a) Expert judgment

b) Risk management plan

c) Interpersonal skills

d) Change requests

169. The output of plan risk management is

a) Cost management plan

b) Risk management plan

c) Scope baseline

d) Risk baseline

170. Which process best describes identify risk?

   a) The process of identifying individual risks as well as sources of overall project risks and documenting their characteristics

   b) Data analysis and interpersonal skills

   c) Project management plan

   d) The process of defining how to estimate, acquire, manage, and utilize physical and team resources

171. A tool and technique that can be used in assessing risk impact is

   a) Project management plan

   b) Project document updates

   c) Risk probability and impact assessment

   d) Risk register

172. Which of the following best describes perform qualitative risk analysis?

   a) The process of prioritizing individual project risks for further analysis by assessing their probability of occurrence and impact

   b) The process of numerically analyzing the effect of identified risks on overall project objects

   c) Identify risks, perform qualitative risk analysis, perform quantitative risk analysis, and plan risk responses

   d) Plan schedule management, define activities, sequence activities, estimate activity resources, estimate activity costs, and develop schedule

173. Which answer is the best description of perform quantitative risk analysis?

   a) The process of numerically analyzing the effect of identified risks on overall project objects

   b) Identify risks, perform qualitative risk analysis, perform quantitative risk analysis, and plan risk responses

   c) Plan schedule management, define activities, sequence activities, estimate activity resources, estimate activity costs, and develop schedule

   d) Estimate costs and determine budget

174. The following are tools and techniques to perform quantitative risk analysis except

   a) Simulations

   b) EEF

   c) Tornado diagram

   d) Facilitation

175. The following are strategies for negative risks/threats except

   a) Avoid

   b) Mitigate

   c) Share

   d) Transfer

176. The following are strategies for positive risks/threats except

   a) Exploit

   b) Mitigate

   c) Share

   d) Enhance

177. All are tools and techniques to plan risk responses except

   a) Expert judgment

   b) Interpersonal and team skills

   c) Contingency response strategy

   d) Change requests

178. Senior management called the project manager into a meeting to talk about cost concerns. Senior management wants the project manager to take as much time as needed. However, they do want the most accurate estimate of the current cost. Which cost management tool and technique will provide the most accurate cost estimates?

   a) Bottom-up estimating

   b) Analogous estimating

   c) Parametric estimating

   d) EVM

179. Terri is a new project manager at a manufacturing firm. Senior management wants her to determine the most accurate costs and the time the project will take. Terri has been instructed to take as long as she needs. What tool and technique would Terri use to satisfy this requirement from senior management?

    a) Prototypes

    b) An oscilloscope

    c) Fishbone

    d) Bottom-up estimating

180. Jim is a top-level project manager at a construction company. During the implementation phase of a project, there was an atypical issue that caused a minor setback for Jim and his team. Then BAC = 150, EV =10, PV = 12, AC = 11. What is the EAC of the project?

    a) 132

    b) 120

    c) 151

    d) 156.2

181. Richard is a junior project manager at a construction company. During the implementation phase of a project, there was an atypical issue that caused a minor setback for Richard and his team. Then BAC = 120, EV =10, PV = 12, AC = 11. What is the ETC of the project?

    a) 132

    b) 120

    c) 110

    d) 156.2

182. Kimberly is a top-level project manager at a construction company. For her project, BAC = 120, EV = 10, PV = 12, AC = 11. What is the EAC forecast earning of the project?

    a) 132

    b) 120

    c) 110.833

    d) 156.2

183. Which is a part of the cost of conformance?

   a) Rework

   b) Testing

   c) Internal failure costs

   d) Liabilities

184. Which is a part of the cost of nonconformance?

   a) Training

   b) Destructive testing loss

   c) Inspections

   d) Lost business

185. All are a part of preventive costs except

   a) Time to do it right

   b) Training

   c) Inspections

   d) Document processes

186. Which is a part of the cost of conformance?

   a) Rework

   b) Testing

   c) Internal failure costs

   d) Liabilities

187. Which is a part of the cost of nonconformance?

   a) Training

   b) Destructive testing loss

   c) Inspections

   d) Lost business

188. All are a part of preventive costs except

    a) Time to do it right

    b) Training

    c) Inspections

    d) Document processes

189. Which of the following is not one of the seven basic quality tools?

    a) Flowcharts

    b) Control charts

    c) Risk management

    d) Check sheets

190. Which answer best describes a communications plan?

    a) The process of developing an appropriate approach and plan for project communication activities based on the information needs of each stakeholder, the available organizational assets, and the needs of the project

    b) The document that includes information on staff acquisition and release, resource calendars, recognition, rewards, compliance, and safety

    c) The process of ensuring timely and appropriate collection, creation, distribution, storage, retrieval, management, monitoring, and the ultimate disposition of project information

    d) The process of ensuring the information needs of the project and its stakeholders

191. What is the output of plan communications management?

    a) Project management plan

    b) Project documents

    c) Communications management plan

    d) Communication baseline

192. What tool and technique can the project manager use to determine the number of communication channels?

 a) EV - AC

 b) PERT

 c) AC + (BAC - EV)

 d) N (n + 1) / 2

193. As a project manager, you are planning the activities in the project schedule. Which of the following depicts the order of activities in risk management?

 a) Collect requirements, define scope, and create WBS

 b) Identify risks, perform qualitative risk analysis, perform quantitative risk analysis, and plan risk responses

 c) Plan schedule management, define activities, sequence activities, estimate activity resources, estimate activity costs, and develop schedule

 d) Estimate costs and determine budget

194. What is the output of plan risk management?

 a) Communication management plan

 b) Configuration management plan

 c) Home improvement plan

 d) Risk management plan

195. What description best identifies plan risk management?

 a) The process of defining how to conduct risk management activities

 b) The process of using existing knowledge and creating new knowledge to achieve the project's objectives and contribute to organizational learning

 c) The process of translating the quality management plan into executable project activities that incorporate the organization's quality policies

 d) Risk baseline

196. Which process best describes plan communications management?

   a) The process of numerically analyzing the combined effects of identified individual project risks

   b) The process of developing an approach and plan for project communications activities based on the information needs of each stakeholder and the project

   c) Plan-Do-Check-Act

   d) The process of prioritizing individual project risks for further analysis by assessing their probability of occurrence and impact

197. Rajish is a new project manager for OpenSystem LLC. Rajish wants to get off to the best start understanding the project, people, and environment. Interpersonal and team skills is a tool and technique of which process?

   a) Meetings

   b) Develop project charter

   c) OPA

   d) Planning

198. All the following are inputs to develop project charter except

   a) SOW

   b) EEF

   c) OPA

   d) Data analysis

199. Henry is a project manager with many years of experience. He wants to understand the objectives of the sponsor of this project. The outputs to develop project charter are

   a) Project management plan and requirements plan

   b) Project charter and assumptions log

   c) Quality management plan and change management plan

   d) Stakeholder management plan

200. What is the output of the plan quality management process?

  a) Project management plan

  b) Project documents

  c) Risk management plan

  d) Quality management plan

Mock Exam Two

200 Questions—4 Hours Solutions

1. Answer: *c.* No, because "the required return on investments is 10%."

2. Answer: *c.*

Estimate at Completion (typical, steady-state or continuous)	(BAC / CPI) = 555,555.56 dollars

3. Answer: *b.* Develop project charter is the only process in this list. Meetings is a tool and technique for many processes. Organizational process assets are input to many processes, and planning is a process group.

4. Answer: *d.* The communication plan is a document for planning the communication of the project.

5. Answer: *c.* Keep informed.

6. Answer: *c.* Project charter, EEF, and OPA are all inputs to the process.

7. Answer: *b.* The project management plan is the output of the process, not a tool and technique.

8. Answer: *d.* The project charter contains the objectives and other information needed to create the PMP. Data gathering and inspection are tools and techniques. The project management plan is the output of the process.

9. Answer: *a.* Enterprise environmental factors are influences out of the project manager's control. Organizational process assets are factors within the organization's and project team's control. And *c* and *d* are not part of the project management plan.

10. Answer: c. The project charter does not contain detailed information of any type. Detailed information is found in the project management plan.

    Note: This is a typical PMP exam question. The problem has nothing to do with the answer. Focus on the "ask" which is "All are found in the project charter except."

11. Answer: *a*. Scope management plan and requirements management plan are outputs to the plan scope management process. The project charter and project management plan are outputs of earlier stages. Answers *c* and *d* are plan quality management and plan risk management, respectively.

12. Answer: b. The benefits management plan is a document outlining the activities necessary for achieving the planned benefits. It shows a time line and the tools and resources necessary to ensure the benefits are fully realized over time.

13. Answer: *b*. The OPA and project management plan are inputs. Data analysis is a tool and technique.

14. Answer: *a*. Answer *b* describes the plan scope management process, *c* describes the create WBS process, and *d* best describes monitoring and controlling a process.

15. Answer: *d*. Gold-plating is work outside the scope of the project deemed necessary by the project team. Answers *b* and *c* are general concepts that help narrow down the scope of the project.

16. Answer: *a*. Code of account is A numbering system used to uniquely identify each component of the work breakdown structure. A chart of accounts is a created list of the accounts used by an organization to define each class of items for which money or its equivalent is spent or received. Control charts are a statistical process control tool used to determine if a manufacturing or business process is in a state of control.

17. Answer: *c*. Organizational process assets is an input. But *a*, *b*, and *d* are all tools and techniques.

18. Answer: *b*. Answer *a* describes project management plan, and *c* is create WBS.

19. Answer: c. Option *a* describes scope management, *b* describes defining risk management, and *d* is cost management.

20. Answer: *a*. Choice *b* describes plan risk management, and *c* is direct and manage projects. As stated earlier, knowing the sequences of the planning group in all knowledge areas is crucial to passing the PMP exam.

21. Answer: *b*. Susan should immediately begin the closing process. Prepare final report is the only answer that is part of the closing process.

22. Answer: *c*. Option *a* describes scope management, *b* defines risk management, and *d* is cost management.

23. Answer: *c*. Decomposition into activities occurs in the define activities process. Decomposition into work packages occurs in the create WBS process. Answer *d* is a typical PMP exam trick to trip you up because it is combining processes like WBS and activities.

24. Answer: *a*. The question clearly states that Jason is still in the planning process, so what process comes after sequence that is in the list of choices and part on the planning process group. Define activities, sequence activities, estimate activity duration, et cetera. Knowing the order of processes in the planning process group is crucial to passing the exam. Memorize the order of processes in the planning process group!

25. Answer: *a*. Gold plating is the practice of making changes to a project that are outside of the original agreed-upon scope.

26. Answer: *b*. The communication management plan is not an input to collect requirements. The communication management plan is a guide on how the project team will send, receive, distribute, store, and dispose of communication material.

27. Answer: *c*. See the order of processes in the planning process group.

28. Answer: *a*. Finish to start (FS) is the most commonly used.

29. Answer: *c*. Answer 'a' is project scope management, answer 'b' is Project risk management and answer 'd' is Project cost management

30. Answer: b. Answer 'a' is project risk management, answer 'c' is project schedule management and answer 'd' is project cost management

31. Answer: *c*. Project documents are inputs to several processes

32. Answer: *a*. Project documents is an input, project plan updates is an output, and rolling wave is a technique in another process.

33. Answer: b). 1000+2000(4) + 3000 / 6=12000
    12000 / 6=2000

34. Answer: *d*. Expert judgments, historical information review, and funding limit reconciliation are all tools and techniques that can be used to determine spending budget.

35. Answer: *a*. Choices *b*, *c*, and *d* are not outputs.

36. Answer: *d*. Choice *a* is an output for develop project plan, *c* is an output for plan risk management, and *b* is not the output for the plan quality management process.

37. Answer: *a*. Choice *b* is monitoring quality, *c* is manage quality, and *d* is not the answer.

38. Answer: *b*. Develop team is the process of improving competencies, team member interaction, and overall team environment to enhance project performance. A team charter is a document that is developed in a group setting that clarifies team direction while establishing boundaries.

39. Answer: *d*. Resource breakdown structure is not used to estimate resources. In project management, the resource breakdown structure is a hierarchical list of resources related by function and resource type that is used to facilitate planning and controlling of project work.

40. Answer: *d*. Team Performance Assessment is defined as teamwork which is key to effective performance in any work group and is a tool and technique.

41. Answer: *d*. Choice *b* is an input, *c* is process, and *a* is an output.

42. Answer: *d*. Change log is an output; project management plan is an input and manage quality is a process.

43. Answer: *b*. Communication technology consists includes shared portals, video and conferencing, chats, databases, social media, email, and websites. Communications model includes encoding and decoding of messages. Communication analysis does not exist in pmbok 6ᵗʰ. Communications requirements analysis combines communications types and formats as needed to maximize value of the information for project stakeholders.

44. Answer: *c*. Start to finish (SF) is very rarely used.

45. Answer: *d*. Estimate costs. 'b' is project risk management, 'c' is project schedule management and 'd' is project cost management.

46. Answer: *b*. Identify risks, perform qualitative risk analysis, perform quantitative risk analysis, and plan risk responses.

47. Answer: *a*. Project documents is an input, decomposition is a tool and technique of create WBS, and define activities and project management plan updates is an output of other processes.

48. Answer: d). a, b, and c are inputs to other processes.

49. Answer: *d*. Answers *a* and *b* are outputs to develop project plan and plan communication management, respectively; *c* is a tool and technique to other processes.

50. Answer: *c*. Risk probability and impact assessment. Project management plan is a document to follow to track project progress. Project document updates include many other documents. Risk register is a document of identified risks.

51. Answer: *a*. Project management plan is an input this process. Alternative analysis is a tool and technique, OPA updates and EEF updates can be output to processes

52. Answer: *a*. It is the process of numerically analyzing the effect of identified risks on overall project objects.

53. Answer: *a*. Risk report. Rolling wave and decomposition are tool and techniques

54. Answer: *d*. Change requests is an output to processes in monitoring and control process group and input to direct and manage project work process.

55. Answer: *a*. Interpersonal skills. Process improvement plan, project management plan and quality management plan are inputs and outputs to their respective processes.

56. Answer: *Plan procurement management*. Data analysis is a tool and technique, Organizational process assets is an input and procurement management plan define activities to be undertaken during the procurement process such as the type of bidding and how the project is funded.

57. Answer: *a*. Procurement management plan. Project management plan is the output of develop project management plan. Conduct procurement and Control procurement are process in the execute process group and monitor and control process group respectively.

58. Answer: *a*. The process of developing approaches to involve project stakeholders based on their needs and expectations, addressing issues, and fostering appropriate stakeholder involvement.

59. Answer: *b*. Stakeholder engagement plan

60. Answer: *d*. Direct and manage project work. Organizational process assets and enterprise environmental factors are inputs to many process groups. Final report is an output of the close project or phase process group.

61. Answer: *d*. The lessons learned register is an input.

62. Answer *b*. Choice *a* is a tool and technique of another process; *c* and *d* are outputs to other processes.

63. Answer: *b*. Quality reports is an output; enterprise environmental factors is not an input in this process, and data gathering is a tool and technique.

64. Answer: *c*. Resource management plan is a document created by the process plan resource management.

65. Answer: *a*. Forming, storming, norming, performing, adjourning is the correct order.

66. Answer: *b*. Project documents updates is an output.

67. Answer: *b*. The process of ensuring timely and appropriate collection, creation, distribution, storage, retrieval, management, monitoring, and the ultimate disposition of project information

68. Answer: *d*. Implement risk responses. The question clearly states ". project team meticulously put together a project plan which captured and strategized for many risks." The risk has been monitored from start of the project and has been ongoing. Once the risk materializes then the project manager must implement the risk responses.

69. Answer: *c*. the project is clearly in the execute phase of the project. The project manager has already estimate durations because the project has entered the execute phase. There is no mention of project close or cancellation. Identifying stakeholders is going on throughout the life cycle. The best answer is control schedule.

70. Answer: *a*. Data analysis is a tool and technique of most processes. Approved changes are an output to performed integrated change control and an input to direct and manage project work. OPA is an input to most processes.

71. Answer: *b*. Conduct procurements is the process of obtaining seller responses, selecting a seller, and awarding a contract. The key benefit of this process is that it provides alignment of internal and external stakeholder expectations through established agreements.

72. Answer: *d*. This is an easy one. Asking your best friend may work in real-world, but always wrong on the PMP exam.

73. Answer: *a*. Manage stakeholder engagement. Monitor communications is reading emails, answering phone calls and responding to chats in social media. Manage communications is the process of creating, collecting, distributing, storing, retrieving, and the ultimate disposition of project information in accordance to the communications management plan.

74. Answer: *b*. Monitor and control project work. Direct and Manage Project Work is the process of leading and performing the work defined in the project management plan and implementing approved changes to achieve the project's objectives. Manage Project Knowledge is the process of using existing knowledge and creating new knowledge to achieve the project's objectives and contribute to organization's learning. Perform Integrated Change Control is the process of reviewing all change requests; approving changes and managing changes to deliverables, organizational process assets, project documents, and the project management plan; and communicating their disposition.

75. Answer: *c*. Ahead of schedule and over budget

Cost Variance	(EV − AC) = (25,000.00) dollars
Schedule Variance	(EV − PV) = 25,000.00 dollars

76. Answer: *b*. change requests can be an input or output, project management plan is a document, and OPA updates is an output.

77. Answer: *c*. Evaluate the impact of the change. Review the order of the closing process.

78. Answer: *a*. Prevent changes from occurring if possible. If change cannot be prevented then evaluate the impact of the change.

79. Answer: *b*. Work performance information

80. Answer: *c*. Change requests is an output to control scope.

81. Answer: *d*. Change requests can be an output or input

82. Answer: *c*. Project management software because costs and schedule can be updated automatically and provides project simulation.

83. Answer: *b*. PERT stands for Program Evaluation Review Technique. PERT is a project management planning tool used to calculate the amount of time it will take to realistically finish a project.

84. Answer: *c*. Fishbone. Prototyping is a method of obtaining early feedback on requirements by providing a model of the expected product before building it. Bottom-up estimating is a project management technique in which the people who are going to do the work take part in the estimating process

85. Answer: *b*. Cause-and-effect diagram

86. Answer: *b*. McGregor's Theory X assumes that the typical worker has little ambition, avoids responsibility, and is individual-goal oriented. McGregor's Theory Y assumes employees are internally motivated, enjoy their job, and work to better themselves without a direct reward in return.

87. Answer: *d*. Forming, storming, norming, performing, and adjourning

88. Answer: *c*. The process of monitoring communications and the process of ensuring the information needs of the project and its stakeholders are met.

89. Answer: *d*. 28
    Solution:
    6 + 2 = 8
    8(7) / 2 = 56
    56 / 2 = 28

90. Answer: *a*. 13
    Solution:
    (8(7) / 2) - (6(5) / 2)
    28 - 15 = 13

91. Answer: *b*. Option *a* describes requirements documentation; *c* is not the choice because you want a risk management plan, and *d* describes the probability impact matrix.

92. Answer: *d*. It is used for mapping the probability of each risk occurrence and the impact on project objectives if the risk occurs.

93. Answer: *c*. The process of managing procurement relationships, monitoring contract performance, making changes and corrections as appropriate, and closing out contracts.

94. Answer: *d*. Claims administration. Project management plan and communication management plan are documents and change request can be an input or output.

95. Answer: *d*. Choice *a* is identifying stakeholders, *b* is manage stakeholder engagement, and *c* does not exist.

96. Answer: *b*. you must never ignore stakeholders.

97. Answer: *b*. Susan should immediately begin the closing process. Prepare final report is the only answer that is part of the closing process.

98. Answer: *a*. Regression analysis. Regression analysis is a technique that involves examining the series of input variables in relations to the corresponding output results. OPA, EEF and deliverables are inputs

99. Answer: *c*. Evaluate the impact of the change

100. Answer: *a*. Prevent changes from occurring

101. Answer: *b*. Acceptable deliverables

102. Answer: *c*. Change requests is an output to control scope.

103. Answer: *d*. Change requests is an output.

104. Answer: *c*. Project management software

105. Answer: *b*. PERT

106. Answer: *c*. Fishbone

107. Answer: *b*. Cause-and-effect diagram

108. Answer: *b*. McGregor's Theory X assumes that the typical worker has little ambition, avoids responsibility, and is individual-goal oriented. McGregor's Theory Y assumes employees are internally motivated, enjoy their job, and work to better themselves without a direct reward in return.

109. Answer: *d*. Forming, storming, norming, performing, and adjourning

110. Answer: *c*. The process of monitoring communications and the process of ensuring the information needs of the project and its stakeholders are met

111. Answer: *d.* 28 Solution:

    6 +2 = 8 (6 current team members plus 2 new team members)

    n = 8

    n(n-1) / 2

    8(7) / 2 = 56

    56 / 2=28

112. Answer: *a.* 13 In this question, you will need to get the new number of channels and subtract the current number of channels from it.

    New - current

    (8(7) / 2 - (6(5) / 2)

    28 - 15 = 13

113. Answer: *d.* Option *a* describes scope management, *b* defines risk management, and *c* is schedule management.

114. Answer: *d.* It is used for mapping the probability of each risk occurrence and the impact on project objectives if the risk occurs.

115. Answer: *c.* The process of managing procurement relationships, monitoring contract performance, making changes and corrections as appropriate, and closing out contracts

116. Answer: *c.* Expert judgments is a tool and technique.

117. Answer: *d.* Claims administration

118. Answer: *d.* Choice *a* is identifying stakeholders, *b* is manage stakeholder engagement, and *c* does not exist.

119. Answer: *b.* Ignoring the stakeholder until they go away

120. Answer: *a.* Regression analysis

121. Answer: *d.* IRR will be 7.93%. On the PMP exam, you should always choose the project with the highest return. In this example, answer '*a*' only gives a dollar value. Answer *b* is just a payback period, which yields no return. And answer *c* is in the negative range.

122. Answer: *d.* Data analysis is a tool and technique, not an input.

123. Answer: *c*. EEF. The order of the closing process is: Obtain acceptance of deliverables, conduct post-project or phase-end review, Record impact of tailoring any process, Document lessons learned, Apply appropriate updates to organizational process assets (OPA), Archive all relevant project documents, Close out all procurement activities and Perform team member assessments.

124. Answer: *c*. Document lessons learned

125. Answer: *b*. Obtain customer satisfaction is not a closing process list. Obtain customer acceptance is in the closing process list.

126. Answer: *b*.

    Project charter and assumptions log

127. Answer: *c*. Expert judgement is always a tool and technique.

128. Answer: *d*. The project charter never states the details of project deliverables.

129. Answer: *a*. The process of monitoring the implementation of the agreed-upon risk response plan, tracking identified risks, analyzing new risks, and evaluating the risk process

130. Answer: *b*. It is the process of defining how to conduct risk management activities for a project.

131. Answer: *b*. The process of how the project and product scope will be defined, validated and controlled throughout the project.

132. Answer: *d*. How the project and product scope will be validated.

133. Answer: *d*. It is a grid for mapping the probability of each risk occurrence and the impact on project objectives if the risk occurs.

134. Answer: *c*. The process of developing detailed descriptions of the project and products, which is what the project includes and excludes

135. Answer: *a*. Determine risks does not exists in Pmbok 6th edition

136. Answer: *c*. The process of ensuring timely and appropriate collection, creation, distribution, storage, retrieval, management, monitoring, and the ultimate disposition of project information

137. Answer: *d*. The process of ensuring the information needs of the project and its stakeholders are met

138. Answer: *d*. 28

139. Answer: *a*. 13

140. Answer: *d*. The process of estimating the number of work periods needed to complete activities with the estimated resources

141. Answer: *c*. Project management plan

142. Answer: *a*. Scope management plan and requirements management plan

143. Answer: a. Enterprise environmental factors are influences out of the project manager's control.

144. Answer: c. Only organization process assets are a valid PMP lexicon and is internal to the organization that affects the project.

145. Answer: *b*. Quality audit

146. Answer: *d*. Precision. Accuracy is measurements are closer to true value.

147. Answer: *d*.
The process of ensuring the physical resources assigned and allocated to the project are available as planned versus actual utilization of resources and taking corrective actions as necessary

148. Answer: *b*. McGregor's Theory X. McGregor stated that those employees who are separated into Theory X need to be micromanaged. Theory X believes that employees are inherently lazy and without constant supervision, they will not complete their work. Conversely, McGregor stated that those employees who are separated into Theory Y should be left to complete their work independently. Theory Y believes that employees are inherently motivated and want to produce quality work.

149. Answer: *d*. Forming, storming, norming, performing, and adjourning

150. Answer: *a*. Avoidance and collaboration

151. Answer: *c*. Staffing management plan

152. Answer: *d.* OPA and EEF are inputs to many process groups. Final report is an output to the close project or phase process group.

153. Answer: *c.* Staffing management plan

154. Answer: *a.* The process of leading and performing the work defined in the project plan and implementing the approved changes to achieve the project objectives

155. Answer: *a.* Active listening. Interpersonal and team skills are used to communicate effectively with team members, sponsors, and others either face to face or via email or other communication methods. Interpersonal and team skills will include conflict resolution methods, facilitation, and meeting management. Interpersonal skills are used in conflict management, facilitation, and meeting management.

156. Answer: *d.* Lessons learned register

157. Answer: *b.* Monitor and control project work

158. Answer *a.* Answer *d* looks tempting, but the key word was *best.* The process of tracking, reviewing, and reporting the overall progress to meet performance objectives defined in the project management plan

159. Answer: *c.* Evaluate the impact of the change

160. Answer: *b.* The process of reviewing all change requests; approving changes; managing changes to deliverables, project documents, and the project management plan; and communicating decisions

161. Answer: *c.* Project management plan updates is an output.

162. Answer: *a.* Avoid is the worst of the four conflict management types.

163. Answer: *d.* Project communications management

164. Answer: *b.* The process of ensuring timely and appropriate collection, creation, distribution, storage, retrieval, management, monitoring, and the ultimate disposition of project information

165. Answer: *d.* Change requests

166. Answer: *d.* Implement risk responses

167. Answer: *a.* The process of implementing the agreed-upon risk response

168. Answer *d.* Change requests

169. Answer *b.* Risk management plan

170. Answer *a.* The process of identifying individual risks as well as sources of overall project risks and documenting their characteristics

171. Answer *c.* Risk probability and impact assessment

172. Answer: *a.* The process of prioritizing individual project risks for further analysis by assessing their probability of occurrence and impact

173. Answer: *a.* The process of numerically analyzing the effect of identified risks on overall project objects

174. Answer: *a.* Simulations

175. Answer: *c.* Share

176. Answer: *b.* Mitigate

177. Answer: *d.* Change requests

178. Answer: *a.* Bottom-up estimating.

179. Answer: *d* Bottom-up estimating

180. Answer: *c.* ATYPICAL: EAC= AC + (BAC-EV) = 11+(150-10) = 151

181. Answer: *c.* ETC = EAC - AC = 11+(120-10) - 11 = 110

182. Answer: *c.* AC + [[BAC-EV)/(CPI*SPI)] = 11 + [[120-10)/ ((10/11) *(10/12))] = 11+ (110/ (.909) *(.833)) = 110.833

183. Answer: *b.* Testing. Rework and Liabilities are part of non-conformance

184. Answer: *d.* Lost business

185. Answer: *c.* Inspections

186. Answer: *b.* Testing

187. Answer: *d.* Lost business

188. Answer: *c.* inspections

189. Answer: *c.*
    Risk management

190. Answer: *c.* The process of ensuring timely and appropriate collection, creation, distribution, storage, retrieval, management, monitoring, and the ultimate disposition of project information

191. Answer: *c.* Communications management plan

192. Answer: *d.* N (n + 1) / 2

193. Answer: *b.* Identify risks, perform qualitative risk analysis, perform quantitative risk analysis, and plan risk responses

194. Answer: *d.* Risk management plan

195. Answer: *a.* The process of defining how to conduct risk management activities

196. Answer: *b.* The process of developing an approach and plan for project communications activities based on the information needs of each stakeholder and the project

197. Answer: *b.* Develop project charter

198. Answer: *d.* Data analysis.

199. Answer: *d.* Project charter and assumptions log

200. Answer: *d.* Quality management plan

Mock Exam Three

200 Questions—4 Hours Advanced

1. Quasar is a project manager who wants to run an efficient project that completes on time and under budget to the client's satisfaction. When performing the develop project plan process, what will be the output document the project manager will want the most?

   a) Project management plan

   b) Project documents updates

   c) Work performance reports

   d) Team performance

2. As the project manager, you have just introduced a new contractor to the project team. What is the correct order of team development according to Tuckerman's ladder?

   a) Forming, storming, norming, performing, and adjourning

   b) Performing, storming, norming, forming, and adjourning

   c) Performing, storming, adjourning, forming, and norming

   d) Forming, norming, storming, performing, and adjourning

3. As a project manager, you have just introduced a new team member to the project. What are the correct elements for Tuckerman's ladder on team development?

   a) Performing, storming, norming, forming, and adjourning

   b) Starting, storming, norming, performing, and adjourning

   c) Performing, storming, adjusting, forming, and norming

   d) Forming, norming, storming, performing, and closing

4. Jonathan is a project manager at a solar car company. Jonathan wants to develop a document that will give him the best chance of managing the project from start to completion. Which document does the project manager need to create next?

   a) Project management plan

   b) Project documents updates

   c) Work performance reports

   d) Team performance

5. Lucia is a new project manager for Razor LLC. Lucia wants to get off to the best start in understanding the project, people, and environment. Meetings are a tool and technique of which process?

   a) Meetings

   b) Develop project charter

   c) Organizational process assets

   d) Planning

6. All are components of tools and techniques in the manage project knowledge process except

   a) Knowledge management

   b) Information management

   c) Interpersonal and team skills

   d) Lessons learned register

7. Barron is a new project manager for Best Cereal Products LLC. Barron wants to get off to the best start in understanding the project, people, and environment. All the following are inputs to the develop project charter process except

   a) SOW

   b) Enterprise environmental factors

   c) Organizational process assets

   d) Data gathering

8. Mila is a project manager at Cool Socks Inc. She is in the planning process for a new project and has completed the sequence activities process. The kickoff of the project occurred three months ago. The project team is currently managing the project. As a project manager, what would Mila do next?

   a) Estimate activity durations

   b) Close the project

   c) Control schedule

   d) Identify stakeholders

9. Candy is a seasoned project manager at a pickle factory. The project manager needs which tool and technique to collect information?

   a) SOW

   b) Enterprise environmental factors

   c) Organizational process assets

   d) Data gathering

10. You are a new project manager for an existing project with issues. What document does the project manager need to determine the project goals, high-level risks, and high-level constraints?

    a) Communication plan

    b) Project management plan

    c) SOW

    d) Project charter

11. The process of communicating and working with stakeholders to meet their needs and expectations, address issues, and foster appropriate involvement is

    a) Manage stakeholder engagement

    b) Monitor communications

    c) Manage communications

    d) Monitor stakeholder engagement

12. Jonathan is the senior project manager for a High-energy company. In the beginning stages of the project, Jonathan spends much of his time conversing with the sponsor and senior management to develop a document that gives the project manager authority to commit resources to the project. What is the output of the develop project charter process?

   a) Project charter

   b) Enterprise environmental factors

   c) Project management plan

   d) Organizational process assets

13. Judy is a superb project manager at her firm. She is currently working on a project in which a fix is necessary. As a project manager, what should Judy do next?

   a) Check the release documents

   b) Notify the sponsor

   c) Evaluate the impact of the change

   d) Implement the risk response plan

14. The following are tools and techniques for the develop project management plan process except

   a) Meetings

   b) Project management plan

   c) Interpersonal and team skills

   d) Expert judgments

15. Harry is a contractor responsible for the refurbishment of an automobile showroom. The estimated refurbishment cost is $500 per square foot. The total showroom area that needs to be refurbished is 1,000 square feet. Based on Harry's experience, he knows his team can refurbish 100 square feet per week. As a project manager, how should Harry report how the project is performing?

   a) On schedule and on budget

   b) Behind schedule and over budget

   c) Ahead of schedule and over budget

   d) Behind schedule and ahead of budget

Cost Variance	(EV - AC) = ($25,000.00)
Schedule Variance	(EV - PV) = $25,000.00

16. Patricia is a top project manager at her firm. She is currently working on a project in which a fix *might be* necessary. As a project manager, what should Patricia do next?

    a) Prevent changes from occurring

    b) Notify the sponsor

    c) Evaluate the impact of the change

    d) Implement the risk response plan

17. Ulysses is a new project manager on an existing project. The project has been in its planning stage. The process that has just been completed is collect requirements. As a project manager, what would you do next?

    a) Define scope

    b) Project management plan

    c) Plan scope management

    d) Expert judgments

18. Danny is a new project manager on an existing project. The project has been in its planning stage. The process that has just been completed is collect requirements. As a project manager, what would you do next?

    a) Project management plan

    b) Define activities

    c) Plan scope management

    d) Expert judgments

19. Deliverables are an output of which process group?

    a) Organizational process assets

    b) Enterprise environmental factors

    c) Final report

    d) Direct and manage project work

20. Luke is a new project manager on an existing project. The project has been in its planning stage. The process that has just completed is define activities. As a project manager, what process did you determine was done previously to define activities?

    a) Define scope

    b) Project management plan

    c) Plan schedule management

    d) Expert judgments

21. Which of the following is a tool and technique of direct and manage project work?

    a) Change requests

    b) PMIS

    c) Project management plan

    d) OPA updates

22. Shaq is a new project manager on an existing project. The project has been in its planning stage. The process that has just been completed is define activities. As a project manager, what process did he determine was done prior to define activities?

    a) Define scope

    b) Project management plan

    c) Data gathering

    d) Create WBS

23. Which process best exemplifies monitoring and control in project integration?

    a) Direct and manage project work

    b) Monitor and control project work

    c) Manage project knowledge

    d) Perform integrated change control

24. Glover is a new project manager on an existing project. The project has been in its execute stage. The process that has just been completed is define activities. As a project manager, which process will he do next?

    a) Define scope

    b) Validate scope

    c) Data gathering

    d) Create WBS

25. You are a new project manager for an existing project with issues. As the project manager, what document do you need to determine how, when, and the level of authority the stakeholders communicate with?

    a) Communication management plan

    b) Project management plan

    c) SOW

    d) Project charter

26. The process of defining how to estimate, acquire, manage, and utilize physical and team resources is

    a) Develop team

    b) Plan resource management

    c) Organizational theory

    d) Team charter

27. Jeffrey is a contractor responsible for the refurbishment of an automobile showroom. The estimated refurbishment cost is $500 per square foot. The total showroom area that needs to be refurbished is 1,000 square feet. Based on Jeffrey's experience, he knows his team can refurbish 100 square feet per week. As a project manager, how should Jeffrey report the forecast estimate at completion to senior management?

    a) $525,000

    b) $375,000

    c) $555,555.56

    d) $516,224.19

28. The process of defining how to estimate, acquire, manage, and utilize physical and team resources is

    a) Develop team

    b) Plan resource management

    c) Organizational theory

    d) Team charter

29. Jonathan is a new project manager at Warm Hands Glove Company Inc. Jonathan does not trust his employees to do their jobs, so he must monitor their every action to make sure he gets the results he wants. Jonathan is practicing

    a) RAM

    b) McGregor's Theory X

    c) Expectancy Theory

    d) McGregor's Theory Y

30. Antonio is a new project manager on an existing project. The project has been is its execute stage. The process that has just been completed is estimate costs. As a project manager, which process will Antonio do next?

    a) Define scope

    b) Control costs

    c) Data gathering

    d) Create WBS

31. What is the correct order of team development?

    a) Performing, storming, norming, forming, and adjourning

    b) Forming, storming, norming, performing, and adjourning

    c) Forming, norming, storming, performing, and adjourning

    d) Performing, storming, adjourning, forming, and norming

32. Sabrina is a new project manager on an existing project. The project has been canceled by senior management without cause. As a project manager, what will Sabrina do next?

    a) Negotiate with management to keep the project going

    b) Negotiate with the sponsor to keep the project going for a few more weeks because things can be turned around

    c) Begin the closing process immediately

    d) Continue the project until she has heard from the sponsor

33. Michelle is a project manager for a bookseller. One of her projects is improving the ways books can be found without assistance from the staff. Michelle needs to introduce a new member to the project team. What is the correct order of team development?

    a) Performing, storming, norming, forming, and adjourning

    b) Performing, storming, adjourning, forming, and norming

    c) Forming, norming, storming, performing, and adjourning

    d) Forming, storming, norming, performing, and adjourning

34. The process of defining how to estimate, acquire, manage, and utilize physical and team resources is

    a) Develop team

    b) Team Charter Plan resource management

    c) Organizational theory

    d) Plan resource management Team charter

35. Mark is a new project manager on an existing project. The project has moved beyond the planning stage. The vendor chosen to complete a portion of the project has started work. As a project manager, what will Mark do next?

    a) Plan what is expected of outside vendors

    b) Ask the vendor for closing reports and place in archives

    c) Control procurements

    d) Continue the project until he has heard from the sponsor

36. Pepper is a new project manager for TF Banking Services. Pepper is in the process of acquiring resources. All are tools and techniques Pepper can use to aid in her search except

    a) Virtual teams

    b) Multicriteria analysis

    c) Resource management plan

    d) Negotiation

37. Sophia is a contractor responsible for the refurbishment of an automobile showroom. The estimated refurbishment cost is $500 per square foot. The total showroom area that needs to be refurbished is 1,000 square feet. Based on Sophia's past experience, she knows her team can refurbish 100 square feet per week. As the project manager, how should Sophia report the steady-state progress of the project?

    a) $525,000

    b) $375,000

    c) $555,555.56

    d) $475,000

Estimate at Completion (typical, steady-state, or continuous)	(BAC / CPI) = $555,555.56

38. All of the following are inputs to manage a team except

    a) Project management plan

    b) Project documents updates

    c) Work performance reports

    d) Team performance

39. Which is an output of the validate scope process?

    a) Work performance data

    b) Acceptable deliverables

    c) Verified deliverables

    d) Work performance information

40. John is a new project manager on an existing project. The project is now in the execute stage. John and his project team know the plan resources they need, what the resources will do, and how long the work will take. As a project manager, what will John do next?

    a) Control resources

    b) Develop team

    c) Manage team

    d) Acquire resources

41. What is the correct order of Tuckman's ladder?

    a) Forming, storming, norming, performing, adjourning

    b) Adjourning, forming, storming, norming, performing

    c) Performing, forming, storming, norming, adjourning

    d) Storming, norming, forming, performing, adjourning

42. As a project manager, Sandy must introduce new team members because either the previous contract did not work out, there was more work than current team members could handle, or the new team members had skills the current team members were lacking. What is the correct order of team development?

    a) Performing, storming, norming, forming, and adjourning

    b) Performing, storming, adjourning, forming, and norming

    c) Forming, norming, storming, performing, and adjourning

    d) Forming, storming, norming, performing, and adjourning

43. Robert is a new project manager at Fresh Minds, Inc. Robert does not trust his employees to do their jobs, so he must monitor their every action to make sure he gets the results he wants. Robert is practicing

    a) RAM

    b) McGregor's Theory X

    c) Expectancy Theory

    d) McGregor's Theory Y

44. Ashley is a new project manager on an existing project. The project has now in the execute stage. Ashley and his project team know the plan resources they need, what the resources will do, and how long the work will take. As a project manager, what will Ashley do next?

   a) Control resources

   b) Train management

   c) Lay out a grand plan for the project

   d) Determine stakeholders

45. Harry is a contractor responsible for the refurbishment of an automobile showroom. The estimated refurbishment cost is $500 per square foot. The total showroom area that needs to be refurbished is 1,000 square feet. Based on his past experience, he knows his team can refurbish 100 square feet per week. As a project manager, how would Harry report how the project is performing?

   a) On schedule and on budget

   b) Behind schedule and over budget

   c) Ahead of schedule and over budget

   d) Behind schedule and ahead of budget

Cost Variance	(EV – AC) = $25,000.00
Schedule Variance	(EV – PV) = $25,000.00

46. Tomas is a junior project manager for a pharmaceutical company. One of Tomas's roles is to assist in the development of a project charter. What document is from the plan stakeholder engagement process?

   a) Assumption and constraint analysis

   b) Stakeholder engagement plan

   c) Project management plan

   d) Process improvement plan

47. The process of defining how to estimate, acquire, manage, and utilize physical and team resources is

    a) Develop team

    b) Organizational theory

    c) Plan resource management

    d) Team charter

48. You are a new project manager for an existing project with issues. What document do you need to determine the project goals, high-level risks, and high-level constraints?

    a) Communication plan

    b) Project management plan

    c) SOW

    d) Project charter

49. Abraham is a project manager on an existing project at the Best Acting Company Inc., which sells dreams. After the project kickoff, Abraham and his project team are managing the team resources process. The project plan has been approved. As a project manager, what will Abraham do next?

    a) Create WBS

    b) Control resources

    c) Perform team development

    d) Monitor stakeholder engagement

50. Samantha is a new project manager on an existing project. After the project kickoff, Samantha and her project team have completed collection of all requirements and determined the scope. The project plan has been approved. As a project manager, what will Samantha do next?

    a) Create WBS

    b) Validate scope

    c) Lay out a grand plan for the project

    d) Negotiate with the sponsor for overtime

51. All the following are inputs to the develop project charter process except

   a) SOW

   b) Enterprise environmental factors

   c) Organizational process assets

   d) Data gathering

52. Which answer best describes the stakeholder engagement plan?

   a) The process of developing approaches to involve project stakeholders based on their needs and expectations, addressing issues, and fostering appropriate stakeholder engagement involvement

   b) The process of monitoring project stakeholder relationships and tailoring strategies for engaging stakeholders through the modification of engagement strategies and plans

   c) The process of communicating and working with stakeholders to meet their needs and expectations

   d) The process of not communicating and working with stakeholders to meet their needs and expectations

53. What is the output of the validate scope process?

   a) Work performance data

   b) Acceptable deliverables

   c) Verified deliverables

   d) Work performance information

54. Luther is a new project manager on an existing project. The project is now in the execute stage. Luther and his project team know the plan resources they need, what the resources will do, and how long the work will take. As a project manager, what will Luther do next?

   a) Control resources

   b) Develop team

   c) Manage team

   d) Determine stakeholders

55. Jesus is a new project manager on an existing project. After the project kickoff, Jesus and his project team have completed the plan stakeholder engagement process and are managing the stakeholder engagements. The project plan has been approved. As a project manager, what will Jesus do next?

    a) Create WBS

    b) Validate scope

    c) Plan stakeholder engagement

    d) Monitor stakeholder engagement

56. Kazem is a project manager with many years of experience. Kazem knows how important customer communication and satisfaction are to project management. What is the best definition of the monitor stakeholder engagement process?

    a) The process of identifying project stakeholders regularly and analyzing and documenting relevant information regarding their interests, involvement, interdependencies, influence, and impact on project success

    b) The process of communicating and working with stakeholders to meet their needs and expectations, address issues, and foster appropriate stakeholder engagement

    c) The process of providing an overview of the project stakeholder management process

    d) The process of monitoring project stakeholder relationships and tailoring strategies for engaging stakeholders through the modification of engagement strategies and plans

57. Joaquim is a very seasoned and energetic project manager. Recently, Joaquim's emails to some stakeholders have gone unanswered. When some stakeholders do respond, Joaquim must decide how to answer their concerns. Joaquim should do all the following in monitor stakeholder engagement except

    a) Managing stakeholder relationships

    b) Ignoring the stakeholders until they go away

    c) Engaging with the stakeholders

    d) Formulating strategies with the stakeholders

58. Jeffrey is a project manager responsible for the delivery of a solar car prototype. There are many moving parts to a project on the cutting edge of technology. Resources such as people and equipment for solar technology are not as common. Jeffrey must learn the language of solar technology to deliver the project successfully. As project manager, which of the following is Jeffery not going to use as an input to manage team?

    a) Project management plan

    b) Project documents updates

    c) Work performance reports

    d) Team performance

59. David is a new project manager for Monorail Enterprises. David wants to get off to the best start in understanding the project, people, and environment. Interpersonal and team skills is a tool and technique of which process?

    a) Meetings

    b) Develop project charter

    c) Organizational process assets

    d) Planning

60. William is a new project manager on an existing project. After the project kickoff, William and his project team have completed the plan procurement management process. The project plan has not been approved. As a project manager, what will William do next?

    a) Create WBS

    b) Validate scope

    c) Plan stakeholder engagement

    d) Negotiate with the sponsor for overtime

61. Emma is a project manager for Guidance Cybernetics, a maker of exoskeletons for those who have lost the use of their limbs or are paralyzed from spinal injuries. Emma's project has suffered both material and people resource setbacks. As the project manager, what should Emma choose as the best tool and technique of the plan communication management process to create the communication management plan document?

a) Change log

b) Project management plan

c) Manage quality

d) Communication technology

62. Robert is a new project manager at No Fear Inc. Robert does not trust his employees to do their jobs, so he must monitor their every action to make sure he gets the results he wants. What is Robert is practicing?

a) RAM

b) McGregor's Theory X

c) Expectancy Theory

d) McGregor's Theory Y

63. One of the duties of a project manager is the process of communicating and working with stakeholders to meet their needs and expectations, address issues, and foster appropriate involvement. As a project manager, what do you do next?

a) Manage stakeholder engagement

b) Monitor communications

c) Manage communications

d) Monitor stakeholder engagement

64. Jerry is a new project manager at Cool Car Seats, Inc. Jerry does not trust his employees to do their jobs, so he must monitor their every action to make sure he gets the results he wants. Jerry is practicing

a) RAM

b) McGregor's Theory X

c) Expectancy Theory

d) McGregor's Theory Y

65. Norman is a project manager for a ventilator company for delivery to hospitals. Norman is replacing a team member because of quality and performance issues. The new team member is getting up to speed quickly to begin producing. As the project manager, in what order will Norman perform the steps of team development?

    a) Performing, storming, norming, forming, and adjourning

    b) Performing, storming, adjourning, forming, and norming

    c) Forming, norming, storming, performing, and adjourning

    d) Forming, storming, norming, performing, and adjourning

66. Miss Jones is a project manager on an existing project at the Best Acting Company, Inc, which sells dreams. After the project kickoff, Miss Jones and her project team are in the managing team resources process. The project plan has been approved. As a project manager, what will Miss Jones do next?

    a) Performing team development

    b) Create WBS

    c) Develop team

    d) Monitor stakeholder engagement

67. Lavell is a new project manager at Prove It to Me Inc. Lavell does not trust his employees to do their jobs, so he must monitor their every action to make sure he gets the results he wants. What is Lavell practicing?

    a) RAM

    b) McGregor's Theory X

    c) Expectancy Theory

    d) McGregor's Theory Y

68. The following describe monitor stakeholder engagement except

    a) Managing stakeholder relationships

    b) Ignoring the stakeholders until they go away

    c) Engaging with the stakeholders

    d) Formulating strategies with the stakeholders

69. Mr. Greene is a project manager on an existing project at the Ultimate Real Estate Company, which sells passports. After the project kickoff, Mr. Greene and his project team are in the manage team resources process. The project plan has been approved. As a project manager, what will Mr. Greene do next?

    a) Control resources

    b) Create WBS

    c) Develop team

    d) Monitor stakeholder engagement

70. Noah is a project manager at Emca, a producer of animated characters for worldwide distribution to children as consumers. Which tool and technique should Noah use next in the plan communications management process to create the communication management plan?

    a) Change log

    b) Project management plan

    c) Manage quality

    d) Interpersonal and team skills

71. Andy is a project manager on an existing project. After the project kickoff, Andy and his project team have completed the acquire resources process. The project plan has been approved. As a project manager, what will Andy do next?

    a) Create WBS

    b) Develop team

    c) Plan stakeholder engagement

    d) Monitor stakeholder engagement

72. Which best describes the manage communications process?

    a) Project management plan

    b) The process of ensuring timely and appropriate collection, creation, distribution, storage, retrieval, management, monitoring, and the ultimate disposition of project information

    c) Work performance reports

    d) Team performance

73. Kazem is a project manager with many years of experience. Kazem knows how important customer communication and satisfaction are to project management. What is the best definition of the monitor stakeholder engagement process?

 a) The process of identifying project stakeholders regularly and analyzing and documenting relevant information regarding their interests, involvement, interdependencies, influence, and impact on project success

 b) The process of communicating and working with stakeholders to meet their needs and expectations, address issues, and foster appropriate stakeholder engagement

 c) The process of providing an overview of the project stakeholder management process

 d) The process of monitoring project stakeholder relationships and tailoring strategies for engaging stakeholders through the modification of engagement strategies and plans

74. The process of communicating and working with stakeholders to meet their needs and expectations, address issues, and foster appropriate involvement is

 a) Manage stakeholder engagement

 b) Monitor communications

 c) Manage communications

 d) Monitor stakeholder engagement

75. Elijah is a project manager at Poor Man's Industries, a maker of economical products that look expensive. As the project manager, Elijah will supply all the inputs to manage a team except

 a) Project management plan

 b) Project documents updates

 c) Work performance reports

 d) Team performance

76. Andy is a project manager on an existing project at the PASSMAX company, which sells passports. After the project kickoff, Andy and his project team are in the managing team resources process. The project plan has been approved. As a project manager, what will Andy do next?

 a) Create WBS

 b) Develop team

c) Control resources

d) Monitor stakeholder engagement

77. Robert is a new project manager at MAX Testosterone Support, Inc. Robert does not trust his employees to do their jobs, so he must monitor their every action to make sure he gets the results he wants. Robert is practicing

a) RAM

b) McGregor's Theory X

c) Expectancy Theory

d) McGregor's Theory Y

78. What is the correct order of team development?

a) Forming, storming, norming, performing, and adjourning

b) Performing, storming, adjourning, forming, and norming

c) Forming, norming, storming, performing, and adjourning

d) Performing, storming, norming, forming, and adjourning

79. Daryl is a project manager on an existing project at the Best Acting Company Inc., which sells dreams. Before the project kickoff, Daryl and her project team are planning to perform qualitative risk analysis. The project plan has not been approved. As a project manager, what will Daryl do next?

a) Plan risk management

b) Create WBS

c) Control resources

d) Monitor stakeholder engagement

80. Joseph is a senior project manager on an existing project for building boats. The project is currently in the execute stage. Which document will Joseph not need as an input to the manage team process?

a) Project management plan

b) Project documents updates

c) Work performance reports

d) Team performance

81. Daryl is a project manager on an existing project at the Best Acting Company Inc., which sells dreams. Before the project kickoff, Daryl and her project team are planning to perform qualitative risk analysis. The project plan has not been approved. As a project manager, what does Daryl do prior to performing qualitative risk analysis?

    a) Implement risk responses

    b) Plan risk responses

    c) Control resources

    d) Plan communication management

82. Ava is a junior project manager learning the ropes for the company Dadcorp. Dadcorp is a company that performs the to-do list for families or single parents and other things around the home of the consumer. Conversations and meetings are part of which tool and technique?

    a) Communications analysis

    b) Communications technology

    c) Communications model

    d) Communications method

83. Daryl is a project manager on an existing project at the Best Acting Company, Inc, which sells dreams. Before the project kickoff, Daryl and her project team are planning to perform qualitative risk analysis. The project plan has not been approved. As a project manager, what will Daryl do next?

    a) Create WBS

    b) Control resources

    c) Monitor stakeholder engagement

    d) Plan risk management

84. David is a project manager on an existing project at the Boat Makers Company, which sells passports. After the project kickoff, David and his project team are in the managing team resources process. The project plan has been approved. As a project manager, what will David do next?

    a) Create WBS

    b) Control resources

    c) Develop team

    d) Monitor stakeholder engagement

85. Daniel is a new project manager for IT Providers LLC. Daniel wants to get off to the best start understanding the project, people, and environment. Interpersonal and team skills are a tool and technique of which process?

    a) Meetings

    b) Develop project charter

    c) OPA

    d) Planning

86. Mia is a new project manager for Warbuck LLC. Mia and her team inherited a project with many assumptions and constraints. All the requirements are not available, and the deliverables do not match up with client expectations. Mia wants to get off to the best start understanding the project, people, and environment. All the following are inputs to develop project charter except:

    a) SOW

    b) Assumptions and constraints

    c) OPA

    d) Data analysis

87. Olivia is a project manager at the corporation MAOHC. MAOHC has numerous affiliates and thousands of ongoing projects. Olivia is introducing a new team member to handle quality assurance on her project. As the project manager, in what order should Olivia perform the steps of team development?

    a) Performing, storming, norming, forming, and adjourning

    b) Performing, storming, adjourning, forming, and norming

    c) Forming, norming, storming, performing, and adjourning

    d) Forming, storming, norming, performing, and adjourning

88. Lucas is a new project manager for a computer company. As a new project manager who documents the develop project charter process, which documents does Lucas needs to examine?

    a) Project management plan and requirements plan

    b) Project charter and assumptions log

    c) Quality management plan and change management plan

    d) Stakeholder management plan

89. David is a new project manager for Unique Homes Corp. David wants to get off to the best start in understanding the project, people, and environment. Interpersonal and team skills are a tool and technique of which process?

   a) Meetings

   b) Develop project charter

   c) Organizational process assets

   d) Planning

90. All the following are inputs to the develop project charter process except

   a) SOW

   b) Enterprise environmental factors

   c) Organizational process assets

   d) Data gathering

91. David is a project manager on an existing project at the Boat Makers Company, which sells passports. After the project kickoff, David and his project team are in the managing team resources process. The project plan has been approved. As a project manager, what will David do next?

   a) Create WBS

   b) Control resources

   c) Develop team

   d) Monitor stakeholder engagement

92. Priscilla is a project manager for an existing project with issues. What document does the project manager need to determine the project goals, high-level risks, and high-level constraints?

   a) Communication plan

   b) Project management plan

   c) SOW

   d) Project charter

93. Daryl is a senior project manager for a book publishing company. Daryl wants to identify all current stakeholders for the project. All the documents below are inputs to the identify stakeholders process except

   a) Project charter

   b) EEF

   c) Expert judgments

   d) Organizational process assets

94. Asheem is a project manager working remotely, so some of his team is in different locations performing their work. As project manager, Asheem determines the output of the develop project management plan process is

   a) Project charter

   b) Enterprise environmental factors

   c) Project management plan

   d) Organizational process assets

95. Pepper is a new project manager for TF Banking Services. Pepper is in the process of acquiring resources. All are tools and techniques Pepper can use to aid in her search except

   a) Virtual teams

   b) Multicriteria analysis

   c) Resource management plan

   d) Negotiation

96. Thomas has been working as a project manager for over 20 years. He has recently acquired his project management professional certificate. Which document does Thomas need to examine that maps the project deliverables to its requirements?

   a) OPA

   b) Requirements traceability matrix

   c) Project management plan

   d) Data analysis

97. Adrianne is a transferred project manager on loan from another department. Adrianne's first task is to develop a schedule management plan. Which order will Adrianne use for inputs to the plan schedule management process?

    a) Project charter, project management plan, scope management plan, development approach, EEF, and OPA

    b) Perform qualitative risk analysis, perform quantitative risk analysis, and plan risk responses

    c) Project management plan, project documents, approved change requests, EEF, and OPA

    d) Project charter, project management plan, quality management plan, project life cycle development, EEF, and OPA

98. Isabella is a project manager for Soylent Purple Corporation. As the project manager, which of the following will she use as an output of the process implement risk response plan?

    a) Change requests

    b) Data analysis

    c) Approved changes

    d) OPA

99. Oliver is a project manager for the Very Tough Corporation of America. As project manager, he will use all the following as inputs to develop project charter except

    a) SOW

    b) Assumptions and constraints

    c) OPA

    d) Data analysis

100. Megan is a new project manager for an existing project with issues. What document does Megan need to determine the project goals, high-level risks, and high-level constraints?

    a) Communication plan

    b) Project management plan

    c) SOW

    d) Project charter

101. Mason is a new project manager for Tube Socks LLC. Mason wants to get off to the best start understanding the project, people, and environment. As the project manager, Mason would choose all as inputs to the identify stakeholders process except

   a) Project charter

   b) EEF

   c) Expert judgments

   d) Organizational process assets

102. Jamis is a new project manager for the World-Eaters Corp. World-Eaters Corp is a company that terraforms planets so humans can live there comfortably. As a project manager, Jamis will use all tools and techniques to determine budget except

   a) Expert judgments

   b) Historical information review

   c) Funding limit reconciliation

   d) Business case

103. Jacob is a contractor responsible for the refurbishment of an automobile showroom. The estimated refurbishment cost is $500 per square foot. The total showroom area that needs to be refurbished is 1,000 square feet. Based on his past experience, he knows his team can refurbish 100 square feet per week. As a project manager, what does Jacob compute the estimate at completion to be?

   a) $525,000

   b) $375,000

   c) $555,555.56

   d) $516,224.19

104. Sophia is a new project manager for Flatliners Inc., a company that makes and sells defibrillators to the medical industry. Sophia wants to get off to the best start understanding the company environment. As the project manager, which output would she choose for the determine budget process?

   a) Cost baseline

   b) Alternative analysis

   c) Business need

   d) Voting

105. Patrick is a new project manager for NoTouchTV LLC. Patrick wants to get off to the best start understanding the project, people, and environment. As a project manager, what process will Patrick perform that contains the project's objectives, assumptions, constraints, and high-level requirements?

    a) Meetings

    b) Develop project charter

    c) OPA

    d) Planning

106. Promise is a project manager at MoreBooks Inc. Promise wants to get off to the best start on her project. Promise will accept all the following as inputs to develop project charter except

    a) SOW

    b) Assumptions and constraints

    c) OPA

    d) Data analysis

107. Paul is a project manager with many years of experience in developing projects, managing personnel, document distribution, and bringing projects in on time and under budget. Paul needs to get started on this project and come up to speed immediately because senior management and the sponsor are getting anxious. As a project manager, what does Paul determine are the outputs of the develop project charter process?

    a) Project management plan and requirements plan

    b) Project charter and assumptions log

    c) Quality management plan and change management plan

    d) Stakeholder management plan

108. Zoey is a new project manager for HoverMobiles. Zoey wants to get off to the best start understanding the project, people, and environment. All are inputs to the identify stakeholder group except

    a) Project charter

    b) EEF

    c) Expert judgment

    d) OPA

109. Logan is a new project manager for iClassified LLC, an internet newspaper company that specializes in online advertisements. Logan wants to understand his new project, so he must secure the right documents and have meetings with the right people. As the project manager, Logan would ask for all documents that pertain to the project charter except those that

    a) Formally authorize the existence of a project

    b) Provide the project manager the authority to apply organizational resources to the project

    c) State the high-level constraints and assumptions of the project

    d) State the details of project deliverables

110. Amelia is a new project manager for Tyronn Toys LLC. Amelia wants to get off to the best start understanding the project, people, and environment. Which best describes the develop project charter process?

    a) The process of developing a document that formally authorizes the existence of a project and provides the project manager with the authority to apply organizational resources to project activities

    b) The process of documenting how the project and product scope will be defined, validated, and controlled throughout the project

    c) The process of developing detailed descriptions of the project and products, which is what the project includes and excludes

    d) The process of estimating the number of work periods needed to complete activities with the estimated resources

111. Frances is starting a new project that involves infrastructure and database migration. Frances needs to create documents for the best plan of communication for the team. Deliverables are an output of which process group?

    a) OPA

    b) EEF

    c) Final report

    d) Direct and manage project work

112. Samuel is a new project manager with good experience in change management to do the necessary work. All the following are inputs to process direct and manage project work except

   a) Approved changes

   b) Project management plan

   c) Deliverables

   d) OPA

113. Charlotte is a senior project manager for Grayson Enterprises. Charlotte wants to avoid scope creep and gold plating on this project. Which choice best describes the direct and manage project work process?

   a) The process of leading and performing the work defined in the project plan and implementing the approved changes to achieve the project objectives

   b) The process of improving the competencies of team members and the overall team environment to enhance project performance

   c) The process of obtaining seller responses, selecting sellers, and awarding a contract

   d) The process of documenting project decisions, specifying the approach, and identifying potential sellers

114. The output of create WBS is

   a) Decomposition

   b) Scope baseline

   c) Project management plan

   d) Product scope statement

115. James is a fresh project manager hired from a competitor. James has a friend who wants to be chosen as a contractor for this project. The bidding for the project does not start until next spring. Which best describes the create WBS process??

   a) The process of developing a detailed description of the project and product

   b) The process of creating a scope management plan that documents how the project and product scope will be defined, validated, and controlled

   c) The process of subdividing project deliverables and project work into smaller, more manageable components

   d) The process of monitoring the status of the project and product scope and managing changes in the scope baseline

116. Harper is a new project manager hired from a competitor. Harper wants to get off to the best start understanding the project, people, and environment. Which are number systems in the WBS dictionary and WBS, respectively?

   a) Code of account identifier and (1.0, 1.1, 1.1.1)

   b) Chart of accounts and (a, ab, abc)

   c) Control chart and (1, 2, 3)

   d) All of the above

117. Henri is a new project manager for the ElitePens Company. Henri wants to get off to the best start understanding the project, people, and environment. What is the output of plan communication management?

   a) Project management plan

   b) Project documents

   c) Communications management plan

   d) Communication baseline

118. Charles is a seasoned project manager and is a wizard at communication management. Which answer below best fits the tools and technique of plan communication management?

   a) Change log

   b) Project management plan

   c) Manage quality

   d) Interpersonal and team skills

119. Ethan is a new project manager for VirtuNext, a maker of virtual games play systems. Ethan wants to get off to the best start understanding the project, people, and environment. What tool and technique of plan communication management would Ethan use next?

   a) Change log

   b) Project management plan

   c) Manage quality

   d) Communication technology

120. Ella is a new project manager for the PlanetEx Corporation. Ella wants to avoid team conflicts in meetings by setting up ground rules. As the project manager, which tool and technique would Ella choose next for the manage communications process?

    a) Change log

    b) Project management plan

    c) Manage quality

    d) Interpersonal and team skills

121. Mateo is a new project manager for the Canopy Corp. Mateo, like all project managers, wants to manage the perfect project: on time, under budget, great quality to the customers' satisfaction. Manage communication is a process of which knowledge area?

    a) Plan communications management

    b) Project quality management

    c) Manage tools and techniques

    d) Project communications management

122. Luna is a new project manager for Clark Enterprises. Luna wants to avoid quality issues that cause defects and require rework. Luna and his team carefully design and monitor quality into the project plan. Which best describes the manage communications process?

    a) Project management plan

    b) The process of ensuring timely and appropriate collection, creation, distribution, storage, retrieval, management, monitoring, and the ultimate disposition of project information

    c) Work performance reports

    d) Team performance

123. Sebastian is a new project manager for Prince International. Sebastian wants to build team cohesiveness, so he schedules team company parties so that the team can bond with games and be better together as workers. Which process would Sebastian use next to communicate and work with stakeholders to meet their needs and expectations, address issues, and foster appropriate involvement?

    a) Manage stakeholder engagement

    b) Monitor communications

    c) Manage communications

    d) Monitor stakeholder engagement

124. Jack is a new project manager for the Stonewall Corp. Jack's team is tasked with improving a business process within the organization. Which answer best describes the manage communications process?

   a) The process of developing an appropriate approach and plan for project communication activities based on the information needs of each stakeholder, the available organizational assets, and the needs of the project

   b) The document that includes information on staff acquisition and release, resource calendars, recognition and rewards, compliance, and safety

   c) The process of ensuring timely and appropriate collection, creation, distribution, storage, retrieval, management, monitoring, and the ultimate disposition of project information

   d) The process of ensuring the information needs of the project and its stakeholders

125. Camila is a new project manager for the Oneil Oil Company. Camila wants to get off to the best start understanding the project, people, and environment. The process of communicating and working with stakeholders to meet their needs and expectations, address issues, and foster appropriate involvement is

   a) Monitor communications

   b) Manage stakeholder engagement

   c) Manage communications

   d) Monitor stakeholder engagement

126. Jackson is a new project manager for the Atlanta Airlines Corporation. Jackson wants to get off to the best start understanding the project, people, and environment. Which answer best describes monitor communications?

   a) The process of developing an appropriate approach and plan for project communication activities based on the information needs of each stakeholder, the available organizational assets, and the needs of the project

   b) The document that includes information on staff acquisition and release, resource calendars, recognition and rewards, and compliance and safety

   c) The process of monitoring communications and the process of ensuring the information needs of the project and its stakeholders are met

   d) The process of ensuring the information needs of the project and its stakeholders are met

127. Aria is a new project manager for Yoda Propulsion Systems. Aria wants to avoid equipment delays and improve worker performance, so Aria registers with a company application that monitors all facets of scheduling from order to delivery. Aria also has daily standup meetings to make sure there is always progress in the project. As the project manager, what description of the resource management plan should best suit Aria?

    a) The process of developing an appropriate approach and plan for project communication activities based on the information needs of each stakeholder, the available organizational assets, and the needs of the project

    b) The document that includes information on staff acquisition and release, resource calendars, recognition and rewards, and compliance and safety

    c) The process of monitoring communications and the process of ensuring the information needs of the project and its stakeholders are met

    d) The process of ensuring the information needs of the project and its stakeholders are met

128. Linda is a new project manager with some experience in risk analysis to do the necessary work. What is the output of plan risk management?

    a) Communication management plan

    b) Configuration management plan

    c) Home improvement plan

    d) Risk management plan

129. Elizabeth is starting a new project that involves infrastructure and database upgrades. What description best identifies plan risk management?

    a) The process of defining how to conduct risk management activities

    b) The process of using existing knowledge and creating new knowledge to achieve the project's objectives and contribute to organizational learning

    c) The process of translating the quality management plan into executable project activities that incorporate the organization's quality policies

    d) Risk baseline

130. Mila is a new project manager for the CyberWorld Corp. Mila wants to impress the managers who hired her by performing well on day one on a massive project that will take a year to complete. As the project manager, which document will Mila create from the plan risk management process?

    a) Cost management plan

    b) Risk management plan

    c) Scope baseline

    d) Risk baseline

131. Benjamin is a new project manager for Anaconda Copper. Benjamin wants to get off to the best start understanding the project, people, and environment. Which process best describes identify risk?

    a) The process of identifying individual risks as well as sources of overall project risks and documenting their characteristics

    b) Data analysis and interpersonal skills

    c) Project management plan

    d) The process of defining how to estimate, acquire, manage, and utilize physical and team resources

132. Kenneth is a new project manager with minimal experience in acquiring proper resources to do the necessary work. Which description best fits perform qualitative risk analysis?

    a) The process of prioritizing individual project risks for further analysis by assessing their probability of occurrence and impact

    b) The process of numerically analyzing the effects of identified risks on overall project objects

    c) Identify risks, perform a qualitative risk analysis, perform a quantitative risk analysis, and plan risk responses

    d) Plan schedule management, define activities, sequence activities, and develop schedules

133. Aurora is a new project manager for Kool Klothes LLC. Aurora wants to get off to the best start understanding the project, people, and environment. Which answer is the best description of perform quantitative risk analysis?

    a) The process of numerically analyzing the effects of identified risks on overall project objects

    b) Identify risks, perform a qualitative risk analysis, perform a quantitative risk analysis, and plan risk responses

c) Plan schedule management, define activities, sequence activities, estimate activity resources, estimate activity costs, and develop schedules

d) Estimate costs and determine budget

134. Kenneth is a new project manager with minimal experience in acquiring proper resources to do the necessary work. Which description best describes perform qualitative risk analysis?

   a) The process of numerically analyzing the effects of identified risks on overall project objects

   b) Identify risks, perform qualitative risk analysis, perform quantitative risk analysis, and plan risk responses

   c) The process of prioritizing individual project risks for further analysis by assessing their probability of occurrence and impact

   d) Plan schedule management, define activities, sequence activities, estimate activity resources, estimate activity costs, and develop schedule

135. Ellie is a new project manager for TinHooks LLC. Ellie's team is tasked with acquiring and installing a new computer and hardware system for use in the organization. Which answer is the best description of perform quantitative risk analysis?

   a) The process of numerically analyzing the effects of identified risks on overall project objects

   b) Identify risks, perform qualitative risk analysis, perform quantitative risk analysis, and plan risk responses

   c) Plan schedule management, define activities, sequence activities, estimate activity resources, estimate activity costs, and develop schedule

   d) Estimate costs and determine budget

136. Carter is a new project manager for Blazed Enterprises. He is managing a project that develops a new pharmaceutical compound to bring to market. As a project manager, which input would Carter choose for the perform qualitative risk analysis process?

   a) Project management plan

   b) Alternative analysis

   c) OPA updates

   d) EEF updates

137. Robert is one of the best project managers the company has. Lately, Robert has seen a switch in management style. SMEs are being switched from one project to another without explanation or permission. Which answer is the best description of perform quantitative risk analysis?

   a) It is the process of numerically analyzing the effects of identified risks on overall project objects.

   b) It is the process by which we identify risks, perform qualitative risk analysis, perform quantitative risk analysis, and plan risk responses.

   c) It is the process by which we plan schedule management, define activities, sequence activities, estimate activity resources, estimate activity costs, and develop schedules.

   d) It involves estimating costs and determining the budget.

138. The project management plan plans the overall activities of the project and contains detailed requirements of the project. The SOW is the statement of work, which contains the objectives of the project. The project charter contains the high-level requirements of the project. All are inputs to the identify stakeholders process except

   a) Project charter

   b) EEF

   c) Expert judgments

   d) Organizational process assets

139. Alysia is a new project manager for Headgear Inc. Alysia wants to show the company they have made the correct decision by asking for the right documents to get up to speed and asking the right questions in meetings. What is the output of plan stakeholder management?

   a) Stakeholder management plan

   b) Stakeholder baseline

   c) Risk register

   d) RBS

140. The process of communicating and working with stakeholders to meet their needs and expectations, address issues, and foster appropriate involvement describes which process?

   a) Manage stakeholder engagement

   b) Monitor communications

   c) Manage communications

   d) Monitor stakeholder engagement

141. Kazem is a project manager with many years of experience. Kazem knows how important customer communication and satisfaction are to project management. What is the best definition of the monitor stakeholder engagement process?

   a) The process of identifying project stakeholders regularly and analyzing and documenting relevant information regarding their interests, involvement, interdependencies, influence, and impact on project success

   b) The process of communicating and working with stakeholders to meet their needs and expectations, address issues, and foster appropriate stakeholder engagement

   c) The process of providing an overview of the project stakeholder management process

   d) The process of monitoring project stakeholder relationships and tailoring strategies for engaging stakeholders through the modification of engagement strategies and plans

142. Avery is a project manager newly hired from a competitor. Avery wants to show the company they have made the correct decision by asking for the right documents to get up to speed and asking the right questions in meetings. The following describe monitor stakeholder engagement except

   a) Managing stakeholder relationships

   b) Ignoring the stakeholders until they go away

   c) Engaging with the stakeholders

   d) Formulating strategies with the stakeholders

143. Grayson is a senior project manager for Nearlight Enterprises. Grayson's team is tasked with modifying a computer software program used in the organization. As the project manager, which definition would Grayson choose as the best description of plan cost management?

   a) The process of defining how the project cost will be estimated, budgeted, managed, monitored, and controlled

   b) The process of defining how to estimate, acquire, manage, and utilize physical and team resources

   c) The process of defining how to conduct risk management activities

   d) The process of identifying the relationships among project activities

144. Abigail is a project manager for a new underwater concept company. Abigail's team is tasked with conducting research to develop a new manufacturing process for the organization. As the project manager, which output of the plan cost management process would Abigail choose?

    a) Risk management plan

    b) Cost baseline

    c) Cost management plan

    d) Schedule baseline

145. Leo is a new project manager for a security software company that protects against hackers and credit card scams. Leo team is tasked with building a complete enterprise system to meet the sponsor's vision. Which is the best description of estimate costs?

    a) The process of analyzing sequences, durations, resource requirements, and schedule constraints to create a project model for project executions, monitoring, and controlling

    b) The process of developing an approximation of the monetary resources needed to complete the work

    c) The process of developing an approach and plan for project communications activities based on the information needs of each stakeholder and the project

    d) The process of defining how to estimate, acquire, manage, and utilize physical and team resources

146. Sofia is a new project manager for a computer animation company. Sofia's team has the task of acquiring resources and computer equipment and installing and configuring software so developers can program. Which of the following depicts the order of activities in project cost management?

    a) Collect requirements, define scope, and create WBS

    b) Identify risks, perform qualitative risk analysis, perform quantitative risk analysis, and plan risk responses

    c) Plan schedule management, define activities, sequence activities, estimate activity durations, and develop schedule

    d) Estimate costs and determine budget

147. As a project manager, you are planning the activities in the project schedule. Which of the following depicts the order of activities in plan cost management?

    a) Collect requirements, define scope, and create WBS

    b) Identify risks, perform qualitative risk analysis, perform quantitative risk analysis, and plan risk responses

    c) Plan schedule management, define activities, sequence activities, estimate activity resources, estimate activity costs, and develop schedule

    d) Estimate costs and determine budget

148. Which is not a tool and technique used in the estimate activity durations process?

    a) Analogous estimating

    b) Bottom-up estimating

    c) Three-point estimating

    d) Duration estimates

149. Mary is a project manager for a real estate company. Using the PERT beta distribution formula, how long will it take Mary to complete the project if most likely = 32, optimistic = 20, and pessimistic = 50?

    a) 44

    b) 33

    c) 34

    d) 32

150. The project manager continues to put numbers together for cost and schedule. Using the triangular distribution method, how long will it take the project manager to complete the project if most likely = 32, optimistic = 20, and pessimistic = 50?

    a) 44

    b) 33

    c) 34

    d) 32

151. The following are all tools and techniques that can be used to determine budget except

   a) Expert judgments

   b) Historical information review

   c) Funding limit reconciliation

   d) Business documents

152. Which is an output of the determine budget process?

   a) Cost baseline

   b) Alternative analysis

   c) Project management plan

   d) Voting

153. As a project manager, you are planning the activities in the project schedule. What is the output of plan schedule management?

   a) Collect requirements, define scope, and create WBS

   b) Identify risks, perform qualitative risk analysis, perform quantitative risk analysis, and plan risk responses

   c) Create the schedule management plan

   d) Estimate costs and determine the budget

154. As the project manager, which inputs would you choose for the plan schedule management process?

   a) Project charter, project management plan, scope management plan, development approach, EEF, and OPA

   b) Perform qualitative risk analysis, perform quantitative risk analysis, and plan risk responses

   c) Project management plan, project documents, approved change requests, EEF, and OPA

   d) Project charter, project management plan, quality management plan, project life cycle development, EEF, and OPA

155. Which of the following depicts the order of activities in schedule management?

   a) Collect requirements, define scope, and create the WBS

   b) Identify risks, perform qualitative risk analysis, perform quantitative risk analysis, and plan risk responses

   c) Plan schedule management, define activities, sequence activities, estimate activity durations, and develop schedules

   d) Estimate costs and determine budget

156. As the project manager in the define activities process, work is decomposed into which of the following?

   a) Work packages

   b) WBS

   c) Activities

   d) WBS and activities

157. Jason is a new project manager who is currently in the planning phase of a project. Jason has defined the activities—what should he do next?

   a) Sequence activities

   b) Estimate costs

   c) Collect requirements

   d) Identify risks

158. Jason is a new project manager who is currently in the planning phase of a project. Jason has defined the activities. As a project manager, what did Jason do before defining the activities?

   a) Sequence activities

   b) Estimate costs

   c) Plan schedule management

   d) Identify risks

159. As the project manager, which of the four types of PDM relationships will you use least often?

   a) Finish to Start (FS)

   b) Finish to Finish (FF)

   c) Start to Finish (SF)

   d) Start to Start (SS)

160. As the project manager, which of the four types of PDM relationships will you use most often?

   a) Finish to Start (FS)

   b) Finish to Finish (FF)

   c) Start to Finish (SF)

   d) Start to Start (SS)

161. As a project manager, you are planning the activities in the project schedule. Which of the following depicts the order of activities in cost management?

   a) Collect requirements, define scope, and create WBS

   b) Identify risks, perform qualitative risk analysis, perform quantitative risk analysis, and plan risk responses

   c) Plan schedule management, define activities, sequence activities, estimate activity resources, estimate activity costs, and develop schedule

   d) Estimate costs and determine budget

162. Which is not a tool and technique used in the estimate activity durations process?

   a) Analogous estimating

   b) Bottom-up estimating

   c) Three-point estimating

   d) Duration estimates

163. As the project manager, when using the PERT beta distribution formula, how long will it take Mary to complete the project if most likely = 32, optimistic = 20, and pessimistic = 50?

    a) 44

    b) 33

    c) 34

    d) 32

164. Mary is a project manager for a biochemical firm. By using the triangular distribution method, how long will it take Mary to complete the project if most likely = 32, optimistic = 20, and pessimistic = 50?

    a) 44

    b) 33

    c) 34

    d) 32

165. Which of the following depicts the order of activities in schedule management?

    a) Collect requirements, define scope, and create WBS

    b) Identify risks, perform qualitative risk analysis, perform quantitative risk analysis, and plan risk responses

    c) Plan schedule management, define activities, sequence activities, estimate activity durations and develop schedule

    d) Estimate costs and determine budget

166. All are tools and techniques of the develop schedule process except

    a) Schedule compression

    b) Data analysis

    c) Project documents

    d) Critical path method

167. Judy is a superb project manager at her firm. She is currently working on a project in which a fix is necessary. As a project manager, what should Judy do next?

   a) Check the release documents

   b) Notify the sponsor

   c) Evaluate the impact of the change

   d) Implement the risk response plan

168. Judy is a top project manager at her firm. She is currently working on a project in which a fix *might be* necessary. As a project manager, what should Judy do next?

   a) Prevent changes from occurring

   b) Notify the sponsor

   c) Evaluate the impact of the change

   d) Implement the risk response plan

169. Mitchell is a project manager for a solar car company on a new project that has not started. He wants to know where he can get information about projects like the one he is about to start. Where would Mitchell go first to get this information?

   a) Program manager

   b) PMO

   c) Portfolio office

   d) Sponsor

170. Jeffrey is a new project manager for Apocrypha Inc., a producer of religious books and artifacts. As the new project manager, he must have a plan in which many criteria are met for the condition of the books and artifacts. As a project manager, what document must Jeffrey create to set guidelines in criteria?

   a) Project management plan

   b) Project documents

   c) Risk management plan

   d) Quality management plan

171. Marshall is a project manager for the Action Solar Company, a maker of sun car parts. Quality is important in the company. Which best describes the plan quality management process?

   a) The process of identifying quality requirements and standards for the project and its deliverables and documenting how the project will demonstrate compliance with quality requirements and standards

   b) The process of monitoring and recording the results of executing the quality management activities to assess performance and ensure the project outputs are complete, correct, and meet customer requirements

   c) The process of translating the quality management plan into executable quality activities that incorporate the organization's quality policies into the project

   d) None of the above

172. Which of the following is an input to the manage quality process?

   a) Quality reports

   b) Quality metrics

   c) Data gathering

   d) Enterprise environmental factors

173. Terri is a new project manager at a manufacturing firm. She has completed the planning stage. Her team has begun implementing the work according to the project plan. One of Terri's team members has noticed a problem with her task but has not yet found a fix. What tools can be used to determine the cause of the problem?

   a) Prototypes

   b) An oscilloscope

   c) Fishbone

   d) Bottom-up estimating

174. David is a new project manager for Voice Activated Systems Enterprises. He wants to get off to the best start understanding ways to deliver a quality product. David and his team are planning for accuracy in quality. Which of the following tools is one of the seven rules of quality control?

   a) Analysis technique

   b) Cause-and-effect diagram

   c) Data representation

   d) Manage quality

175. Emma is a project manager at a paper factory. Before the project starts, she requests information about political influence and public opinion. Which of these are influences out of the project manager's control?

   a) Enterprise environmental factors

   b) Organizational process assets

   c) Evolution environmental factors

   d) Extreme environmental factors

176. Susan is a project manager with many years of experience. Her current project is especially difficult because of problems with the timeline getting extended many times. This could be because the scope is not well defined, and the delays are causing increases in cost because of increased hours of work on the project for fixes. Susan can find all of the following in the project charter except

   a) Project purpose

   b) High-level requirements

   c) Detailed requirements

   d) Key stakeholder list

177. Bradford is the new project manager at Green Thumb Nursery. His current project has constantly run into delays because of new deliverables that must be added for the project to be a success. As a project manager, which documents should Bradford check first to determine deliverables?

   a) Scope management plan and requirements management plan

   b) Project charter and project management plan

   c) Quality management plan and process improvement plan

   d) Risk management plan and risk response plan

178. Jamerson is the project manager of Aqua Rooms, which are short-term underwater apartments. The project Jamerson is managing is consistently encountering incomplete requirements. As a project manager, he would use all tools and techniques to collect requirements except

   a) Data analysis

   b) Decision-making

   c) Organizational process assets

   d) Interpersonal skills and team skills

179. Jamal is a senior project manager at a major pharmaceutical company. The project involves the testing of a new drug to halt aging. The project data is currently being collected. As a senior project manager, which requirement will Jamal not capture as an input to collect requirements?

    a) Project management plan

    b) Communication management plan

    c) Project documents

    d) EEF

180. Maria is a newly hired contract project manager who wants all documents related to the current project. Which document will Maria most want to map deliverables to their respective requirements?

    a) OPA

    b) Requirements traceability matrix

    c) Project management plan

    d) Data analysis

181. Which answer best describes the define scope process?

    a) The process of developing a detailed description of the project and product

    b) The process of creating a scope management plan that documents how the project and product scope will be defined, validated, and controlled

    c) The process of subdividing project deliverables and project work into smaller, more manageable components

    d) The process of monitoring the status of the project and product scope and managing changes in the scope baseline

182. Work that is outside the scope of the project is demanded by a sponsor, senior management, or stakeholders other than the project team. Which answer best describes this scenario?

    a) Gold plating

    b) Work that is necessary

    c) Work that is unnecessary

    d) Scope creep

183. There is work performed outside the scope of the project and suggested by the project team. Which answer best describes this action?

   a) Gold plating

   b) Work that is necessary

   c) Work that is unnecessary

   d) Scope creep

184. Which process best exemplifies monitoring and control in project integration?

   a) Direct and manage project work

   b) Monitor and control project work

   c) Manage project knowledge

   d) Perform integrated change control

185. Harry is a contractor responsible for the refurbishment of an automobile showroom. The estimated refurbishment cost is $500 per square foot. The total showroom area that needs to be refurbished is 1,000 square feet. Based on his past experience, he knows his team can refurbish 100 square feet per week. As the project manager, Harry will report the steady-state value of the project as

   a) $525,000

   b) $375,000

   c) $555,555.56

   d) $475,000

186. David has been a project manager for many years. David has been communicating with the sponsor and senior management, combining SOW, assumptions, initial stakeholders, and high-level risk into one document. As the project manager, which of the following documents is he creating?

   a) Data gathering

   b) Project management plan

   c) Inspection

   d) Project charter

187. Jeffrey is a project manager and wants to define how to estimate, acquire, manage, and utilize physical and team resources. Which process fits the definition for Jeffrey?

   a) Develop team

   b) Plan resource management

   c) Organizational theory

   d) Team charter

188. Priscilla is a project manager who transferred from another department. One of the documents Priscilla must create is vital to the success of the project in meeting its deliverables. Which document is created from the output of the develop project management plan process?

   a) Project charter

   b) Enterprise environmental factors

   c) Project management plan

   d) Organizational process assets

189. Robert is a new project manager at Use It or Lose It! Inc. Robert does not trust his employees to do their jobs, so he must monitor their every action to make sure he gets the results he wants. As a project manager, what management type is Robert practicing?

   a) RAM

   b) McGregor's Theory X

   c) Expectancy Theory

   d) McGregor's Theory Y

190. David has been a project manager for many years. David has been communicating with the sponsor and senior management, combining SOW, assumptions, initial stakeholders, and high-level risk into one document. As the project manager, which of the following documents is he creating?

   a) Data gathering

   b) Project management plan

   c) Inspection

   d) Project charter

191. Carmen is a new project manager who wants to impress everyone with how good her skills and knowledge are. When a new contractor is added to the team, she wants to use the correct order of team development. Which is the correct order of team development, according to Tuckerman's Ladder?

    a) Performing, storming, norming, forming, and adjourning

    b) Performing, storming, adjourning, forming, and norming

    c) Forming, norming, storming, performing, and adjourning

    d) Forming, storming, norming, performing, and adjourning

192. Which answer best describes the process to manage communications?

    a) Project management plan

    b) The process of ensuring timely and appropriate collection, creation, distribution, storage, retrieval, management, monitoring, and the ultimate disposition of project information

    c) Work performance reports

    d) Team performance

193. David is a new project manager for New Brand Cola LLC. David wants to get off to the best start in understanding the project, people, and environment. As a project manager, David has discovered interpersonal and team skills as a tool and technique of which process?

    a) Meetings

    b) Develop project charter

    c) Organizational process assets

    d) Planning

194. Frank is a project manager with Carmon Lip Balm LLC. He and his project team meticulously put together a project plan that captured and strategized for many risks. One of the risks has just materialized. As a project manager, what should Frank do next?

    a) Plan risk management

    b) Monitor risks

    c) Use his interpersonal and team management skills

    d) Implement risk responses

195. Debbie is a project manager at Cool Socks Inc. She is in the planning process for a new project and has completed the sequence activities process. The kickoff of the project occurred three months ago. The project team is currently managing the project. As a project manager, what would Debbie do next?

  a) Estimate activity durations

  b) Close the project

  c) Control schedule

  d) Identify stakeholders

196. Olivia is a new project manager at World of Crowe Inc. Olivia trusts her employees to do their jobs, so she does not monitor their every action to make sure she gets the results she wants. What is the project manager practicing?

  a) RAM

  b) McGregor's Theory X

  c) Expectancy Theory

  d) McGregor's Theory Y

197. Which of the following is an output of the process implement risk response plan?

  a) Change requests

  b) Data analysis

  c) Approved changes

  d) OPA

198. Joseph is a project manager with Carmon Lip Balm LLC. He and his project team meticulously put together a project plan that captured and strategized for many risks. One of the risks has just materialized. As a project manager, what should Joseph do next?

  a) Plan risk management

  b) Monitor risks

  c) Use his interpersonal and team management skills

  d) Implement risk responses

199. Which of the following is an output of the process implement risk response plan?

  a) Change requests

  b) Data analysis

  c) Approved changes

  d) OPA

200. Which of the following is an input to the manage project knowledge process?

  a) Alternative analysis

  b) Deliverables

  c) OPA updates

  d) Project management plan updates

Mock Exam Three

200 Questions—4 Hours Advanced Solutions

1. **Answer: a.** The project management plan is the document the project manager will want most.

2. **Answer: a.** Only a is in the correct order.

3. **Answer: a.** Only a has all the correct elements. Starting, adjusting, and closing are not part of Tuckerman's ladder.

4. **Answer: a.** Jonathan needs to create a project management plan which is used by the project manager to manage the project from start to completion. Project documents is not used to track project from start to completion. Work performance reports is a document that shows how well project is performing.

5. **Answer: b.** Develop project charter is the only process on this list. Meetings is a tool and technique for many processes. Organizational process assets are input to many processes, and planning is a process group.

6. **Answer: d.** The lessons learned register is an input.

7. **Answer: d.** Data gathering is a tool and technique, not an input.

8. **Answer: c.** We are clearly in the execute phase of the project. We have already estimated durations because we have entered the execute phase. There is no mention of project close or cancellation. Identifying stakeholders is going on throughout the life cycle of the project. The best answer is control schedule.

9. **Answer: d.** Data gathering is a tool and technique. SOW, enterprise environmental factors, and organizational process assets are inputs for develop project charter.

10. **Answer: d.** The communication plan is a document for planning communication of the project. The project management plan plans the overall activities of the project and contains detailed requirements of the project. The SOW is the statement of work, which includes the objectives of the project. The project charter contains the high-level requirements of the project.

11. **Answer: a.** The difference between monitoring and managing is that monitoring is watching or observing. Managing is an action in which you are actually doing something. In this case, it is the "process of communicating and working with stakeholders."

12. **Answer: a**. The project management plan is the output of the process to develop the project management plan. EEF and OPA are inputs of other processes.

13. **Answer: c**. If the fix is necessary, then checking release documents has already occurred. Implementing the risk response plan would occur if a risk previously planned had occurred. Notifying sponsor might occur if a fix was not previously planned for, and the issue that necessitated the fix would impact the project adversely either in cost, schedule, or quality.

14. **Answer: b**. The project management plan is the output of the process, not a tool and technique.

15. **Answer: c**. Harry will report the project ahead of schedule and over budget.

Cost Variance	(EV - AC) = ($25,000.00)
Schedule Variance	(EV - PV) = $25,000.00

16. **Answer: a**. The project manager would want to prevent the change from occurring and seek alternative solutions. However, if the change must occur, then evaluate the impact of the change. Implement the risk response plan would occur if a risk previously planned had occurred. Notify sponsor might occur if the fix was not previously planned for, and the issue that necessitated the fix would impact the project adversely, either in cost, schedule, or quality.

17. **Answer: a**. Define scope is the planning process that would be performed next. The project management plan is an output of develop project management plan. Plan scope management would have been done previously to collect requirements. Expert judgments is a tool and technique.

18. **Answer: b**. Define activities is the planning process that would be performed next. The project management plan is an output of develop project management plan. Plan scope management would have been done previously to collect requirements. Expert judgments are a tool and technique.

19. **Answer: d**. Organizational process assets and enterprise environmental factors are inputs to many process groups. The final report is an output of the close project or phase process group.

20. **Answer: c**. Plan schedule management is the planning process that would have been performed prior to define activities. The project management plan is an output of develop project management plan. Plan scope management would have been done previously to collect requirements. Expert judgments is a tool and technique.

21. **Answer: b**. Change requests are an output of perform integrated change control process, the project management plan is an output of develop project plan process, and OPA updates are outputs of other processes. Only b is a tool and technique.

22. **Answer: d**. Create WBS is the planning process that would have been performed prior to define activities. The project management plan is an output of develop project management plan. Plan

scope management would have been done prior to collect requirements. Data gathering is a tool and technique.

23. **Answer: d**. Choices a, c, and d are not the best exemplification of monitoring and control in project integration.

24. **Answer: b**. Validate scope is the process that would be performed next because the project is in the execute phase. When execute starts, then the monitor control process starts. Project management and plan scope management are planning processes. Data gathering is a tool and technique.

25. **Answer: a**. The communication management plan is a document for planning communication of the project. The project management plan plans the overall activities of the project and contains detailed requirements of the project. The SOW is the statement of work, which includes tMhe objectives of the project. The project charter contains the high-level requirements of the project.

26. **Answer: b**. Plan resource management is part of the planning stage and answers the question of how to estimate, acquire, manage, and utilize physical and team resources. Develop team is also a process but in the execute stage and would best fit training a resource. Choices c and d are not processes.

27. **Answer: d**. Jeffrey should report the estimate at completion as $516,224.19.

28. **Answer: b**. The keyword here is "how," which describes the plan—in this case, plan resource management.

29. **Answer: b**. McGregor's Theory X assumes that the typical worker has little ambition, avoids responsibility, and is individual-goal oriented. McGregor's Theory Y assumes employees are internally motivated, enjoy their jobs, and work to better themselves without a direct reward in return.

30. **Answer: b**. Control costs is the process that would be performed next since the project is in the execute phase; money is being spent, so the cost must be controlled. When execute starts, then the monitor control process starts. Data gathering is a tool and technique. Define scope and create WBS are planning processes.

31. **Answer: b**. Only b is in the correct order.

32. **Answer: c**. Once the project manager has been notified by senior management or the sponsor that the project is being canceled, then the closing procedure must begin immediately.

33. **Answer: d**. Only d is in the correct order.

34. **Answer: d**. The fact that the question asks "how to" indicates the project is in the planning stage. Develop team is a process in the execute stage. Organizational theory and team charter are not processes.

35. **Answer: c.** Once the contractor has started work, they will be monitored and tracked to make sure the results are being established according to the project plan and the vendor contract. Closing reports for archive comes in the closing phase. Planning what is expected of the vendor would have been performed in the planning stage.

36. **Answer: c.** The resource management plan is a document and is the output of plan resource management.

37. **Answer: c.** Sophia will report the steady-state as $555,555.56.

Estimate at Completion (typical, steady-state, or continuous)	(BAC / CPI) = $555,555.56

38. **Answer: b.** Project document updates is an output.

39. **Answer: b.** The output of validate scope is acceptable deliverables. Validate scope formalizes the acceptance of the completed project deliverables. Verified deliverables are the output of the project tasks. Work performance data is raw data that is reported on change requests. Work performance information is the work performance data that has been transformed for example, number of change requests or forecast estimates.

40. **Answer: d.** Since the project is now in the execute stage, the order of what occurs next is acquire resources, develop team, and manage resources.

41. **Answer: a.** Choices b,c, and d are not in the correct order.

42. **Answer: d.** Only d is in the correct order.

43. **Answer: b.** McGregor's Theory X assumes that the typical worker has little ambition, avoids responsibility, and is individual-goal oriented. McGregor's Theory Y assumes employees are internally motivated, enjoy their jobs, and work to better themselves without a direct reward in return.

44. **Answer: a.** Control resources will be the project manager's next task. Since the project is now in the execute stage, the order of what occurs next is acquire resources, develop team, and manage resources. However, since none of these options are there, the choice that best answers the question is control resources.

45. **Answer: c.** As a project manager, you report the fact at the time and not what you know or assume will happen later. Harry would report the project as ahead of schedule and over budget.

Cost Variance	(EV - AC) = $25,000.00
Schedule Variance	(EV - PV) = $25,000.00

46. **Answer: b.** Assumption and constraint analysis is a tool and technique. Choices c and d are outputs of other processes.

47. **Answer: c.** Plan resource management defines how to estimate, acquire, manage, and utilize physical and team resources.

48. **Answer: d.** The communication plan is a document for planning communication of the project. The project management plan plans the overall activities of the project and contains detailed requirements of the project. The SOW is the statement of work, which includes the objectives of the project. The project charter contains the high-level requirements of the project.

49. **Answer: c.** Performing team development is the next step for the project manager. After the project kickoff the project is in the Execute phase. Create WBS is in the planning phase. Control resources and stakeholder engagement are in the monitoring and control phase.

50. **Answer: b.** Validate scope is the best option here. Create WBS is performed in the planning process, in which the project plan has already been approved. Answer c is the approved project plan. The negotiation with a sponsor for overtime response is already answered in the project plan with the creation and approval of the schedule baseline.

51. **Answer: d.** Data gathering is a tool and technique, not an input.

52. **Answer: a.** If the question asks for a plan, then b is not the answer. Answer c is executing the plan. Answer d is not correct because you always want to communicate in project management. The process of developing is a "plan" type of answer.

53. **Answer: b.** Acceptable deliverables is the output of the validate scope process.

54. **Answer: c.** Develop team will be the project manager's next task. Since the project is now in the execute stage, the order of what occurs next is acquire resources, develop team, and manage resources.

55. **Answer: d.** The next thing the project manager will do is monitor the stakeholder engagement as part of the project plan.

56. **Answer: d.** Option a is identifying stakeholders, b is manage stakeholder engagement, and c does not exist.

57. **Answer: b.** You would think answer b would be common sense, but it is surprising how many testers will miss a question like this on the exam. You never ignore stakeholders because communication, collaboration, and compromise are primary tools of a project manager.

58. **Answer: b.** Project document updates is an output. All others are inputs to one or more processes.

59. **Answer: b.** Develop project charter is the only process on this list. Meetings is a tool and technique for many processes. Organizational process assets are an input to many processes, and planning is a process group.

60. **Answer: c.** The next step in the planning stage after plan procurement management is to plan the stakeholder engagement process. Create WBS happens earlier in the planning stage, and validate scope is in the execute stage. Project managers will not negotiate with the sponsor.

61. **Answer: d.** Change log and project management plan are never a tool and technique. Manage quality is a process.

62. **Answer: b.** McGregor's Theory X assumes that the typical worker has little ambition, avoids responsibility, and is individual-goal oriented. McGregor's Theory Y assumes employees are internally motivated, enjoy their jobs, and work to better themselves without a direct reward in return.

63. **Answer: a.** The difference between monitoring and managing is that monitoring is watching or observing. Managing is an action in which you are actually doing something. In this case, it is the "process of communicating and working with stakeholders."

64. **Answer: b.** McGregor's Theory X assumes that the typical worker has little ambition, avoids responsibility, and is individual-goal oriented. McGregor's Theory Y assumes employees are internally motivated, enjoy their jobs, and work to better themselves without a direct reward in return.

65. **Answer: d.** Only d is in the correct order.

66. **Answer: d.** Develop team is the next step for the project manager.

67. **Answer: b.** McGregor's Theory X assumes that the typical worker has little ambition, avoids responsibility, and is individual-goal oriented. McGregor's Theory Y assumes employees are internally motivated, enjoy their jobs, and work to better themselves without a direct reward in return.

68. **Answer: b.** You would think answer b would be common sense, but it is surprising how many testers will miss a question like this on the exam. You never ignore stakeholders because communication, collaboration, and compromise are primary tools of a project manager.

69. **Answer: a.** The next thing the project manager will do is control resources as part of the project plan. At this time, the resources have already been trained and developed. The team is producing results. As a project manager, you want to make sure the results are per the project plan.

70. **Answer: d.** Option a is an output, b is an input, and c is a process.

71. **Answer: b.** The next thing the project manager will do is develop a team as part of the project plan.

72. **Answer: b.** The project management plan describes the project, work performance reports describe the status of the project, and team performance is the evaluation of the effectiveness of the team.

73. **Answer: d.** Option a is identifying stakeholders, b is manage stakeholder engagement, and c does not exist.

74. **Answer: a.** The difference between monitoring and managing is that monitoring is watching or observing. Managing is an action in which you are actually doing something. In this case, it is the "process of communicating and working with stakeholders."

75. **Answer: b.** Project document updates is an output.

76. **Answer: c.** The next thing the project manager will do is control resources as part of the project plan. At this time, the resources have already been trained and develop. The team is producing results. As a project manager, you want to make sure the results are per the project plan.

77. **Answer: b.** McGregor's Theory X assumes that the typical worker has little ambition, avoids responsibility, and is individual-goal oriented. McGregor's Theory Y assumes employees are internally motivated, enjoy their jobs, and work to better themselves without a direct reward in return.

78. **Answer: a.** Only a is in the correct order.

79. **Answer: a.** Plan risk management is the next step for the project manager.

80. **Answer: b.** Project documents updates is an output.

81. **Answer: b.** Plan communication management is the step that comes before planning to perform qualitative risk analysis.

82. **Answer: b.** Communications analysis describes what is needed to maximize the value of information for project stakeholders. Communications technology includes shared portals, emails, and databases. The communications model is the encoding and decoding of messages. And the communication method is the interaction of information, such as one-way or multidirectional conversations.

83. **Answer: d.** Plan risk management is the next step for the project manager.

84. **Answer: b.** The next thing the project manager will do is control resources as part of the project plan. At this time, the resources have already been trained and developed. The team is producing results. As a project manager, you want to make sure the results are per the project plan.

85. **Answer: a.** Meetings are the only tool and technique on this list. Develop project charter is a process. OPA is input, and planning alone is a word, not a tool and technique.

86. **Answer: d.** SOW, assumptions, and constraints and OPA are all inputs to the project charter. Data analysis is a tool and technique.

87. **Answer: d.** Only d is in the correct order.

88. **Answer: b.** The output when developing a charter is a project charter and assumptions log.

89. **Answer: b.** Develop project charter is the only process on this list. Meetings is a tool and technique for many processes. Organizational process assets are an input to many processes, and planning is a process group.

90. **Answer: d.** Data gathering is a tool and technique, not an input.

91. **Answer: b.** The next thing the project manager will do is control resources as part of the project plan. At this time, the resources have already been trained and developed. The team is producing results. As a project manager, you want to make sure the results are per the project plan.

92. **Answer: d.** The communication plan is a document for planning communication of the project. The project management plan plans the overall activities of the project and contains detailed requirements of the project. The SOW is the statement of work, which includes the objectives of the project. The project charter contains the high-level requirements of the project.

93. **Answer: c.** Expert judgments is a tool and technique.

94. **Answer: c.** Project charter, EEF, and OPA are all inputs to the process.

95. **Answer: c.** The resource management plan is an output of plan resource management.

96. **Answer: b.** The requirements traceability matrix maps the project deliverables to its requirements. The OPA and project management plan are inputs. Data analysis is a tool and technique.

97. **Answer: a.** Choice b describes plan risk management, and c describes direct and manage projects. As stated earlier, knowing the sequences of the planning group in all knowledge areas is crucial to passing the PMP exam.

98. **Answer: a.** Data analysis is a tool and technique of most processes. Approved changes are an output of performed integrated change control and an input to direct and manage project work. OPA is an input to most processes.

99. **Answer: d.** Data analysis is a tool and technique. Statement of work, assumptions and constraints, and organizational process assets are inputs to the project charter.

100. **Answer: d.** The project management plan has the overall activities of the project and contains detailed requirements of the project. The SOW is the statement of work, which contains the objectives of the project. The project charter contains the high-level requirements of the project.

101. Answer: c. Expert judgments is always a tool and technique.

102. Answer: d. Expert judgments, historical information review, and funding limit reconciliation are all tools and techniques that can be used to determine the budget.

103. Answer: d. The estimate at completion formula is (AC + (BAC-EV)) / (CPI * SPI). (AC + (BAC-EV)) / (CPI * SPI) = $516,224.19

Complete table solutions below:

Estimated refurbishment cost	$500.00 per square foot
Total showroom area	1,000.00 square feet
Refurbishment pace	100.00 square feet per week

Term	Value
Budget at Completion	($500 x 1,000) = $500,000.00
Planned Value	(4 / 10 x BAC) = $200,000.00
Earned Value	(45% x BAC) = $225,000.00
Actual Cost	$250,000.00
Cost Variance	(EV - AC) = $25,000.00
Schedule Variance	(EV - PV) = $25,000.00
Cost Performance Index	(EV / AC) = 0.90
Schedule Performance Index	(EV / PV) = 1.13
Estimate at Completion (atypical)	(AC + (BAC - EV)) = 525,000
Estimate at Completion (forecast)	(AC+ (BAC - EV)) / (CPI * SPI) = 516,224.19
Estimate at Completion (typical, steady-state or continuous)	(BAC / CPI) = $555,555.56
Estimate to Complete	(EAC - AC) = $305,555.56
Variance at Completion	(BAC - EAC) = $55,555.56

Total duration (1,000 / 100)	= 10.00 weeks
Duration Elapsed	= 4.00 weeks
Percentage completion	= 45%

104. Answer: a. Options b, c, and d are not outputs.

105. **Answer: b.** Develop project charter is the process that creates the project charter document, which contains the project's objectives, assumptions, constraints, and high-level requirements. Meetings is a tool and technique. OPA is the organization policies, procedures, and practices, and planning is not a process. Develop project plan is a process.

106. **Answer: d.** Data analysis is a tool and technique. SOW, OPA, and assumptions and constraints are used in the develop project charter process.

107. **Answer: b.** The project charter and assumptions log are the outputs of the develop charter process.

108. **Answer: c.** Expert judgment is a tool and technique. Project charter, EEF, and OPA are inputs to most identify stakeholder processes.

109. **Answer: d.** The project charter does not have detailed information. Options a, b, and c all describe the project charter.

110. **Answer: a.** Choice b better describes plan scope management. Choice c, develop charter, does process detailed information. Choices b, c, and d are performed in the planning stage of the project.

111. **Answer: d.** OPA and EEF are inputs to other processes, and the final report is an output of close process.

112. **Answer: c.** Deliverables is an output of direct and manage the project work process. Options a, b and c are inputs to direct and manage project work.

113. **Answer: a.** Choice b is the develop team process, and c and d involve procurements.

114. **Answer: b.** Decomposition is a tool and technique. The project management plan is an output of develop project plan process

115. **Answer: c.** Option b describes plan scope management and d describes monitor and control project work.

116. **Answer: a.** Code of account identifier and (1.0, 1.1, 1.1.1) are the correct number systems.

117. **Answer: c.** The project management plan is the output of develop project plan. Communication baseline does not exist in PMBOK.

118. **Answer: d.** Interpersonal and team skills are the only tools and techniques in the list. The project management plan is an output of the develop project plan. Manage quality is a process. The change log is an output of perform integrated change control.

119. **Answer: d.** Communication technology is the only tool and technique on the list. The project management plan is an output of the develop project plan. Manage quality is a process. The change log is an output of perform integrated change control.

120. **Answer: d**. Interpersonal and team skills are only tool and technique on the list. The project management plan is an output of develop project plan. Manage quality is a process. The change log is an output of perform integrated change control.

121. **Answer: d**. There are ten knowledge areas in the *PMBOK* 6th edition. You can get a quick glance at all ten knowledge areas in *PMBOK*, page 25.

122. **Answer: b**. Manage communications is the process of ensuring timely and appropriate collection, creation, distribution, storage, retrieval, management, monitoring, and the ultimate disposition of project information.

123. **Answer: a**. Manage stakeholder engagement is the correct response. Revisit glossary for definitions.

124. **Answer: c**. Manage communications is the process of ensuring timely and appropriate collection, creation, distribution, storage, retrieval, management, monitoring, and the ultimate disposition of project information.

125. **Answer: b**. The process described is manage stakeholder engagement.

126. **Answer: c**. This choice best describes monitor communications.

127. **Answer: b**. Option b best describes the resource management plan.

128. **Answer: d**. The risk management plan is the output of plan risk management.

129. **Answer: a**. Option a best describes plan risk management. Option c is plan quality management, and d does not exist in PMBOK.

130. **Answer: b**. Answer a is the output of plan cost management. Answer c is the output of define scope, and d does not exist in PMBOK.

131. **Answer: a**. Option b is a tool and technique, c is a document, and d is plan resource management.

132. **Answer: a**. Choice b is perform quantitative risk analysis. Answer c is project risk management, and d is project schedule management.

133. **Answer: a**. Option a best describes perform quantitative risk analysis.

134. **Answer: c**. Choice c best describes perform qualitative risk analysis.

135. **Answer: a**. Option a best describes perform quantitative risk analysis.

136. **Answer: a**. Choice b is a tool and technique. Choices c and d are outputs to other processes.

137. **Answer: a**. Choice a is the best description for perform quantitative risk analysis.

138. **Answer: c**. Expert judgments is a tool and technique.

139. **Answer: a**. Answer b does not exist in PMBOK. Answer c is an output of identify risks. Answer d could be either a risk breakdown structure or resource breakdown structure, neither of which is the answer.

140. **Answer: a**. The difference between monitoring and managing is that monitoring is watching or observing. Managing is an action in which you are actually doing something. In this case, it is the "process of communicating and working with stakeholders."

141. **Answer: d**. Option a is identifying stakeholders, b is managing stakeholder engagement, and c does not exist.

142. **Answer: b**. You would think answer b would be common sense, but it is surprising how many testers will miss a question like this on the exam. You never ignore stakeholders because communication, collaboration, and compromise are primary tools of a project manager.

143. **Answer: a**. Option b is plan resource management. Option c is manage risks.

144. **Answer: c**. Option b is an output of plan risk management. Option c is an output of plan cost management. Option d is an output of define scope.

145. **Answer: b**. Option a is plan schedule management. Option d is plan resource management.

146. **Answer: d**. The order is plan cost management, estimate costs, and determine budget.

147. **Answer: d**. Option a describes scope management, b defines risk management, and c is schedule management.

148. **Answer: d**. Analogous, bottom-up, and three-point estimating are tools and techniques for the estimate activity durations process.

149. **Answer: b**. (20 + 32(4) + 50) / 6 = 33

150. **Answer: c**. (32 + 20 + 50) / 3 = 34

151. **Answer: d**. Expert judgments, historical information review, and funding limit reconciliation are all tools and techniques that can be used to determine the budget.

152. **Answer: a**. Options b, c, and d are not outputs.

153. **Answer: c**. Option a describes scope management, b describes defining risk management, and d is cost management.

154. **Answer: a**. Choice b describes plan risk management, and c describes direct and manage projects. As stated earlier, knowing the sequences of the planning group in all knowledge areas is crucial to passing the PMP exam.

155. **Answer: c.** Option a describes scope management, b defines risk management, and d is cost management.

156. **Answer: c.** Decomposition into activities occurs in the define activities process. Decomposition into work packages occurs in the create WBS process. Answer d is a typical PMP exam trick to trip you up because it combines processes like WBS and activities.

157. **Answer: a.** The question clearly states that Jason is still in the planning process, so what process occurs after the sequence that is in the list of choices and part of the planning process group? Define activities, sequence activities, estimate activity duration, et cetera. Knowing the order of processes in the planning process group is crucial to passing the exam. *Memorize the order of processes in the planning process group!*

158. **Answer: c.** See the order of processes in the planning process group.

159. **Answer: c.** Start to Finish (SF) is very rarely used.

160. **Answer: a.** Finish to Start (FS) is the most commonly used.

161. **Answer: d.** Option a describes scope management, b defines risk management, and c is schedule management.

162. **Answer: d.** Analogous, bottom-up, and three-point estimating are tools and techniques for the estimate activity durations process.

163. **Answer: b.** (20 + 32(4) + 50) / 6 = 33

164. **Answer: c.** (32 + 20 + 50) / 3 = 34

165. **Answer: c.** Choice a is plan scope management, b is plan risk management, and d is plan cost management.

166. **Answer: c.** Project documents are inputs.

167. **Answer: c.** She should evaluate the impact of the change.

168. **Answer: a.** She should prevent changes from occurring.

169. **Answer: b.** Answer b is the best choice. Answer a is an option as the **project manager** can go to the program manager; however, the program manager will go to the PMO and then give the information to the PM. There is no portfolio office. The sponsor would not be an option.

170. **Answer: d.** Option a is the output of develop project plan, b is not the output of the plan quality management process, and c is the output of plan risk management.

171. **Answer: a.** Option b is monitoring quality. Option c is managing quality, and d is not the answer.

172. **Answer: b.** Quality reports are an output; enterprise environmental factors are not input in this process, and data gathering is a tool and technique.

173. **Answer: c.** An oscilloscope is outside the scope of PMP. Prototypes are used to find problems in the design, and bottom-up estimating is used to estimate the time and cost of a project.

174. **Answer: b.** Only the cause-and-effect diagram is one of the seven rules of quality control.

175. **Answer: a.** Enterprise environmental factors are influences outside the project manager's control. Organizational process assets are factors within the organization's and project team's control. And c and d are not part of the project management plan.

176. **Answer: c.** The project charter does not contain detailed information of any type. Detailed information is found in the project management plan.

177. **Answer: b.** The project charter will contain the vision of what is expected from the project. The project management plan will include the WBS, which will include project deliverables.

178. **Answer: c.** Organizational process assets are inputs. But a, b, and d are all tools and techniques.

179. **Answer: b.** The communication management plan is not an input to collect requirements. The communication management plan is a guide on how the project team will send, receive, distribute, store, and dispose of communication material.

180. **Answer: b.** The requirements traceability matrix maps deliverables to their respective requirements. The OPA and project management plan are inputs. Data analysis is a tool and technique.

181. **Answer: a.** Answer b describes the plan scope management process. Answer c describes the create WBS process. Answer d best describes monitoring and controlling a process.

182. **Answer: d.** Gold plating is work outside the scope of the project but deemed necessary by the project team. Answers b and c are general concepts that help narrow down the scope of the project.

183. **Answer: a.** Gold plating occurs when project team members make unnecessary and unwanted changes to the project.

184. **Answer: b.** Direct and manage project work is in the execute process groups and describe the performance of work. Manage project knowledge manages documents found, generated, compiled, or created because of the work. Perform integrated change control is a process that occurs when the original work plan must deviate with an approved change.

185. **Answer: c.** The steady-state value of the project is computed with the formula below.

Estimate at Completion (typical, steady-state, or continuous)	(BAC / CPI) = $555,555.56

186. **Answer: d.** The project charter contains the objectives and other information needed to create the PMP. Data gathering and inspection are tools and techniques. The project management plan is the output of the process.

187. **Answer: b.** The keyword here is "how," which describes the plan—in this case, plan resource management. Develop team is in the execute process group, and you would see terms such as "manager," "administer," "train," and "translate." Organization theory and team charter describe the organization and the team, respectively, and would not utilize "how."

188. **Answer: c.** Project charter, EEF, and OPA are all inputs to the process.

189. **Answer: b.** McGregor's Theory X assumes that the typical worker has little ambition, avoids responsibility, and is individual-goal oriented. McGregor's Theory Y assumes employees are internally motivated, enjoy their jobs, and work to better themselves without a direct reward in return.

190. **Answer: d.** The project charter contains the objectives and other information needed to create the PMP. Data gathering and inspection are tools and techniques. The project management plan is the output of the process.

191. **Answer: d.** Only d is in the correct order. All others are not in the correct order, according to Tuckerman's ladder.

192. **Answer: b.** The project management plan describes the project, work performance reports describe the status of the project, and team performance is the evaluation of the effectiveness of the team.

193. **Answer: b.** Develop project charter is the only process on this list. Meetings is a tool and technique for many processes. Organizational process assets are input to many processes, and planning is a process group.

194. **Answer: d.** Plan risk management is a process to first create the risk management plan document. Interpersonal skills is a tool and technique. Risks are being monitored to see if any occur. If a risk does occur, the next step as a project manager is to implement the risk response strategy.

195. **Answer: c.** We are clearly in the execute phase of the project. We have already estimated durations because we have entered the execute phase. There is no mention of project close or cancellation. Identifying stakeholders is going on throughout the life cycle of the project. The best answer is control schedule.

196. **Answer: d.** McGregor's Theory Y assumes employees are internally motivated, enjoy their jobs, and work to better themselves without a direct reward in return. McGregor's Theory X assumes that the typical worker has little ambition, avoids responsibility, and is individual-goal oriented.

197. Answer: a. Data analysis is a tool and technique of most processes. Approved changes are outputs of performed integrated change control and inputs to direct and manage project work. OPA is an input to most processes.

198. Answer: d. Plan risk management is a process to first create the risk management plan document. Interpersonal skills is a tool and technique. Risks are being monitored to see if any occur. If a risk does occur, the next step as a project manager is to implement the risk response strategy.

199. Answer: a. Data analysis is a tool and technique of most processes. Approved changes are outputs of performed integrated change control and inputs to direct and manage project work. OPA is an input to most processes.

200. Answer: b. Choice a is a tool and technique of another process; c and d are outputs to other processes.

Glossary

Acceptable deliverables are the verified deliverables from performing quality control that has been approved by the Customer / Stakeholders to fulfill the acceptance criteria;

Acceptance acknowledges the existence of the threat; however, no action is taken.

Accuracy is an assessment of correction.

Activity attributes will contain sequenced information along with predecessor and successor information. It also defines the duration of the activity, lead, lag, and logical relationships.

Adaptive life cycles are agile—sometimes the processes within their iterations can be going on in parallel. Adaptive life cycles are used in application areas such as IT where there is rapid change.

Advertising is a way to reach out to companies or individuals who can perform the work needed.

Affinity diagram is a business tool used to organize ideas and data.

Agile release planning provides a high-level summary time line of the release schedule (typically 3 to 6 months) based on the product road map and the vision for the product's evolution. Agile release planning also determines the number of iterations or sprints in the release

Agreements are the intentions for the project (Service Level Agreement [SLA], Memorandum of Understanding [MOU], letters of intent, verbal agreements, contracts, or emails).

Alternative analysis is a diverse way of capturing duration information whether the analysis is manual or automatic.

Analogous estimating is the historical estimating from a very similar or same-size project.

Approved change requests, which are an output to project integrated change control, are executed in this process.

Audits are the review of the procurement process. While inspection checks whether the outcome of a product, deliverable or result is correct, auditing checks whether the process was performed responsibly for the end product, deliverable, or result.

Avoidance is when the project team acts to eliminate the threat or protect the project from its impact. In this case, the project team will attempt to remove the threat, extend the schedule, change the project schedule, or reduce the scope.

Backward pass is a critical path method technique for calculating the late start and late finish dates by working backward through a schedule model from the project end date.

Balanced Matrix is a two-dimensional management structure (matrix) in which employees are assigned to two organizational groups

Basis estimates support how the cost or schedule estimates were determined. Basis of estimates is necessary to support the estimated costs. A basis of estimates might include how estimates were developed, how assumptions were made, known constraints, identified risks, the range of costs for the estimate, and your level of confidence in the estimates.

Benchmarking is a process of measuring the performance of a company's products, services or results against those of another business considered to be the best in the industry.

Benefits management plan includes the target benefits of the project, such as net present value calculations and the time frame for realizing the benefits.

Bidder conferences are the meetings between buyer and prospective seller prior to proposal submittal.

Bottom-up estimating is the most exact way to determine activity duration. Bottom-up estimating gets analysis information from the lower-level components of the WBS. Bottom-up estimating takes longer but is the most accurate method for schedule and cost estimation.

Brainstorming uses the combined creative efforts of the project team, experts, and consultants to develop the quality management plan.

Business case describes why the project is necessary and includes information on funding the project.

Business documents describe the necessary information from a business standpoint and whether the expected outcomes justify the investments. Business documents will contain the business case and the benefits management plan. The benefits case contains the project's objectives, and the benefits management plan will describe the expected plan for realizing the benefits that are claimed in the business case."

Change requests may be necessary if you find that some activities were not initially discovered through progressive elaboration.

Closed procurements, the buyer, through formal notice issued by the authorized procurement administrator, notifies the seller that the contract has been completed.

Closing process group is to conclude all activities across all project management process groups and formally complete the project, phase, or contractual obligations. A key word in this definition is formally, which means that the conclusion of the project must be documented. (Whenever you see the word formally, think "in writing.")

Collect requirements process determines, documents, and manages stakeholder needs and requirements to meet project objectives

Communication methods are interactive (multidirectional conversations), push (emails), and pull (shared storage, portals, or websites).

Communication models include encoding, which is transmitting the message, and decoding, which is receiving the message

Communication technology includes shared portals, video and conferencing, chats, databases, social media, email, and websites.

Communications management plan is the how-to guide that explains what type of communication

technology, communication models, and communications methods will be used to engage stakeholders.

Communications requirements analysis combines communications types and formats as needed to maximize the value of the information for project stakeholders.

Conduct procurements process obtains seller responses, selects sellers, and awards a contract. Contractors can be selected by SMEs, advertising, bid conferences, interpersonal and team skills, or data analysis.

Configuration management plan defines items that are configurable and require a formal change control and the process for controlling changes to the items.

Context diagram is a visual tool that depicts the scope of the product, showing the business system and how it relates to and interacts with the other systems as well.

Contingent Response Strategies is the type of response only executed under predetermined conditions. When the risk does occur, there will be sufficient warning to implement the response plan, such as missing a milestone or a task gaining higher priority with the seller.

Contractual obligations cover two sets of obligations:

1. If the organization doing the project is a buyer receiving some component from a supplier to make the finished product, the contractual obligation to the supplier is to compensate the supplier according to the agreed-upon terms of the procurement contract.

2. If the organization doing the project is providing the finished product to a customer, the contractual obligation to the customer is to provide the customer with the finished product according to the agreed-upon criteria for acceptance.

Control chart is a graphic display of process data over time and against established control limits that has a centerline that assists in detecting a trend of plotted values toward either control

Control quality process monitors and records the results of executing the quality management plan activities to assess performance and ensure project outputs are complete, correct, and meet customer expectations.

control resources process ensures the physical resources assigned and allocated to the project are available as planned versus actual utilization of resources and taking corrective actions as necessary.

control scope is the process of monitoring the status of the project and product scope and managing changes to the scope baseline.

Controlling—Controlling PMOs provide support and require compliance through various means. Compliance may involve adopting project management frameworks or methodologies; using specific templates, forms, and tools; or conforming to governance.

Cost aggregation is defined as summing up the cost for the individual work package to control the financial account up to the entire project level.

cost baseline is used as an example in which cost performance is measured and monitored to gauge the importance of the project. This cost baseline is created by estimating the costs by the period in which the project would be completed.

Cost estimates are determined for activities within a work package. Cost estimates include quantitative assessments and contingency amounts for identified risks. The estimates include direct labor, equipment, services, facilities, and information technology as well as the cost of financing, inflation allowance, exchange rates, or a cost contingency reserve.

cost management plan document will determine what to charge, how to charge, when to charge, what denomination to use, and who makes decisions on costs. This document will be the guideline to managing the cost of the project in order to control overcharging, overspending, and out-of-control cost management.

Cost of quality (COQ) refers to the total costs needed to bring products or services up to standards defined by project management professionals. To determine the cost of quality, combine the costs of conformance and the costs of nonconformance. Cost of quality associated with the project determines what happens when quality procedures are followed and when they are not. Cost of quality is the additional cost that includes conformance versus nonconformance.

cost performance index (CPI) is a measure of the financial effectiveness and efficiency of a project. It represents the amount of completed work for every unit of cost spent. As a ratio it is calculated by dividing the budgeted cost of work completed, or earned value, by the actual cost of the work performed.

Cost plus award fee contracts (CPAF): With a CPAF, the seller is paid for all his or her legitimate costs plus an award fee. This award fee is based on achieving satisfaction with the performance objectives described in the contract.

Cost plus fixed fee contracts (CPFF): With CPFF, the seller is paid for all the costs he or she incurs plus a fixed fee, which will not change, regardless of his or her performance. This type of contract is used in projects where risk is high and no one is interested in bidding. The seller is reimbursed for completed work plus a fee representing his or her profit. Consider using a CPFF when there is uncertainty about the scope or the risk is high.

Cost plus incentive fee contracts (CPIF): With a CPIF, the seller is reimbursed for all costs plus an incentive fee based on when performance objectives mentioned in the contract are met.

Cost Variance is a process of evaluating the financial performance of your project. Cost variance compares your budget set before the project started and what was actually spent.

Crashing shortens schedule duration by adding resources, such as approving overtime or paying to expedite delivery to activities on the critical path.

create work breakdown structure (WBS) process subdivides project deliverables and project work into smaller, more manageable components. The WBS decomposes work information into work packages. This decomposition helps the project manager identify risks, resource assignments, and estimate resources; gets team buy-in; prevent changes; and improve quality.

critical path is the sequence of activities that represents the longest path through a project, which determines the shortest duration. The critical path method is used to estimate the minimum project duration and determine the amount of schedule flexibility on the logical network paths within the schedule model. The critical path is the path with zero total float. (Total float is the amount of time an activity can be delayed without delaying the project completion date.) On a critical path, the total float is zero.

Data analysis includes the stakeholder analysis of its interests, legal rights, ownership, knowledge, and contribution. It may also include analyzing documents from previous projects.

Data analysis tools used in this process may include simulations, sensitivity analysis, decision tree analysis, and influence diagrams.

Data gathering includes brainstorming, problem-solving, and meeting management, to give a few examples.

Data gathering techniques are used to collect data and information from a variety of sources such as questionnaires and surveys like the Delphi technique are used. The Delphi technique is used to solicit information anonymously and gather honest feedback by eliminating intimidation from other team members. Brainstorming sessions among the project team members bring ideas to the project to solve problems and issues affecting the project.

Data representation includes a probability and impact matrix showing the likelihood a risk might occur and hierarchical charts, such as bubble charts. Essentially, bubble charts are like XY scatter graphs except that each point on the scatter graph has an additional data value associated with it that is represented by the size of a circle or "bubble" centered around the XY point. Bubble charts are often used in business to visualize the relationships between projects or investment alternatives in dimensions such as cost, value, and risk.

Decision-making at this stage includes such activities as voting and multicriteria analysis.

Decomposition is the technique for dividing and subdividing the project scope and project deliverables into smaller, more manageable components.

define activities process identifies and documents the specific actions to be performed to produce the project deliverables.

define scope process involves developing a detailed description of the project (what it includes and excludes) and its products. This process determines what is and is not in scope. By excluding unnecessary requirements, we save on time, cost, and the complexity of the project.

Definitive estimate is after project initiation, you may check for the cost of past projects using analogous or parametric estimating. Once you apply a formula (PERT) to information discovered about the project, you'll get a definitive estimate, which is a more accurate answer of -5% to +10%.

Deliverables are unique and verifiable products, results, or services that are required to be completed.

Design for X is a set of technical guidelines that can be applied during the design for the optimization for a specific aspect of the design. The X can be for reliability, deployment, assembly, cost, service, usability, safety, or quality. Using design for X can result in a product that has reduced costs, improved quality, better performance, and customer satisfaction.

determine budget process aggregates the estimated costs of individual activities or work packages to establish an authorized cost baseline.

develop project management plan process lays out what needs to be done to define, prepare, and coordinate all subsidiary activities to produce a document that defines the project. This document will be the project management plan

develop schedule process analyzes sequences, durations, resource requirements, and schedule constraints to create a project model for project executions, monitoring, and controlling.

develop team process improves competencies of team members' interactions and the overall team environment to enhance project performance.

development approach can be an estimating technique, scheduling approach, or tools and techniques for controlling the schedule. development approach defines the approach used in the project management plan: waterfall, iterative, adaptive, agile, or hybrid.

direct and manage project work process leads and performs the work defined in the project plan and implements the approved changes to achieve the project objectives.

Direct costs are costs related to the production of specific goods.

Directive is where PMOs take control by directly managing the project.

Discounted cash flow (DCF) is a valuation method used to estimate the value of an investment based on its future cash flows.

Discretionary dependency, also referred to as preferred logic, is established based on knowledge of best practices.

Enhancement is used to increase the probability or impact of an opportunity. Examples of enhancing opportunities are increasing resources such as fast-tracking and crashing to finish faster.

Enterprise environmental factors are the things out of the project team's control. Examples are war, weather events, and economic conditions.

Escalating is appropriate when the threat is outside the scope of the project and at the program, portfolio, or another organizational level, but not at the project level.

estimate activity durations process estimates the number of work periods needed to complete activities with the estimated resources.

estimate activity resources process estimates team resources and the quantity of materials, equipment, and supplies necessary to perform project work.

Estimate at Completion (EAC) Estimate at completion is the forecasted cost of the project, as the project progresses

estimate costs process develops an approximation of the monetary resources needed to complete project activities. This process determines the cost to complete the project work.

Estimate to Complete is the amount of money required to complete the remaining work from a given date.

executing process group occurs after the approval of the project plan and the kickoff meeting for the project. The executing process group is when the activities in the project plan are executed and managed until completion.

Expert judgments are considerations provided by an individual or group with specialized knowledge or training available for many resources. Expert judgments can come from consultants, customers, or sponsors; professional or technical organizations; industry groups; subject matter experts (SME); and PMO.

Exploitation is appropriate with high-priority opportunities where the organization wants to make sure the opportunity is realized, such as using a more talented resource to increase the chances that a task completes sooner.

External dependencies involve the relationship between project activities and those that are not related to the project.

Facilitation drives the agenda of the meeting, which in this case is identifying risks.

Fast-tracking is when activities normally done in sequence are performed in parallel for at least a portion of their duration.

Financing means obtaining funding for the project.

Finish to finish (FF) is a logical relationship in which a successor activity cannot finish until a predecessor activity has finished.

Finish to start (FS) is a logical relationship in which a successor activity cannot start until a predecessor activity has finished.

Firm fixed price contracts (FFP): The FFP is the simplest type of procurement contract because the fee is fixed, and the seller must complete the job for an agreed amount of money and within an agreed amount of time. The seller must pay any cost overruns because of inferior performance or time. This type of contract is mostly used in government or semi-government contracts, in which the scope of work is specified with every detail. Both parties know the scope of the work and the total cost of the task before the work is started. Any cost increase due to substandard performance of the seller will be the responsibility of the seller.

Fixed costs are the business expenses not dependent on the level of goods or services produced, such as rent paid by the month

Fixed price incentive fee (FPIF): In the FPIF, the price is fixed; however, the seller is given an added incentive based on his or her performance. Both parties know the scope of the work and the total cost of the task before the work is started. This incentive lowers the risk borne by the seller."

Flowcharts or process maps display the sequence of steps and the branching possibilities that exist that transform one or more inputs into one or more outputs. (See "The Seven Basic Quality Tools.")

Forecasts may be used to determine if the project is still within defined tolerance ranges and identify any necessary change requests.

Formulas for PERT are:

Triangular Distribution = (O + M + P) / 3 or simple average Beta Distribution = (O + 4M + P) / 6 or PERT formula Standard Deviation = (P - O) / 6"

Forward pass is the critical path method technique for calculating the early start and early finish dates by working forward through the schedule model from the project start date or a given point in time.

Functional Matrix. This is the practice of managing individuals with more than one reporting line Funding limit reconciliation can result in the rescheduling of work to level out the rate of expenditure.

Gold-plating occurs when a project team member adds requirements or deliverables that were not a part of the original approved project plan or approved scope baseline. Gold-plating of items, requirements, or deliverables to the project may cause the sponsor not to accept the project at closing.

Grade is a category assigned to a deliverable having the same functional or technical use.

histogram chart is a bar graph that illustrates the frequency of an event occurring using the height of the bar as an indicator.

identify risks process identifies individuals' risks as well as sources of overall project risks and documents their characteristics. Identifying risks, assessing the risk probability of those outcomes, quantifying the loss because of a risk occurring, and designing a risk response strategy are all very important parts of project management.

Identify project stakeholders regularly and analyzing and determining relevant information regarding their interests, involvement, interdependencies, influence, and potential impact on project success.

implement risk response process implements the agreed-upon risk response. When the agreed-upon risk response is implemented, the overall project risk exposure is addressed, threats are minimized, and opportunities are maximized. This process is performed throughout the project.

Independent cost estimates are estimates from a third party that has no stake in the project. Independent cost estimates are said to be more objective or truthful than those generated in house.

Indirect costs are costs not related to a particular project, such as heat or lighting (overhead).

Individual and team assessments are needed to evaluate performance and to look for areas of improvement or change.

Information management is used to connect people to information, such as the lessons learned register, library services, web searches, reading published articles, and PMIS.

Inspection is when the contractor performs the structural review of the work—either a review of the deliverables or a physical review.

Internal dependencies involve the relationship between different project activities that are within the control of the project team.

Internal rate of return (IRR) is the interest rate at which the net present value (NPV) is zero. This state is attained when the present value of outflow is equal to the present value of inflow.

International Organization Standardization (ISO) is intended to provide generic guidance and explain core principles and what constitutes good practice in project management.

Interpersonal and team skills are used to communicate effectively with team members, sponsors, and others either face to face or via email or other communication methods. Interpersonal and team skills will include conflict resolution methods, facilitation, and meeting management. Interpersonal skills are used in conflict management, facilitation, and meeting management.

Interviews are informal, formal, implicit, and explicit.

Invitation for bid (IFB) is an invitation to contractors or equipment suppliers to submit an offer on a specific project to be realized or product or service to be furnished. The IFB is focused on pricing and not on ideas or concepts.

Invitation for negotiation is merely a preliminary discussion or an invitation by one party to the other to negotiate or make an offer.

Iterative life cycle, the scope is not determined ahead of time at a detailed level but only for the first iteration or phase of the project. Once that phase is completed, the detailed scope of the next phase is worked out, and so on.

Knowledge management connects people so they can work together to create new knowledge, share tacit knowledge, and integrate the knowledge of various team members. The connection occurs via networking, practice communities, physical and virtual meetings, shadowing others on the team, workshops, storytelling, fairs, cafés, and training.

Lag is the amount of time a successor activity will be delayed with respect to a predecessor activity.

Lead is the amount of time a successor can be advanced with respect to a predecessor activity. lessons learned register is used to improve performance and avoid repeat mistakes.

Make-or-buy analysis determines which is best for project needs. As explained before, a make-or-buy analysis is used to determine whether the project team can accomplish work or deliverables. For example, do we have the necessary professional to perform the work within the organization, or does it make more sense to buy software on the market or write our own code?

manage communications process ensures timely and appropriate collection, creation, distribution, storage, retrieval, management, monitoring, and ultimate disposition of project information.

manage quality process translates the quality management plan into executable project activities that incorporate the organization's quality policies.

manage stakeholder engagement is the process of communication and working with stakeholders to meet their needs and expectations, address issues, and foster appropriate stakeholder involvement.

manage team process tracks team member performance, provides feedback, resolves issues, and manages team changes to optimize project performance.

Mandatory dependency refers to tasks that are stipulated in the contract; thus, they are inherent in the project.

Meetings are organized by the project manager, either as leader, facilitator, or participant only. If the meeting is to gather requirements, the project manager is definitely the leader; however, if the meeting is very technical and beyond the project manager's expertise, the project manager participates, taking minutes or notes to share with stakeholders later. The project manager is the organizer, leader, manager, creator, and coordinator of meetings.

milestone list is a list of significant points or events in a project. It is important to remember that milestones have zero duration because they are significant points or events.

Mind mapping is a technique that is used to collect and consolidate ideas created through brainstorming sessions with the team members. Mind maps are great tools for project managers and their teams. The most important benefit they provide is a way of expressing ideas visually and communicating these ideas to the rest of the team members

Mitigation is action taken to reduce the probability the risk will occur, such as designing redundancy into the system that may reduce the impact of failure.

monitor and control project work is the process of tracking, reviewing, and reporting the overall progress to meet performance objectives defined in the project management plan.

monitor communications process ensures the information needs of the project and its stakeholders are met.

monitor risks process monitors the implementation of the agreed-upon risk response plan, tracking identified risks, analyzing new risks, and evaluating the risk process.

monitor stakeholder engagement process monitors project stakeholder relationships and tailors' strategies for engaging stakeholders through modification of engagement strategies and plans.

Monitoring and Controlling process oversees all the tasks and metrics necessary to ensure that the approved and authorized project is within scope, on time, and on budget so that the project proceeds with minimal risk. Monitoring and Controlling process is continuously performed throughout the life of the project.

Monte Carlo simulation is a quantitative risk-analysis technique used to identify the risk level of completing the project. The simulation involves taking multiple work packages in the WBS with a diverse set of assumptions, constraints, risks, issue, or scenarios and using probability distributions with the probability of achieving a certain target date.

Most likely (M) is the realistic expectation of the duration.

Multicriteria analysis is a method of assigning weighted scores for a more qualitative evaluation method of which resource to choose. Multicriteria analysis is a tool that is used to identify key issues and suitable alternatives, which are prioritized as a set of decisions for implementation. Decide which criteria in quality management are important in this project. Then prioritize the criteria. Give each criterion a numerical score. Now a mathematical score can be obtained for each alternative.

Net present value (NPV) is the difference between the present value of cash inflows and the present value of cash outflows over a period of time. NPV is used in capital budgeting and investment planning to analyze the profitability of a projected investment or project. The NPV must always be positive.

When selecting a project, the one with the higher NPV is a recommended option.

Number of communication channels can be calculated using the formula N (N - 1) / 2; where N = the number of people.

Operations constitute an organization's ongoing, repetitive activities, such as accounting or production.

Opportunity cost is a cost that is being given up when choosing another project. During project selection, the project that has the lower opportunity cost is selected.

Optimistic (O) is the best-case scenario for the duration.

Organizational process assets are the policies, procedures, and practices of the organization. Examples are best practices, templates, and organizational procedure documents. OPA are used to produce the most successful project within the organization's guidelines.

Organizational theory provides information on the way that people, teams, and organizational units behave. Organizations are defined as social units of people that are structured and managed to meet a need or to pursue collective goals.

overlapping phase relationship, a phase starts before the completion of the previous one. Overlapping phase relationship is sometimes applied when the project team is using schedule compression techniques and fast-tracking, both of which are discussed more in the project planning section in schedule management.

Parametric estimating is also the historical estimating from a very similar project; however, it is from a project of a different size.

Pareto diagram is a chart that consists of a vertical bar and sometimes a bar-and-line graph. The vertical bar represents the frequency of defects from most to least, and the line represents a cumulative percentage of the defects.

Payback period is the ratio of the total cash to the average per period inflow cash. In simpler terms, it is the time necessary to recover the cost invested in the project.

perform integrated change control process reviews all change requests, approves changes, and manages changes to deliverables, project documents, and the project management plan and communicating decisions.

Perform qualitative risk analysis process prioritizes individual project risks for further analysis by assessing their probability of occurrence and impact as well as other characteristics.

Perform quantitative risk analysis process numerically analyzes the combined effect of identified individual project risks.

Pessimistic (P) is the worst-case scenario for the duration.

Physical resource assignments are the material, equipment, supplies, and location of physical resources that will be used during the project.

Plan communications management process develops an approach and plan for project communications activities based on the information needs of each stakeholder and the project.

plan cost management process defines how the project cost will be estimated, budgeted, managed, and monitored and controlled.

Plan procurement management process documents project decisions, specifying the approach and identifying potential sellers. Each project might have a unique procurement plan for how nonstaff workers can do the work and make physical resources the company cannot do or make.

plan resource management process defines how to estimate, acquire, manage, and use team resources. The resources can be either physical (like equipment) or people.

plan risk management is the process of conducting risk management activities for a project. plan risk responses process develops strategies and actions to address project risk exposure.

plan schedule management process establishes the policies, processes, and documentation for planning, developing, managing, executing, and controlling the project schedule. This process provides guidance and direction on how the project schedule will be managed throughout the project.

plan scope management process documents how the project and product scope will be defined, validated, and controlled throughout the project.

plan stakeholder engagement process develops approaches to involving project stakeholders based on their needs, expectations, interests, and potential impact on the project.

planning package is above the work package but below the control account and has known work content but does not have detailed schedule activities.

planning process group consists of those processes performed to establish the total scope of the effort, define and refine objectives via progressive elaboration, and develop the course of action required to attain those objectives.

portfolio manager can manage programs, projects, and components of programs and projects, such as separate phases or process groups.

portfolio refers to projects, programs, subportfolios, and operations managed as a group to achieve strategic objectives. The projects or programs of the portfolio may not necessarily be interdependent or directly related

Pre-assignment of resources will be stated in the project charter. Pre-assignment is a physical or team resource determined in advance before the resource manage plan has been completed.

Precision is a measure of exactness.

Predictive life cycles are fully plan driven. In a predictive life cycle, the three major constraints of the project—the scope, time, and cost—are determined ahead of time, not just at a high level but in detail in the planning stage, and the project is split up into phases that can be either sequential or overlapping.

probability impact matrix is the process of assessing the probabilities and consequences of risk events if they are realized. The results of this assessment are then used to prioritize risks to establish a most-to-least-critical importance ranking

Procurement documentation updates may include all approved change requests, requested but unapproved contract changes, and supporting schedules.

Procurement documents used are the bid documents, procurement statement of work, independent cost estimates, and source selection criteria.

procurement management plan defines activities to be undertaken during the procurement process such as the type of bidding (local, national, or international) and how the project is funded.

Procurement request are issued to potential sellers to submit a proposal or bid is normally done in newspapers, in trade journals, in public registries, or on the internet.

procurement statement of work (PSOW) is developed from the project scope baseline and defines a part of the project scope and describes the procurement items in sufficient detail to allow prospective sellers to determine if they are capable of providing the products, services, or results. The PSOW should be clear, concise, and complete so the seller or contractor knows what is expected in satisfying each requirement, the physical resources meet all specifications, and deliverables are per the contractual agreement. Each PSOW item requires a SOW; however, multiple products or services can be grouped as one procurement item within a single SOW.

procurement strategy is used to determine the project delivery method, type of contract, and how the procurement will move forward through phases.

Product analysis is a tool that is used to define the scope of the product. It basically means that when analyzing the product through its scope, questions can be asked about it.

program in PMBOK is a group of related projects, subprograms, and program activities managed in a coordinated way to obtain benefits not available from managing them individually

program manager directing all efforts of the projects and project managers

Progressive elaboration involves continuously improving and detailing a plan as more detailed and specific information and more accurate estimates become available.

project as "a temporary endeavor undertaken to create a unique product, service or result. Project calendars are the working days and shifts that are available for the scheduled activities.

Project Charter is the process of developing a document that formally authorizes the existence of a project and provides the project manager with authority to apply organizational resources to project activities.

Project integration includes processes and activities to identify, define, combine, unify, and coordinate the various processes and project management process groups.

project life cycle description determines the phases a project passes through from one inception to another.

Project life cycle is the phases that a project passes through from its start to its completion

project management office (PMO) is the natural liaison between the organization's portfolios, programs, and projects and the corporate measurement systems. There are three types of PMOs: supportive, controlling, and directive.

project management plan is a how-to guide on how the project will be designed, managed, monitored and controlled, and closed. The project management plan starts with the high-level information contained in the project charter. It also includes the scope baseline, schedule baseline, and cost baseline.

project management team are members of the project team who are directly involved with project management activities. In other words, the project management team is a subset of the project team and may include project management staff, project staff, supporting experts, customer representatives, sellers, business partners, and so on

project manager is a person who has the overall responsibility for the successful initiation, planning, design, execution, monitoring, controlling, and closure of a project.

Project Phases is a collection of logically related project activities that culminates in the completion of one or more deliverables.

Project reporting for the project team, stakeholders, sponsor, and senior management is strongly recommended for stakeholder engagement. Project team members want a status so they know when their involvement is needed, stakeholders want to be informed on how the project affects them, the sponsor wants to know the status and how the project is progressing, and senior management want a summary and the percent completion of the project.

project schedule is the output of the schedule mode with linked activities of planned dates, durations, milestones, and resources. Project schedule is the planned start and end dates of the activities.

project schedule network diagram is a graphical representation of relationships between project activities, also referred to as dependencies. The project schedule network diagram can be created either manually or using project management software.

project scope statement provides detailed descriptions of the project deliverables, such as the project scope, major deliverables, assumptions, and constraints. The project scope statement will include all work that will need to be done and exclude the work that will not need to be done.

Project selection methods offer a set of time-tested techniques based on sound logical reasoning to arrive at a choice of project and filter out undesirable projects with a very low likelihood of success.

Project team assignments contain the project team directory and the roles and responsibilities of team member recorded in the project plan.

project team is defined as a set of individuals (such as the project management team, the sponsor, and senior management) who support the project manager in performing the work of the project to achieve its objectives.

Prompt lists are predetermined lists of categorized risks to help guide meetings.

Prototypes are project management tools that are used in getting early feedback related to the project requirements. This is done by providing a working model of the product even before building it.

Purchase order (PO): This type of contract is used to buy commodities.

Quality is the degree of performance to which a deliverable will fulfill requirements.

quality management plan contains policies and procedures on how quality policy, methodologies, and standards are executed on the project. quality management plan defines the activities and resources necessary for the project management team to achieve the quality objectives of the project.

Quality reports can be graphical, numerical, or qualitative. These reports are used by other processes and departments to take corrective actions to achieve quality expectations. Other outputs include test and evaluation documents and change requests.

Recognition and rewards are needed to show team members how important they are to the project and to say thanks for a job well done.

Representations of uncertainty such as representations of risk in duration, cost, or resource requirement use a probability distribution such as triangular, normal, lognormal, beta, uniform, or discrete distributions.

Request for information (RFI) is a standard business process to collect written information about the capabilities of various suppliers.

Request for proposal (RFP) is a document that solicits a proposal from potential suppliers. An RFP is often made through a bidding process by an agency or company interested in procurement of a commodity, service, or valuable asset.

Request for quotations (RFQ) is a standard business process to invite suppliers into a bidding process to bid on specific products or services. RFQ generally means the same thing as IFB (invitation for bid).

requirements documentation contains all the requirements that are necessary to achieve deliverables and the objectives of the project. Some unnecessary requirements will be filtered out in the next process, define scope.

requirements management plan is used to document the information required to efficiently manage

the project requirements from their definition through traceability to delivery. It will also explain how configuration management (change requests) will be initiated, how requests will affect analysis, and what is required to approve changes

requirements traceability matrix links product requirements from their origins to the deliverables that satisfy them

Reserve analysis estimates include contingency reserves. As more information becomes available through progressive elaboration, the contingency reserve is changed, reduced, and possibly eliminated.

Reserve analysis is used to figure out the amount of contingency and management reserve necessary for the project. The contingency reserve is associated with knowns-unknowns. Management reserve is associated with unknowns-unknowns.

Residual risks are the leftover risks, the minor risks that remain. The PMBOK guide defines residual risks as "those risks that are expected to remain after the planned response of risk has been taken, as well as those that have been deliberately accepted."

resource breakdown structure (RBS) is a list of necessary people, equipment, and supplies by category

resource calendar identifies working days and shifts, start and end of normal business hours, and holidays and vacation for available resources.

Resource leveling is used when shared or critically required resources are only available at certain times or in limited quantities or are overallocated, such as when a resource has been assigned to two or more projects during the same time. Resource leveling can often cause the original critical path to change, usually by increasing the CP.

Resource management plan is a component of the project management plan that guides how project resources will be acquired, developed, allocated, managed, and released. Resource management plan may identify areas of resources that may be at risk due to constraints and assumptions.

Resource optimization is used to adjust the start and finish dates of activities to match adjusted planned resource availability. For example, if it is determined that a resource will not be available on the date. Planned the start and finish dates of an activity can sometimes be adjusted, extending the time line. Adjusting the schedule for resource optimization includes either resource leveling or resource smoothing.

Resource smoothing does not change the critical path, and the completion date may not be delayed because with resource smoothing, the activities are adjusted on the schedule model so the requirements for resources on the project do not exceed certain predefined resource limits.

Risk categorization or grouping of risks is usually structured with a risk breakdown structure (RBS). RBS is a hierarchal structure of potential resources to risk. Risk is categorized to determine areas of the project most exposed and common root causes. Grouping risks this way can lead to a more effective risk response plan.

risk management plan is a document that a project manager prepares to foresee risks, estimate impacts, and define responses to risks. Risk management plan is a document that a project manager prepares to foresee risks; estimate impacts; and define responses to issues, roles, and responsibilities.

Risk register has information on the aggregated costs of foreseen risk.

Rolling wave planning is a technique wherein work to be completed in the near term is planned in detail, while work further in the future is planned at a higher level.

Rough order of magnitude is when a project is at or near its birth stage and someone asks what it may cost for the project, the project manager may give the sponsor or senior management a rough order of magnitude, which is -25% to + 75%.

Scatter diagrams allow you to analyze the relationship between two variables.

Schedule baseline, is the approved version of a schedule that can be changed only through formal change control procedures and is used as a basis for comparison to actual results.

Schedule compression is used to shorten the schedule duration without reducing the project scope to meet imposed constraints.

Schedule data is the raw start date, end date, and schedule milestones along with activity attributes, schedule activities, and all identified constraints and assumptions.

schedule management plan is the document developing, maintaining, and communicating schedules for time line and resources. Schedule management plan is the document used in developing, maintaining, and communicating schedules for time and resources.

Schedule network analysis is the technique used to generate the project schedule for which we use the critical path method, resource optimization, and other modeling techniques to plan and manage the schedule.

Schedule Performance Index (SPI) is a measure of schedule efficiency, expressed as the ratio of earned value to planned value." The Schedule Performance Index gives you information about the schedule performance of the project.

Schedule variance (SV), which measures the difference between the earned value (EV) (the value of work actually performed) and the planned value (PV), so $SV = EV - PV$

scope baseline is the approved version of a project scope statement, WBS, and WBS dictionary. The scope baseline can only be changed with formal change control procedures.

Scope creep occurs when the sponsor or other stakeholder adds requirements or deliverables that were not a part of the original approved project plan or approved scope baseline. Scope creep causes additional cost and time to the project. Any changes to the scope must be approved by the sponsor.

scope management plan documents what will be used to prepare the project scope statement, the creation of the WBS, the scope baseline, and formal acceptance of the deliverables.

secondary risks as "those risks that arise as a direct outcome of implementing a risk response." In simple terms, you identify risk and have a response plan in place to deal with that risk. Once this plan is implemented, a new risk that may arise from the implementation tactics.

Seller proposals will have basic information on how a seller is selected.

sequence activities process identifies the relationships among project activities. sequential phase relationship, one phase starts once another phase is completed.

Share risk involves transferring ownership to a third party. Examples of sharing actions include partnerships, teams, and joint ventures.

SIPOC (suppliers, inputs, process, outputs, customers) diagram is a visual tool for documenting a business process from beginning to end.

Source selection criteria should offer the best quality of service based on selection criteria such as capability, product cost, life-cycle cost, delivery dates, technical expertise, specific experience, et cetera. The project team or subject matter experts should be relied on heavily in determining selection criteria.

Tuckman's ladder describes the stages of team formation and development. These stages are: 1. Forming - The team meets and learns about the project. 2. Storming - The team begins to address the project work. 3. Norming - The team begins to work together. 4. Performing - The team is efficient and works through issues. 5. Adjourning - The team completes the work and is released.

Stakeholder engagement plan provides a method for documenting the stakeholders' needs and expectations. Stakeholder engagement plan includes strategies formal or informal for engaging stakeholders. The stakeholder engagement plan also contains methods for engaging stakeholders such as face-to-face

meetings, status reports, or any communication designed in the communications plan.

Stakeholder is an individual, group, or organization that may affect, be affected by, or perceive itself to be affected by a decision, activity, or outcome of a project. Stakeholders include all members of the project team as well as all interested entities that are internal or external to the organization.

stakeholder register contains information about stakeholders such as their names, profiles, and interest.

Start to finish (SF) is a logical relationship in which a successor activity cannot finish until a predecessor activity has started.

Start to start (SS) is a logical relationship in which a successor activity cannot start until a predecessor activity has started.

Strong Matrix or Project Matrix. The project manager has most of the power, resources, and control over the work. The functional manager is there to add support and technical expertise and to look after HR issues

Supportive PMOs provide a consultative role to projects by supplying templates, best practices, training, access to information, and lessons learned from other projects. This type of PMO serves as a project repository

SWOT analysis analyzes the project's strengths, weaknesses, opportunities, and threats. The technique starts with identification of strengths and weaknesses of the organization, the project, or the business. The analysis examines the threats and opportunities that may arise because of weakness or strengths respectively

Team charter is a document that establishes team values, team agreements, and operating guidelines for the team. The team charter will contain information on how to handle conflict resolution, decision-making, and communication.

Tender notice invites bids for a project or to accept a formal offer such as a takeover bid. Tender usually refers to the process whereby governments and financial institutions invite bids for large projects that must be submitted by a finite deadline.

activity list includes scheduled activities needed for the project.

Three-point estimating is more of an exact science using a tested formula to estimate activity duration.

Time and materials contracts (T&M): T&M are a hybrid of fixed-price and cost-reimbursable contracts. Use this type of contract when the scope is incomplete or not determined. T&Ms are also used when the deliverable is "labor hours."

To Complete Performance Index (TCPI) is a comparative Earn Value Management (EVM) metric used primarily to determine if an independent estimate at completion is reasonable. It computes the future required cost efficiency needed to achieve a target Estimate at Completion (EAC).

Training is necessary for team members very close to the needed skill set but missing a certain tool or discipline.

Transference involves shifting ownership to a third party, such as payment of insurance premiums so that if the risk occurs, its impact will be minimized.

validate scope process formalizes acceptance of the completed project deliverables. When validating the scope of the project, the project manager is validating the success of completing the approved requirements, whether for a product, service, or result.

Variable costs are expenses that change in proportion to the level of activity of a business, such as the purchase of more or less raw material

Variance at Completion (VAC) is a projection of the budget surplus or deficit. It is expressed as the difference of the Budget at Completion (BAC) to the Estimate at Completion (EAC)

Verified Deliverable is the output from project tasks that meets by quality control measures as specified in Quality Management Plan.

Virtual teams are resources that are not collocated.

Voting is used to select for best response involving project team members when discussing cost estimates.

Waterfall model is a relatively linear sequential design approach as progress flows in largely one direction through the phases of conception, initiation, analysis, design, construction, testing, deployment, and maintenance"

Weak Matrix: In this form of organization, the functional manager retains most of the power; they "own" the people and resources. In a weak/functional matrix, the project manager is not very powerful.

What-if scenario analysis is the process of changing the values in cells to see how those changes will affect the outcome of formulas on the worksheet.

work package is the lowest level of the WBS and has a unique identifier associated with it called the code of account identifier. The identifier will contain summation of costs, schedule, and resource information. The work package is part of the control account.

Work performance data is raw data that is reported on change requests, such as the number of change requests received and accepted as well as deliverables verified, validated, and completed.

Work performance information is work performance data that has been transformed. Examples of work performance information are deliverables, implementation status for change requests, and forecast estimates to complete.

Work performance report is a compilation of work performance information for consumption for some purpose such as status or decision-making.

Appendix B—Common Confusions

1. Project statement of work versus project scope statement

   a) Project statement of work (SOW) is an input to the project charter. Project statement of work contains three things: business need, high-level scope description, and the organization's broad strategic plan. It is important to remember that the SOW contains *high-level description and lacks any detail*.

   b) Project scope statement provides a *detailed description of the deliverables* being created and identifies all work required to create those deliverables. Project scope statement tells you "what's in and what's out."

2. Business case versus business need

   a) Business case is the generic *reason for the project*, such as market demand, strategic opportunity, customer request, technological advance, legal requirement, ecological impact, or social need.

   b) Business need describes what the organization *needs to accomplish* and how that fits in with the overall organizational strategy.

3. Sign-off on the charter versus sign-off on the project plan

   a) Sign-off on the charter should be sign-off by the sponsor.

   b) The entire project team and key stakeholders sign off on the charter.

4. Project scope versus product scope

   a) Project scope describes ways in which the deliverables will be created. It sets forth things like scheduling, budgeting, quality, resources, et cetera.

   b) Product scope refers to the deliverable being created and *outlines design specifications and features*.

5. Work performance data versus work performance information

   a) Work performance data, which is an output of direct and manage work is raw data showing the status of a particular project area.

   b) Work performance information is a broader and more descriptive indicator of project status, provides project performance results such as actual versus planned values in the earned value management formulas.

6. Work package versus activity list

    a) Work package is the lowest level of project work decomposed in WBS. Work packages can be further decomposed in the process define activities.

    b) Activities lists are discrete activities necessary to complete the project. The project team can the estimate the resources and duration needed to complete the project.

7. Analogous estimating versus parametric estimating

    a) With analogous estimating, we are looking to a past project that is similar to that being estimated and simply plugging that number into our current estimate while adjusting for any known differences. For example, if we know it took 3 months to deploy software to 500 users during a prior software upgrade, we can use that 3-month time frame as an estimate to deploy new software.

    b) Parametric estimating requires us to scale the figures we take from our historical information. For example, if we know it previously took 6 months to construct a 6,000 square foot building, but in this case, we are constructing a 10,000 square foot building that is similar, we could use parametric estimating to determine that it will take 10 months to construct the new building.

8. Critical chain method versus critical path method

    a) Critical path method reveals the long chain of activities throughout your schedule network diagram which adds up to the longest total duration.

    b) Critical chain method uses "buffers" in the project to protect against schedule delay from resource constraints such as a team member being away or unavailable for a critical time in the project.

9. Baselines (cost baseline, scope baseline, schedule baseline). When baseline is used in PMBOK language, it means it has been approved

    a) Cost baseline is the approved budget for the project.

    b) Scope baseline are the approved requirements necessary to complete the project.

    c) Schedule baseline is the approved time line it will take to complete the project.

10. Cost of Quality

Cost of Conformance	Cost of Nonconformance
Preventive costs	Internal Failure Costs
Training	Rework
Document processes	Scrap
Equipment	
Time to do it right	External Failure Costs
Appraisal cost	Liabilities
Testing	Warranty work
Destructive testing loss	Lost business
Inspections	

11. Contingency reserve versus management reserve

   a) Contingency reserves are buffers that project managers add to the project cost estimates to account for uncertain events that we know might happen (also called known-unknowns). These costs are included in the cost baseline.

   b) Management reserves are not set by the project manager but instead established by senior management reserves and are called (unknowns-unknowns). These costs are not part of the cost baseline.

12. Control quality versus manage quality

   a) Control quality is concerned with ensuring correctness of the deliverables. Do the deliverables meet the requirements? Did the deliverables come out as planned? For example, on a car, we would test for brakes stopping as designed or crash worthiness.

   b) Manage quality looks to the process and methods of how the quality check was done, such as using proper metrics when we perform the testing. Manage quality is an audit of the quality process.

13. Communication method versus communication technology

   a) Communication method—interactive, push and pull

   b) Communication technology—email, fax, telephone

14. Risk management plan versus risk register

    a) Risk management plan is a document that describes how risk will be managed, controlled, and monitored.

    b) Risk register is a list of specific risks facing the project.

15. Qualitative risk analysis versus quantitative analysis

    a) Qualitative risk analysis uses tools such as probability and impact matrix analysis and risk urgency assessment. Looks to rank the risk.

    b) Quantitative risk analysis looks to quantify the impact of the potential risk events on our project objectives. Provides a numerical assessment of the risk.

16. Corrective actions versus preventive actions

    a) Corrective actions are where a failure has already occurred, so we want to fix the problem and ensure it does not happen again.

    b) Preventive actions are where a failure has not yet occurred, so we want to prevent failures from occurring in the first place.

17. Team performance assessments versus project performance appraisals

    a) Team performance assessments are assessments of the team performance, such as schedule performance or staff turnover. Team performance assessment is an output of the develop team process.

    b) Project performance appraisals are a tool and technique and are individual assessments, such as an annual review at work.

18. Requirements versus constraints

    a) Requirements are features and functionality that a deliverable must include.

    b) Constraints are anything that limits the project team's options, such as a date deadline.

19. The EAC formula and when to use it:

    a) Atypical: $EAC = AC + (BAC - EV)$

    b) Typical: $EAC = BAC / CPI$

    c) Forecast: $EAC = AC + (BAC - EV) / (CPI*SPI)$

20. EAC versus BAC

    a) EAC is a forecast. This is what our project will end up costing

    b) BAC is the current cost of the project. This is the cost performance baseline. We want BAC to be lower than EAC.

21. Verified deliverables versus accepted deliverables

    a) Verified deliverables have gone through the control quality process and are deemed to be correct.

    b) Accepted deliverables have gone through the validate scope process and have been accepted by the sponsor.

22. Procurement performance reviews versus procurement audits

    a) Procurement performance reviews are a tool and technique of control procurement and used to assess the seller's performance in regard to scope, quality, cost, schedule, et cetera.

    b) Procurement audits focus on the entire procurement process. Procurement audits the successes and failures from plan procurement onward throughout the project. Procurement audit is a tool and technique of the close process.

Index

Made in the USA
San Bernardino, CA
03 July 2020